Ruby Langford Ginibi (19. . _ _ ,.
Bundjalung people, was born on Box Ridge mission
at Coraki in northern New South Wales. She grew up
in Bonalbo and later Casino. Her tribal name 'Ginibi'
(black swan) was given to her in 1990 by her aunt,
Eileen Morgan, a tribal elder of Box Ridge mission. Her
autobiographies *Don't Take Your Love to Town* (1988)
and *Real Deadly* (1992) describe her life in the bush and
later in Sydney raising a family of nine children. She has
also published *My Bundjalung People* (1994), *Haunted by
the Past* (1999) and *All My Mob* (2007). Recognised as
a spokesperson for and educator of Koori culture, she
travelled and lectured in Australia and abroad, and her
essays were widely published.

First Nations Classics

DON'T TAKE YOUR LOVE TO TOWN

RUBY LANGFORD GINIBI

First published 1988 by University of Queensland Press
PO Box 6042, St Lucia, Queensland 4067 Australia
Reprinted 2010, 2014, 2018, 2021
This First Nations Classics edition published 2023

University of Queensland Press (UQP) acknowledges the Traditional Owners
and their custodianship of the lands on which UQP operates. We pay our
respects to their Ancestors and their descendants, who continue cultural and
spiritual connections to Country. We recognise their valuable contributions
to Australian and global society.

uqp.com.au
reception@uqp.com.au

Cover design by Jenna Lee
Typeset in 11.5/16 pt Bembo Std by Post Pre-press Group, Brisbane
Printed in Australia by McPherson's Printing Group

  First Nations Classics are assisted
by the Australian Government through
the Australia Council, its arts funding
and advisory body.

This project is supported by the Copyright Agency's Cultural Fund.

A catalogue record for this book is available from the National Library of Australia.

ISBN 978 0 7022 6600 3 (pbk)
ISBN 978 0 7022 6791 8 (epdf)
ISBN 978 0 7022 6792 5 (epub)

MIX
Paper | Supporting
responsible forestry
FSC
www.fsc.org   FSC® C001695

You've painted up your lips
and rolled and curled your tinted hair
Ruby, are you contemplating
going out somewhere
The shadow on the wall tells me
the sun is going down
Oh Ruby, don't take your love to town.
KENNY ROGERS, 'Don't Take Your Love to Town'

black women are on the way 'up'
you now must ponder
who will babysit the kids
while you make your (un-paid) t.v. appearance
you must try not to let your bitterness
be construed as 'black racism'
as you recall the abuses
heaped upon you all your life
and you view your 'liberation'
with a scepticism born of poverty,
corrugated-iron shacks, no water,
four children from six live births
and the accumulated pain of two centuries
black woman black woman black woman black woman black
BOBBI SYKES

I swear the earth shall surely be complete to him or her who shall be complete
The earth remains jagged and broken only to him or her who remains jagged and broken.

WALT WHITMAN, 'A Song of the Rolling Earth'

Contents

INTRODUCTION
by Nardi Simpson

*For Aunty Ruby Langford Ginibi
and Aunty Georgina Williams*

A month before Christmas 2022 our family lost its matriarch. She was the eldest of eleven children belonging to my grandparents, Bertha and George. Georgina Simpson was born in Walgett, north-west New South Wales, in 1940. My Aunty George passed away after a short and aggressive illness. With seven children, forty grandchildren, the same number of great-grandchildren and hundreds of extended family and kin connections, us Simpsons found ourselves reeling. Aunty George had always kept us together: she was our pillar – our living link to our family's ancestral and cultural memories. When she passed, she took a huge part of us with her.

In her early life, Aunty George lived on several properties and stations taking work as a domestic, cook and caregiver as she and her husband and their growing family followed the work. Aunt never spoke openly about those times, and we didn't much ask. We knew the reality of prejudice that shaped New South Wales country towns. We also knew our old fullas would rather crack a joke or tell a funny yarn than go over difficult stuff. This was common in our and many other Aboriginal families; when given the choice between sad sorry business or a joke, a laugh always won out in the end. As a result, we could sit around and laugh for hours at ourselves and others, but mostly shy away from the details of the hardships that our own family endured. It's not the version of the story we naturally look to share.

So my knowledge of my Aunt's life revolves around long, late-night laughs; star-studded nights on ancient river bends; spread-eagled over cousins on a mattress dragged into her front yard; around suffocatingly hot kitchen tables drinking tea and listening to stories about family or friends or people in the town.

In the later years of her life, she took to jewellery making; so I took to listening to her speak as she threaded exquisitely painted gumnuts and quandong seeds into elaborate handmade necklaces (all of which she would eventually gift or give away.) During these times she increasingly wanted to talk about her early life with me. She told me she had written down many stories and incidences – the parts none of us really knew about. She said she had notebooks planted around her house. 'I could never bring myself to tell my children some of the things I went through,' she said to me once, not too long ago. 'Maybe if they find them and read them when I'm gone, they will finally know what it was like for me.'

The preciousness of these notebooks strikes me now that the storyteller herself has gone. They are diamonds or, more appropriately for us, opals: deposited in the earth, shaped by the moving waters and formed by the extreme pressures inherent in the landscape.

Aunty Ruby Langford Ginibi's *Don't Take Your Love to Town* is already a sparkling gem glinting around our matriarchs' necks. It is, of course, a publishing literary success. But for us, the daughters and granddaughters of women such as Aunty Ruby and Aunty Georgina, the life within the narrative – its inhalations of love and exhalations of culture – are its true triumph. The author lived the life she wrote; she birthed and raised the characters in it. Its heartbeats and heartbreaks ruminated through her body before making it onto the page. We read the story as black women's truth – existing as best she can upon Australia's cultural landscape and wastelands.

Don't Take Your Love to Town is extraordinary to me in that it is brave enough to confront challenges rather than laugh them away. In this way, it is the appendage to my own family's archive. Aunty Ruby wrote truth so that I could experience the joy of laughter with family, and with my Aunty George.

What can we possibly be without the example of such women? Without their differences and similarities? Without their complications and simplicities, their challenges and invitations, their secrets and truths? Their life waters our spirit. We grow because they breathe. We thrive in the shade that they so generously cast.

We sustain ourselves on their defiance, resourcefulness and sovereignty. And this is how the black matriarchy and black storying works: each action providing a foundation, a stepping stone for another black woman or girl to follow; success and achievement not measured by awards or sales or reprints but by the kindnesses, generosities and strengths passed down the line. May we always uphold and uplift the stories of our black matriarchs – the published and unpublished – the written as well as the lived.

Names

I was called after my great aunt Ruby. In the mission photo, she's sitting beside her identical twin, Pearl. They're dressed in Victorian fashion, high collars and pinched waists. Their dresses are white. Ruby and Pearl are black.

When I was six, Mum left us. My sisters were four and two. The person who took over our mothering was an Aboriginal cleverman, Uncle Ernie Ord. He's telling us our totems. He says my totem is a willy wagtail, he says I'll always know if there's trouble because the wagtail will warn me. Many years later I'm living in Alexandria. There are sparrows and crows here, also a rain bird calls out when it's going to rain. There are no wagtails. One day I hear a wagtail outside my window. That afternoon I heard my brother had died.

After Mum left, Dad took us to stay with Aunty Nell and Uncle Sam in Bonalbo. I am nine years old. Aunty Nell has boiled up flour bags and made our pants. Our dresses are made of cheesecloth, starched. Also the rag hats. It's my job to damp the starched clothing down,

I hate it. I shinny up the tree outside our bedroom and hide in the leaves. Uncle Sam is calling me. Everything's quiet in the house. 'Where's the Big Noise?' he calls. I start to sing. I'm singing as loud as I can.

I am in high school, thirteen going on fourteen. My best friend is Olga Olive. She's the only girl in her family and one of her brothers, Bruce, races us home from school. He can always outrace us, he belts us on the head with his father's newspaper to make us run faster. Sometimes Olga and I climb a tree and hide till he goes past. I'm so so good at climbing Olga calls me *rangi*, short for orangutang. 'Hey Rangi,' she calls, 'give me a leg up, here he comes.'

Ruby Anderson. My maiden name. I had a bad crush on a boy called Reggie Gordon who called me Ando all the time instead of Ruby. I got my first proposal when I was fifteen years old. It wasn't from Reggie but from Mervyn Kenny, a boy I called pug mug because of his nose.

I'm fifteen now. I finished high school and I'm working for a family called the Bulls. Their farmhouse overlooks Gorge Creek. I clean the house and look after two little girls. At weekends I borrow the chestnut pony and ride home singing, 'Yippi hi oh, yippi hi ay.' When I come to our gate Uncle Sam is on the back steps. 'Hey mother, here comes our little heifer who works for the Bulls,' he calls.

At Christmas Dad arrives at Uncle Sam and Aunty Nell's. He's taking my sister Gwen and me to Sydney.

Our younger sister, Rita, stays, she's too young. We get to Redfern and my stepmother, Little Mum Joyce, takes me to Brachs and I'm put on as an apprentice trousers machinist. My best mate is Betty Williams. On Sunday nights we go to the dance at the Ironworkers Union, down in Sussex Street. When we're broke we borrow money from Dad. He keeps the money in a big old woman's handbag in the wardrobe, he doesn't believe in banks. 'Come on Andy,' says Betty after we've borrowed a pound. 'Let's go Willy,' I say. Off to the dance. We weren't wallflowers for long.

I had my first three kids with Sam Griffin (Koori), but I didn't change my name. Bill, Pearl and Dianne are Andersons, named after me. The next three I had with Gordon Campbell (gubb), Nobby, David and Aileen. They're registered in his name. Then I married Peter Langford (gubb), and Ellen and Pauline were born. Now I'm Mrs Langford. My only legal name change. Later I had Jeff, my youngest, with Lance Marriot (Koori), who took on all my kids and loved them all. But I stayed Langford, by now things were complicated enough.

You can think of me as Ruby Wagtail Big Noise Anderson Rangi Ando Heifer Andy Langford. How I got to be Ruby Langford. Originally from the Bundjalung people.

1

You are my Sunshine

Coraki and Bonalbo

I was born on Australia Day, the twenty-sixth of January 1934, at Box Ridge, Coraki, on the far north coast of NSW. It was a reserve or Aboriginal mission. My father was a log-cutter and later he drove trucks carting logs out of the Taloome scrub.

Dad was a tall and proud man, a family man, and he watched after my mother. They were married when I was six months old and my mother was sixteen. A year later we moved to Stoney Gully mission near Kyogle, where Dad worked as a handyman for the manager. Sister Gwen was born when I was two.

In the afternoons Dad sat four or five of us on Bonnie, the mission horse, and we took her to the creek. One of the older kids sang 'My Bonnie Lies over the Ocean'. In the mornings Dad hitched a slide behind the horse and went under the culvert to the dairy for milk cans and delivered them to the mission houses.

The houses were four-roomed, no lining, open fire for cooking, and the windows were wooden slats that you prop open with a stick. Mum looked after old man Ord, who we called nyathung. I sat on the step and watched his grey beard moving as he talked, he was telling me stories in Bundjalung. Sometimes he sang.

One night I was woken by movement in the room. I opened my eyes slowly to sounds coming from a mattress in the corner. It was my mother moaning. Other women were there with her, shapes near the hurricane lamp. One of them noticed me awake. She turned me over and covered me up, 'Go ngudam,' she said, but I rolled over and watched. It sounded like my mother was hurt. In a while I saw them holding up a baby and heard the new cry. Then I went back to sleep. I forgot I had seen this, and forty years later the memory came back.

After sister Rita was born I started at the schoolhouse. It was on a hill overlooking the mission. There was a railway track and a culvert we went under to get to school. Our chickens laid eggs in the long bladegrass, which grew everywhere. Old folk hunted for bandicoot and bunning in this grass. Dad also grew corn and pumpkin.

One day he came in with a gramophone so tall I had to stand on a chair to wind it. We played country-and-western records. I was about to climb on the chair one afternoon when Mum told me to come into Grandfather Ord's back room. He was lying quiet on the bed. 'Go and kiss grandfather goodbye, he's going away.' I leaned over and kissed his cold head. The men came and wrapped him in a tarp and took him out. I didn't know where he was going, I sat under the verandah and cried. Later Grandfather's son, Uncle Ernie Ord, came to stay.

We left Stoney Gully and went to live on the bank of the Richmond River outside of Casino. We rented a wooden house on the Lismore Road. Uncle Ernie Ord and my father must surely have wanted boys in the family, Santa always brought us boys' toys. We never got dolls and prams, instead we would get rubber daggers, cricket bats, wind-up motorbikes.

I started school again. My mother took me by the short cut along the river bank. She came half way, to a place called the Bamboos, and met me there after school.

The teacher's name was Miss Pie, and she taught us to sing. When I went on messages to the other teachers I'd give my message and sing a song. One day, it had been raining for a week, I sang songs about the rain.

That day, when I was walking home, the river was pretty high. I got as far as the Bamboos, carrying my lunch pail, and my mother wasn't there. I went on by myself, in and out of the trees and staying on the track. A slippery sensation, and I was in the river.

I reached out but there was nothing to grab onto, the current sucked me under and when I came up I was out in the river. I took a breath. The current took me under again forcing the lunch pail out of my hand and I could hear a strange soothing music ringing in my ears. The river rushed me back near the bank and this time I grabbed a willow branch and hung on tight. It swept me in and I grabbed the reeds on the bank and pulled myself up. I sat there shaking.

Further up there was a fall in the river and I could hear it roaring. I climbed up the bank and ran hard, in my head the music and the water roaring.

My mother was making mulberry pies and my father was out in the scrub. I had a bath and calmed down. The Olives came over, Mrs Olive with her hair in a bun and one of the kids dragging a chaff bag he'd found in the bush. Mrs Olive went inside and the kids sat me on the chaff bag so they could drag me up and down the verandah. I got a big splinter in my bundung and my mother had me down on the bed cutting it out with a razor blade. The Olive kids' faces appeared at the window and I could hear them laughing as I yelled.

Uncle Ernie Ord had made a three-pronged spear for catching mullet. 'Come on,' he said one afternoon, 'I'll show you how to catch fish. See this piece of string?' He reached into his pocket and laid some string on the table. He tied a bent pin to it. 'Now you try.' Then we made dough for bait and went to the fishing hole. Uncle Ernie threw some dough on the water and we could see schools of garfish and mullet rising. We came home with about six mullet, 'a good feed', Uncle Ernie said.

A few nights later he almost used his three-prong spear on our neighbour, Eddie Webb, who he heard on the verandah. When Dad came home and wanted an explanation, Eddie said he'd just called in to get some tea and sugar.

We didn't know it then, but Eddie Webb was sneaking after Mum. 'Nyaiwanyi bumanyi,' Dad said, and Eddie cleared off. After that we moved back to the mission at Coraki. Much later I realised we were moving away from Eddie Webb, that his visits were more important than we thought.

One morning I heard a noise outside and went out to see a tall man on a horse riding into the mission. This was my Grandfather Sam, Dad's father. At this time I was a grumpy and pouty child and I wouldn't talk. Grandfather was a fine horseman. He hoisted me onto his seventeen hands high stock horse, Kangaroo, and I soon yelled out, 'Get me down Poppy, get me down.' He came into the house loping and bandy-legged from riding and sat down with my mother. He'd been away droving – Coraki, Dairy Flat, Kyogle. He stayed till Dad and Uncle Ernie came in from their log-cutting job a few days later and then he went away on Kangaroo. After he left, the men talked about cricket games they'd seen him play, how he was known as the Bungawalbyn crack and could bowl anyone out. I didn't take much notice at the time, I was more interested in why Mum was so upset and quiet all the time.

There were days when she seemed happy and other times when she seemed to be waiting for something to happen. We now had a new baby brother, George. Dad and Uncle Ernie hardly ever came home.

It was a pitch dark night. I could hear Mum moving around in the room, talking in a low voice to the baby.

I saw her wrap him up in a blanket and then I called out, 'Mum, where are you going?' 'I'll be back,' she said.

I went to the door and watched her walking down the track to the gate. In the darkness the only thing you could see was the light on the top of a taxi. She got into the car. We didn't know where she'd gone, though I looked out for her and kept thinking she'd be back.

I was six, Gwen was four, Rita was two. The Breckenridges had got word to Dad and he came in a borrowed car and took us out into the scrub. Uncle Ernie was with him. They were like brothers, always wrestling and shaping up and biffing each other good-naturedly. We lived in a tent and played around the camp all day. Uncle Ernie boiled corned beef in a big boiler on the open fire, and cooked damper in the ashes. When Dad came into the camp at night I asked a few times, 'Where's Mum?' and he said, 'She's gone. She won't be back.'

The days were hot and clear. Uncle Ernie had a tom-axe in his belt and a beer bottle with water in it. 'Let's go for a walk, see if we can get some bush tucker,' he said. He rolled his trouser leg up. We headed off into the scrub, big timber all around us; we could hear the axes ringing from where Dad and the others were, further up. Not far into the scrub Uncle Ernie pointed, high up in a tree. At first I couldn't see it. He squatted down next to me and pointed again, and there it was. A big old grey bugger, goanna. 'Watch this,' he said.

He took the tom-axe and threw it hard. It landed in the back of the goanna's head with a thunk, and there was a silence, and then the goanna fell down right near our feet. Then next thing he had it on the hot coals back at the camp, and when it was cooked he offered some to us, but we wouldn't eat it. I remember the flesh was white like fish.

The next day he fed us on boiled swan's eggs. A half one was enough for each person. Later he gave us cobra, worm-like things that were embedded in waterlogged willows in the Richmond River.

Later on we moved back to Box Ridge. As you came through the main gate of the mission there was a church and then, in the shape of a square, a school and about ten houses. This was our place, this was where the Kooris lived, about fifty of us. We stayed with some people called Breckenridge. In the middle of the square was a tennis court.

Out the back was Uncle Ernie's hut, which he'd made from a few pieces of galvanised iron and hessian bags, with a single bed in it and his tin trunk with all his belongings. There was a fire-bucket too. To keep warm he sat in front of the fire-bucket and told us stories about bush animals·: binging, jarahny, guyahny, burbi, also kangaroos, cranes, emus, possums.

He started to doze and we poked him in his big belly and woke him up. He went on with the story. One night he told me my totem was the willy wagtail. Years later I think about that small bird. I am a very large woman with a bird singing inside me, good news and bad.

Uncle Ernie was an Aboriginal cleverman, that is he knew magic. When Mrs Breckenridge got sick and didn't seem to be getting any better, Uncle Ernie was sent for. I watched him go to his tin trunk and take out an old tobacco tin where he kept the hair of his dead father. He warmed it on the fire-bucket by rubbing his hands together.

Then he went back inside, and hunted everyone out of the sick room. I looked through the window and I saw him put his hand with the hair on it, to her forehead. He sang and chanted in the lingo and stayed there for about an hour. When he came out he told us to be quiet, she was sleeping. She slept for a few hours and then she got up and set about doing her work.

A few months later an old lady came to visit. Uncle Ernie told her that he was asleep one night in his shack and he heard his dead father's voice calling him to wake up. When he did he saw a hole in the hessian bag around his hut, and he knew someone was watching him. He sneaked around the back in the dark and saw a man walking away towards the bush. He followed and the man disappeared in front of him.

We all ate in the kitchen of the house. It was my job to do the washing up and pack the table. The cups were made of jam tins or Sunshine Milk tins, which were called pannikins. One night Uncle Ernie was sitting at one end of the table and he said, 'Do you want to see that pannikin move up here? Watch this.' He waved his hand towards himself and the pannikin moved across the table and stopped right in front of him. We looked under the table to see if he had strings tied to it, but there were no strings. 'How did you do that?' we said, and he laughed, and his whole body shook.

The headmistress at the school was Mrs Hiscock. She taught us to cook, sew and grow vegetables in the schoolyard.

Every Monday morning we were given a big tablespoon of sulphur and molasses to clean our systems out. Behind the school was a field of millet belonging to Mr Breckenridge, who was a broom maker. One day Rita fell on a squaring axe and needed about ten stitches, but they didn't take her to a doctor. They bathed us in the water that had been used to wash the linen, with handfuls of caustic soda added. Did she want us to go white? Instead we had burning skin.

To get from the mission to the town of Coraki you went across a common where the cows were kept. In wet weather the common turned into a swamp. On the other side of the swamp was a gate, a shop where the Kooris went, then the town. In the main street, which ran parallel to the river, was a baker with a crow in a cage on the counter. When the baker was out the back, the crow called out, 'There's blackfellers in the shop!' Further up the street was the Masonic Hall where we went to the pictures: Hopalong Cassidy, Tom Mix, Charlie Chaplin. Only a few times we went in to the pictures – three miles – the adults piggybacking kids home after. The pictures had segregated seating, one side for us, the other side for the whites. At the hospital they had special wards for Kooris, down the back.

One afternoon I was sent to stoke the fire. It was down to coals so I put chips on and brambles and fanned it with a piece of cardboard. It still wasn't lit so I poured kero on and the rings were still on top and it blew up in my face with a loud boom. I was in pain for weeks, I had no eyebrows and all my face was blistered. They didn't take me to the doctor.

Not long after this some kind person must have got word to Dad about the way we were being treated. He came in the truck and packed our things. Uncle Ernie was the only one who knew we weren't coming back. He helped us into the truck and kissed us goodbye then walked away from us with his head down crying.

It was a long ride from the mission at Coraki to Dad's brother's place. Bonalbo was a small town nestled in dairy hills, and we were to stay here for the next four years. Uncle Sam came out to the verandah to meet us, and took us inside to meet eight or nine other relatives who lived there. Dad stayed a few days, and then went back to the Taloome scrub, timber cutting. We settled in and went to school.

Aunt Nell was a big woman who wore an apron with pockets where she kept clothes pegs and a pencil and notepad for the shopping list. From the cowbales where I was milking I could pick up the drifting smells of suet pastry, steak and kidney pie, the warm sweet smell of stew. In winter we came in from school and squatted on the woodbox near the stove. There was a fountain of water always boiling, and a tap at the bottom for making tea.

The house was the original station house, on a property eight miles long. Aunt Nell was a Hinnett, and the house was left to her family by the original owners who the Hinnetts had worked for.

Aunt Nell had a daughter before she married Uncle Sam. Her name was Shirley (Midge). She was two years older than me and she washed our faces and combed our hair and put ribbons in it. I was nine years old.

Dad was away all week and came home at weekends. We watched for the lights of his truck coming around the hills outside of town; we swarmed all over him as soon as he arrived. We jostled to see who'd get to sit on his knees first. The two little ones always managed to beat me.

When the job cut out, Dad went to Sydney to find work. He left us in the care of Uncle Sam and Aunt Nell and then we only saw him at Christmas time. He sent money to Aunt Nell for our keep.

Uncle Sam and Aunty Nell always referred to each other as mother and father. She was ten years older than him but it didn't matter to them at all. They were the best parents we could have had, and I promised myself if I ever had kids I'd never leave them.

Eventually there were nine people at the table.

At tea time Midge and we three sat on a long stool, the others had their own chairs. Uncle Sam at one end,

Aunty Nell at the other. Aunty Nell's sister Aunty Flo and her brother Uncle Willy on one side and their nephew John on the other. Later Aunty Nell had a baby girl, Judy.

At mealtimes only the grown-ups could speak and make conversation. The kids cleaned the table when the meal was finished, then we did our homework by candle-light. There was a big lamp which Aunt Nell kept in her bedroom at night. Their room was next to ours, and she checked us in the night to see if we were covered properly. It was very cold in winter.

We did our chores before we went to school. My job was to milk three or four cows before breakfast. I separated the milk by hand, so by the weekend I had a big bowl of cream in the icebox. Then I'd make butter for the next week. It was the days of the Second World War – sugar, tea and butter were rationed. Gwen's job was to polish the dining room table. One morning Aunty Nell came in and said, 'Put some more elbow grease into that!' I was going through from the milking to get dressed for school. When I came into the kitchen I found Gwen on all fours looking into a cupboard. 'What are you doing?' I said. She was looking for the elbow grease.

The twenty-five-pound flour bags Aunt Nell bought were washed and boiled and then cut up to make our pants. She made our dresses and hats from starched cheesecloth. It was my job to damp the starched clothing down and I hated doing it. When I was called to do some chore I shinnied up the crepe myrtle outside our bedroom and hid in the leaves. Uncle Sam called me the Big Noise because when I wasn't hiding I was singing as loud as I could.

When I stopped, I heard chooks making their small noises, pecking around in the vegetable garden and under the fruit trees. Down near the cowbales were two orange trees and a big mulberry tree. There was also a passionfruit vine growing in a cow pat, and at the side of the house a grapevine. It was an old weatherboard house with rafters in the kitchen.

At the back of the house was a big paddock with suckers in among the gum trees. I went down to the biggest tree and climbed up. You had to watch out for spitfires, grubs that sting. At the end of the paddock was a fence then the stock route. On sale days I watched cattle coming down here like a river, heard the calls of the Indian cowboys, the Khan brothers, who lived up the back.

From this tree I could see the whole town – Marty Askew's shop, the hardware, the feed and grain store, Jim McQueen's butcher shop. Behind the hotel were the cattle saleyards, the butter factory, the track to the swimming-hole. Soon I knew who lived in every house that I could see.

Aunty Nell was having a baking day. From the cowbales, or the creek, or up the tree I could smell the cakes cooking. When I went to the back door I saw Uncle Sam palming a few cupcakes. He hobbled out and handed them to us. Soon Aunt Nell said, 'Father, where're all those cakes gone to?' 'I don't know,' he said, 'must be fairies taking them.' As soon as we heard this, we ran like blazes, leaving him to take the blame.

He had a gammy leg and when we asked him how it was stiff and why, this was his story. He said when he was younger he was a horse-breaker and the horse threw him and he was a flying angel.

Later we found out he'd had polio. It never stopped him from playing cricket and working on the Shire Council. He was a grader driver for twenty years. He liked to dance around the kitchen imitating how we danced with our boyfriends. 'Look at how Gwennie dances with Cippi Hannan,' and he threw his gammy leg out and danced in the big kitchen. Once he stuck oranges down his flannel shirt and walked around like Betty Stubbins. He half-limped half-danced towards us. 'Look out,' he said, 'these bosoms'll knock your eyes out. Specially when you're comin' round the corner.'

The people in the town were friendly, there was no prejudice against us. It felt different from the atmosphere in Coraki. We went to Sunday School and church, we sang at concerts and church festivals. At the festival we bought a watermelon for sixpence and there was enough to go around eight people. The harvest festival was held when the corn was in. We were getting the church ready. Uncle Willy was the gardener at our place, and he brought in squash and marrows. The farm people came in with stacks of corn and put them all around the church walls. In a little room at the back the women unwrapped homemade cakes and put the urns on to boil. Mrs Bull arrived with the draughthorse and sulky. The Browns and the Grays came in their utes with pumpkin the size of watermelon, grey-white skin, and sweet and dry inside. We called them cow pumpkins. I was presented by the Bishop of Grafton with a prayerbook and a scroll, which Aunt Nell hung in the dining room.

After the harvest festival we went to the nearest farm, about six hundred yards from the town, Mac McQueen's place. We showed him the chaff bag and asked if we could have some corn for the cookout. We had fried corn, fricasseed corn and then corn fritters. In the end Aunty Nell was pouring castor oil down our throats.

A couple of days before Christmas we were sitting on the back steps watching through the suckers of the trees. We saw the bus pull in at Marty Askew's shop, we saw Dad, tall, coming across the footbridge towards the church. We ran down to meet him. He had one suitcase slung on his shoulder and one down beside him. We knew the suitcases were packed with things for us, clothes and toys and bags of nuts for the Christmas table.

We opened our presents at the same time, and the family watched. We started with the biggest parcels first. Pale blue skirts and blouses to match with sailor suit collars, packets of scented soaps and talcum powder, crackling presents that opened up to be lollies and liquorice, and then the last ones, tiny combs and mirrors.

When we were quiet again, Gwen went over and stood near Dad's knee. 'When you're away so long,' she said, 'what are you doing all the time?' Dad said he drove a bulldozer. 'What's a bulldozer?' she said. Rita looked up from her presents and said, 'Oh Gwen, don't be silly. Don't you know it's a bull that dozes.'

The next morning I was in the kitchen and Dad sent me to get his shaving gear out of his suitcase. I opened the lid and lifted up some clothes and there was a photograph of a beautiful lady in a big white picture hat, sitting on a chair. I stared at the photo and then turned it over. The words said, *You are my Sunshine, love Evelyn.*

Dad came in with a towel around his neck and said, 'Haven't you found my shaving gear yet?' When he saw the photo I said, 'Is that our mother?'

'Yes,' he said.

I stared at the picture. 'Isn't she beautiful,' I said.

'Yes,' he said. 'She's very beautiful.' He closed the lid of the suitcase.

2

Chiefy Pie and the Ballet Lesson

Bonalbo

'Mrs Richards from the fruit shop called in today,' Aunt Nell said one evening. 'She wants to know if she can borrow you to look after Jan.' The story was, I'd get Jan from the kindergarten after school, we'd go to my place and I'd get changed, then up the hill about three hundred yards to the Richards' place. Now I'd light the fire, bath Jan, and put the vegetables on for their tea. At five o'clock Mrs Richards would shut the shop and come home, and I could go. Mr Richards was away a lot. He went to Brisbane to get the fruit and vegetables.

I looked out the classroom window at the horses tethered near the gate, waiting for the farm kids to ride them home. I looked in the direction I thought Sydney was and wondered how long it would take to ride there. Mr Tyler came into the room and told us that King George the Sixth was talking on the radio. He switched it on. 'The war has ended,' the king said. 'All school children can have the day off.'

We ran outside and banded together. Someone said,

'Let's go and have a cookout at Gorge Creek.' The farm kids had to get home to their jobs, and the rest of us – about thirty kids – went home, raided the icebox and met out at the creek. We built a big fire and had a rowdy day.

The following afternoon Mrs Richards showed me where the vegetables were kept, and where the towels were. As I did each job I said, 'Okay, Chief?' and she grinned. Later she took me into another room and showed me how to work the gramophone.

A few weeks after that I worked out the jobs so I'd be finished by four thirty. I went into the lounge room and lifted the lid on the gramophone. I put on 'Pedro the Fisherman' and sang to that, then I played 'Jeannie with the Light Brown Hair'. I started to dance around the big room, past the cane lounge where Jan sat in her pyjamas, round the flowers on the coffee table and across to the door. As I was raising my arms for the dance to the final chorus, Mrs Richards appeared in the doorway and started to clap.

'I could hear you singing,' she said coming into the room, 'from way down the bottom of the hill.'

Jan went to her and hugged her legs. I kept dancing.

In a while she came back into the room with a box under her arm.

'Sit down here,' she said, patting the lounge.

I sat down beside her. 'What's this, Chief?'

She handed me the box and I opened the lid. Inside was a pair of ballet shoes, made of satin.

'I want you to have them,' she said. She showed me how to put them on.

I looked at my black feet in the pink shoes. 'Oh, Chiefy Pie,' I said, and I could hardly speak. I tucked myself under her arm and hugged her.

'Now,' she said. 'First. I'll teach you how to stand on your toes. Then the arm movements. Then some steps you can practise by holding onto the chair. After Christmas, I'll teach you how to pirouette.'

I stood up. For some reason, I could keep my balance. Chiefy Pie put Richard Tauber on the gramophone, and in the house with its windows open on the hill and the cows and chooks outside and the horses munching, he sang, 'You are my heart's delight' and 'Come be my love, when no-one else can end this yearning', and I joined in and the highest note was on the word 'love' and I could reach the note easily.

Chiefy Pie showed me some steps and she watched while I danced. I moved into another world and another time.

The following week Grandfather Sam rode in on Kangaroo. He'd come to stay for a while. Twice a week he went over to the slaughterhouse with a sugar bag and came back with the guts of the bullock, the heart, liver and intestines. He washed the innards thoroughly then cut it into small rings like washers, rolled them in flour and fried them. They were very tasty and white. He called them moggi, meaning ghost in the Bundjalung language.

He took us out on the flat and taught us to googly bowl, and how to hold the ball and wicketkeep, and how to hold the bat. He gave us hot peppermint lollies and he had the habit of saying 'goodfulla, goodfulla'.

The slaughterhouse had a fascination for us. The butcher went there and killed his bullocks, sheep and pigs, then he cut them up and put them in the window of his shop. What did they do with the blood?

Sunday was the day for slaughtering. I was at the swimming-hole talking to Audrey Lee and the other kids about the slaughterhouse. We could hear noises from up there. We decided to go up the creek bank and hide in the tall grass and watch.

There was a yard beside a covered-in section, and a chute where the bullock was run in and wedged between the rails so it couldn't move. There were three men. One climbed on top of the chute with a large spear-like piece of iron, and as the bullock was wedged in, the man rammed the spear into the bullock's brain behind the ears. Its knees sank then the whole body dropped to the ground. Another man in a big apron cut its throat and then they wound it up on a winch with pulleys. The butcher cut the stomach open and the guts tumbled out onto the floor. Everything was bloody. We sat quietly terrified.

In a while Audrey Lee got up and we followed her back to the swimming-hole. Nobody said anything. We got in the water and thrashed about as if we were washing the blood off ourselves. When we were sitting on the bank again Audrey Lee said, 'I'll never eat meat again. I can't believe it's so cruel.'

That didn't stop us tucking into the lamb chops a few days later but I never wanted to go near the slaughterhouse again. When we had bull calves Grandfather Sam and Dad and Uncle Sam hunted us away so we couldn't see what they were doing. The calves bellowed like mad. I didn't find out till I was older that they were knackering them and making them into steers. Uncle Sam fattened them up and sold them at the cattle sales each month.

Aunt Nell was an expert with a stockwhip. Every now and then she'd leave off her jobs in the house and come out and give us a demonstration. Slowly she lifted the whip then *crack*! It snaked in the air – *crack*! And spun the dust near us in a circle. 'Think you can do that?' she'd say, laughing, then she'd go back inside.

I didn't dare try the whip but since we'd seen the Khan brothers practising buckjumping for the show, I wanted to try that. Midge was keen. We took Gwen too and went into the cowyard. We put a flank-rope on one of the bull calves and tightened it to make it buck. We made Gwen be the rider. The calf was bellowing and bucking all around the yard. Gwen hung on then Aunty Nell looked out a window and came out cracking the stockwhip. Midge and I ran off and left Gwen bucking in the yard and the whip cracking round her ears.

I was coming home from Chiefy Pie's one afternoon when Audrey Lee came out of her house and pulled me up. She wanted to go looking for fruit at Lillypilly Creek.

'We'll make sandwiches and take the billy and go up Sunday,' she said. 'Tell all the kids.'

Audrey Lee and I had a habit of long hikes. We sometimes came across empty farmhouses and big trees still fruiting, we knew by now where to find things, and in what season.

When we turned up at her place on Sunday she said, 'Come in and see Joey.' In the backyard was their pet, a huge kangaroo they'd raised from a baby. Audrey Lee's father was bent over Joey's feet cutting his claws so he couldn't scratch us. In the silence of the early morning all you could hear was the metal of the clippers meeting and Joey making low noises in his chest. When Mr Lee bent down to do the back legs, Joey put his arms on Mr Lee's shoulders.

While we waited for Audrey's brothers and sisters to get ready for the picnic, we wandered around the yard looking at things, and being followed by Joey who was twice our height. When we stopped he'd stop. Sometimes he scratched himself under the arm like a thoughtful old man.

When the little kids were ready we trekked off. Over the hill from Chiefy Pie's place about half a mile out of town, we came to an old farmhouse near a creek bed with oranges and lemons, wild cherries, lilly pilly and willow trees growing. Audrey and I cut willow branches and tied them around our waists, draping them to make hula skirts. We put wild cherries and flowers in our hair and danced around singing 'To You Sweetheart, Aloha'.

26

The boys made a fire and boiled the billy. Hawaiian queens sat down and ate their sandwiches and then we played in the creek bed. In the afternoon we walked home with our billycans full of cherries for Aunt Nell to make pies.

Audrey tapped me on the shoulder and pointed behind us. I saw a dingo moving from bush to bush, following us. We didn't tell the little kids. We herded them in front of us all the way back up the hill to town, the bigger boys carrying lumps of wood and stones in case it came at us. But it was only curious, it probably had a mate and some young nearby. When we were off its territory, it stood and watched us silently.

Three weeks later Dad got off the bus at Marty Askew's shop with two suitcases. We climbed all over him and finally he put us down and opened the biggest case. There was a winter coat for me with fur around the cuffs and collar, there were dresses and pants for the others.

I didn't care that it was hot. I took the coat out to the front verandah and put it on. I reached my arms around the wistaria vine, thick as a tree trunk, and leaned back so all I could see when I looked up was the wistaria spreading on its trellis and bits of sky showing through. Then I sat on the step and looked out under the vine to two huge poplars at either side of the trellis, and the climbing roses around their trunks. The air was full of a sweet perfume, a cow mooed from down in the cowbale.

When I went inside Dad laughed and said, 'You'll be working up a sweat in that coat now Ruby, take it off.'

He stayed with us for two weeks and left for the Warragamba Dam.

In the summer time Aunty Nell sat in the hessian fold-up chair under the wisteria and fanned herself with her apron. We sat on the grass. Uncle Sam came out with a watermelon and cut it up. Later he got up from his chair and started to wrestle with us, then he jumped on Aunty Nell and rubbed watermelon in her face and then his sharp beard.

'Father, father,' she yelled, 'stop being such a torment!'

In March we heard from Dad that he'd got a job in Sydney. The letter was from his new place in Great Buckingham Street, and he was working at a furnace where they made springs. I knew my mother was somewhere in Sydney too, but there was no news of her. I wondered whether she and Dad would find each other, or whether he was looking for her. I knew she was living with another man, and would have other children by now. I tried not to imagine what they looked like, where they lived, what kinds of things my mother said to them.

Chiefy Pie came up to the house to ask if I could stay overnight. 'Mr Richards is away in Brisbane,' she said to Aunty Nell. 'He's gone to get the fruit and vegetables.' She didn't want to be on her own at night.

I took Jan home in the afternoon and did my chores.

I could hear the creak creak of her wooden horse on the verandah, then the sound of Jan's feet on the boards and Chiefy Pie's voice. She came in and said, 'Now I hope you don't mind. I get frightened at night.' She got out a flannel nightie for me and said I could sleep in the bed with her and Jan.

The next morning was a Saturday. I got up early and went outside to light the copper. Grey Marco appeared from round the corner of the house and nuzzled at my hand, looking for bread. He was the pony stallion champion of Bonalbo, and the other horse, Jack, had a hard mouth. He was never mouthed when he was broken in, and had to be ridden with a curbed bit.

In a while Chiefy Pie came out to boil up the clothes in the copper. She had her jodhpurs on, and stood there in the steam poking at the clothes with the pot stick. I was practising standing on my toes.

'Where did you learn to do ballet?' I said.

'In Gladesville, where I grew up.'

'Where's that?'

'Sydney, the big smoke.' She scooped the washing out with the stick and put it in the rinse water. I sloshed the sheets around and started to wring them out.

'How many people live there?' I said.

'In Sydney? I dunno. It's a very big place. There's the harbour, and a big bridge across it shaped like this –' (she drew an arc in the air) '– and tall buildings and Bondi Beach.'

'Do you know where Great Buckingham Street is?'

'No.'

I imagined Dad going off to work every morning at Henderson's Federal Springs, walking past the tall buildings and the Harbour Bridge.

I put the first load of wash in the basket and took it out to the line. As I reached up to hang the sheets I felt something butting at my back. He nudged and butted me towards the back steps, and pushed till I went inside to get him some bread. I could hear Chiefy Pie laughing.

After we finished the washing she decided to peroxide Grey Marco's mane for the show. The hair was already pale, but she wanted it silver blond. I sat on the steps and watched her get everything ready.

Past Chiefy Pie's shoulder I could see McQueen's dairy and the cows at the fence. Voices floated across from over the back, shouts and calls from the Khans' place where the boys were practising buckjumping for the show. They were an Indian family, and old Jimmy Junga was dead. His boys were the champion buckjump riders and they also did cattle draughting. I could see them in my mind, Jimmy and Johnny Khan in their cowboy clothes and Stetsons, their skin dark like ours.

When I looked back at Grey Marco, his mane was turning silver. Chiefy Pie stood there in her jodhpurs, watching, then turned to me and held out her hand. I walked across to her, took her hand, and we danced around the horse on our toes, flinging out our arms and legs, the hills circling us as we turned until everything was a blur of green and silver.

When I got back home that night, there was a mail order catalogue on the table. I always read these things. On the second page there was a mother-of-pearl brooch made in the shape of a leaf, with MOTHER written in gold lettering and underneath hanging by a small chain was a tiny heart, on which the Lord's Prayer was written so small you practically needed a microscope to read it. I thought to myself that this was the ideal present for Mother Nell, so I got a pen and paper and wrote away for it cash on delivery. The price was fourteen and sixpence.

It took me nearly a month of working for Chiefy Pie and running messages for threepence and sixpence till I'd saved enough. It'd be Mother's Day in a while. I never mentioned a word about it to anyone, and on the day it arrived I'd been waiting for the postman and I took it and hid it in a secret place. And it was worth all the secrecy, to see the look on Mother Nell's face when I gave it to her. 'Oh, Ruby.'

Behind her on the dresser were rows of jam and preserves ready to be put in boxes and taken to the show. Midge came in and said, 'Come and help me catch the bantams.'

'Midge, look at this.' Aunt Nell showed her the brooch and then we went outside and started to chase the bantams. There were two particular hens and two roosters we wanted to catch so we could oil their feathers and have them ready for the show.

The hens were brown with speckles on them and feathery legs. They had keen eyes and sharp beaks.

The two roosters were something else, their tail feathers were long and black and each one had yellow-and-rust coloured feathers and bright red cocks combs. Their spurs could draw blood and they were hard to catch.

Chiefy Pie was planning a picnic with her friend Margaret who lived on the next hill. She packed the things and knowing I liked to ride, sent me on ahead with the picnic basket on Jack. I went bareback, the basket in one hand and the reins in the other. Jack was a gelding and usually when horses are gelded they're more tame. Not Jack. He took the bit in his mouth and bolted.

I dug my knees in and pulled hard on the reins but as he galloped the basket banged hard on his flanks which made him go faster, until the basket rose up and opened mid-air and hard-boiled eggs, cordial, cake and sandwiches flew out across the hill.

From her verandah Chiefy Pie had seen Jack bolt, and when she saw her picnic in the air she jumped on Grey Marco and came after me.

I'd grown up all my life around horses and cattle – Grandfather Sam was a drover, Uncle Willie and his father old Tom Hinnett were horsemen, and Uncle Sam was the original flying angel, but I was shaken up that day.

Aunt Nell came in with a letter in her hand and sat down at the big table and looked at me.

'This is from Aunt Mary,' she said, 'my sister in Ballina. She's very sick, she needs someone to stay with her for company. So would you like to go and stay with her, because she's bedridden, you know, and can't do for herself.'

I looked up from my seat on the woodbox and said I'd go. 'It might only be for a few months. You know where Ballina is? It's right next to Cabbage Tree Island, where your people come from.'

I was enrolled in a convent school close to where Aunt Mary lived. I couldn't believe how many prayers we had to say. As soon as we came into the class and every time before we went out to morning lunch, and in the afternoon we said Hail Marys. If there was a burial service all the Sisters took off to the chapel and we had to pray till they came back.

I stayed with Aunt Mary for about six months. She knew she didn't have long to live, so she got the ambulance to take us all the way back home to Bonalbo, and she was admitted to the hospital there.

From the gate I could see the kids running up towards me, Midge and then the little ones. I hugged them all. In the house I laid my head on Aunty Nell's big apron and I heard Uncle Sam hobble in saying, 'What's this, mother? Is this the Big Noise home?'

I went out the side to the cowyard. There was my yellow cow Daisy and my black one Hobby, they were my favourites. There was a fawn one called Pansy and a red one, Strawberry, they came up to be patted too. The cows made it feel like home again and even though it was hard work, milking – and constant – I realised I'd missed the animals and tried not to think about them. I laid my head in their hides and breathed in.

One morning I sat up in bed and Midge threw a pillow at me. Soon the others had joined in, pillows and legs flying around on the big double bed, and we were making a hell of a racket. Aunt Nell appeared in the room and stood there till we stopped. 'Please be quiet,' she said, 'Aunt Mary's in the next room, she passed away last night.'

She unlocked the door and took us in to say our last goodbyes. The coffin was on a stand with the lid open. Aunt Mary looked like she was sleeping, we kissed her forehead and left the room.

I didn't know Aunty Nell was pregnant. Nothing about women's matters ever got mentioned, even between the women. The first thing I knew about the pregnancy was when Aunty Nell got off the bus at the end of Dyrabba Street with a baby in her arms.

When I was twelve going on thirteen I found some blood on my underdackers. I used to ride a boy's bike and I'd fallen on it a few times, I thought I'd hurt myself. When Aunty Nell was doing the washing she called me into her bedroom and told me a few pieces of information. Midge was there too, the younger kids got shunted away.

'You'll be getting these every month now. They're called monthlies, you have to wear pads and a belt. Now Ruby, you're not to mess around with boys, or you'll get into the family way.'

I looked up at her.

'You mustn't mention this to anyone.'

Midge was sitting on the bed smirking, she knew all about this women's business.

'Come here,' Aunty Nell said to Midge. She gave her some money and said to take me in to Mrs Brownfield the chemist and buy a packet of Modess and a sanitary belt.

When we got to the chemist Midge gave me the money and pushed me in the door. 'You get 'em,' she said. 'I'll wait here.'

There were a few people in the shop, waiting for scripts. Mrs Brownfield looked straight at me and said, 'Yes, Ruby.' I was trying to remember the words for the things I needed.

'One now, my box of Modess and one – uh, one dunnycan belt.' I said the word quick so it sounded like 'dunnygin', I knew it was something like that. The people in the shop laughed, Mrs Brownfield too.

When I got outside I whacked Midge on the side of the head with the Modess and took off up the street. In my head I called her every name I could think of.

One morning I was sitting in the tree when I heard a noise and looked down. It was Midge coming through the suckers. She was too big to climb up, so she called, 'Sst sst, Ruby!' This was the signal for me to tell her what was going on and who I could see.

The Khan brothers were riding down the stock route in their cowboy clothes and Stetsons, soon they'd pass the vacant lot heading into town. I told Midge to hide in the suckers and warned her when they were getting close. She let out a wolf whistle then a muffled giggle. 'Go on Ruby, you whistle.' I tried it too, and I could see the tops of their cowboy hats turning, trying to work out where the whistles were coming from. We laughed so much I had to hang on to my branch to stop rolling off.

That night Father Sam was late getting home from the pub and he came in hungry. 'Mother Nell, where's my tea?' he asked, and she said, 'It's out in the icebox, I'm not getting up to get it for you.' He hobbled out to the kitchen with a candle in his hand and he'd just opened the door of the icebox when he heard a noise over in the corner at the stove. He turned around to see what it was and nearly dropped the candle with fright.

Aunt Nell's mother's spirit was sitting at the stove stirring something in a pot, as much as to say, 'I'll get your tea, Sam.' And he took off back into the bedroom and was gasping for breath. He told Aunt Nell what had happened and she said, 'Well come home late again, Sam.'

That Christmas as usual we were on the back steps watching out for the bus to pull up at Marty Askew's shop. Suddenly Dad was there, and it looked like he had another little girl with him. We ran to meet him, we were amazed to see it wasn't a little girl but a little woman, who he told us was his lady friend. We were very shy with her at first. By the end of the day we could see she was a friendly person and we were happy for Dad. He'd been lonely for too long, and the little woman became our stepmother, Mum Joyce.

I'd finished sixth class and there was no high school in Bonalbo, so Dad had organised for me to be boarded with a family in Casino. While Dad and Mum Joyce were in the kitchen with Uncle Sam and Aunt Nell, I packed my new serge tunic, the white blouse, black stockings, and the sports tunic with white braid at the hem.

I went outside and looked at the cows. The milking would be Gwen's job now. I found her under a tree and sat down next to her.

'You worried about goin' away?' she said.

I didn't know whether I was or not. I couldn't think about Casino till I got there.

'Don't forget to rug the cows in winter,' I said. 'You know which rug belongs to which cow.'

She nodded.

'And if you can't find the cows in the afternoon they'll be out with Nowland's bull.'

'I know. I know where to find 'em.'

At six the next morning we left on the bus for Casino. Dad settled me in with Aunty Amy and Uncle Harry Pentland and they introduced me to the other four Koori kids who boarded there.

Dad took me out on the verandah and told me to write to him any time I needed money for books or clothes. He was still working at the Warragamba Dam and I was to write to him c/o Wallacia Post Office.

Back inside, he gave Aunty Amy some money for my board and then we waved him off. I felt a bit lost, I didn't want to talk to the other kids yet.

Uncle Harry took me into the lounge room and pointed up at a big photograph. It showed a man with feathers in his hat, a tall solidly built man in a uniform sitting on a horse.

'That's me,' he said, 'when I was a Light Horseman in the War.' He told me to call him Uncle Pent.

3

Ghost Riders in the Sky

Casino

The Pentlands' house was about two and a half miles out of town. I went out the door with Leila and Neil. They were in Primary and I was being enrolled in high school by the Hogan girls, Beatrice and Patty and Ethel. They lived over the road with their mother in a shack in Imerson's paddock where the steers were kept to slaughter. On the way I said to Neil and Leila, 'Where are your Mum and Dad?' and they said their Mum was dead and their father was away working.

When we climbed through the fence Neil said, 'You have to be careful going through here, the steers'll chase you. Make sure they're a long way off before you go across.' As soon as we got through the wire they started to run at us. We took off for the Hogans' place pretty fast. Neil introduced me to the three girls. Ethel was my age, and we were starting first year together.

The way to school was along the river bank. I knew that soon we'd be coming to the Bamboos, the place where I nearly drowned. 'This place is our swimming-hole,' Ethel said.

'I've been here a few times,' I said.

The high school was a big building across the road from the police station. The primary, where Neil and Leila went, was next door. Beatrice took Ethel and me to Mr Rubenach the Headmaster and we were enrolled. Then she took us to the tuckshop. I ordered one homemade meat pie and two boiled saveloys and it came to sixpence. You could also get iceblocks with chopped up fruit and coconut in for a penny. In the playground I met up with Olga Olive again. I'd known her when we were living up the river.

We walked home past the Bamboos every day, we hid our swimming togs there and went for a swim on the way home. Mango and guava trees grew everywhere and we ate the fruit as we walked.

The water was so clear you could see mullet and garfish swimming. In summer, at weekends, a whole bunch of us lived in the water. When it rained and the river was up, we waited till a big log came down and rode on it for miles downstream and then walked home. Sometimes there were platypus and snakes on the logs and we jumped off, swam for our lives to the bank.

Our class teacher was called Tiger McGee because he growled a lot. 'Now Ruby,' he'd growl when I handed in another ten-page composition, 'you're not here to write whole books. Two pages will do.' But he always read my stories and he also taught us how to tan hides. He sent some of the boys over to the abattoir to get some cattle hides. We put our aprons on and soaked the skins in wattle-bark solution and pegged them out. Now our project was to make toys out of these hides. Tiger McGee drafted out patterns for koalas and baby kangaroos and we set to work.

While we cut and sewed, he recited poems in the hot afternoons, or in the rain, and the poems nearly always matched the weather.

'Core of my heart, my country!' (he'd yell)
'Her pitiless blue sky –'

And we'd join in:

'When, sick at heart, around us
We see the cattle die –'

(Though ours weren't dying) – and later when we began to doze off (most of us had been up early milking.)

'How sleep the brave,' (he'd say)
'Who sink to rest …'

On my way home one afternoon I was passing the Rink Picture Show, which overlooked the riverbank, when I saw Grandfather Sam waiting on a seat bench under the trees in the park.

'Hello Grandfather, what are you doing here?'

'Hello goodfulla.' He patted the seat beside him and I

sat down. In a while he took some peppermints from his shirt pocket and offered me one.

'Good for your colds,' he said. We looked out at the park, white people with their children on the swings, the few black people around, the river passing under the willows. I chewed on my lolly and took another one.

'Where've you been?' I said.

'Droving. Kyogle. Dairy Flat. Down Coraki way. Listen goodfulla, I want you to write a letter to Dad, ask him to send me some money.'

I tore a few pages out of my exercise book and wrote for him, and posted it the next day. Grandfather Sam would wait around Casino until he heard from Dad, then he'd be gone and I wouldn't see him again until he wanted me to write another letter. He always appeared in the park, and then disappeared.

Sometimes I rode home from school on the bar of Olga Olive's bike. She was a year older than me. We went to the rollerskating rink, which was made of wooden boards. The next morning I had to press my serge tunic and I stood there with the tweezers countless times, plucking the splinters out of the cloth.

Olga was the only girl in her family and her brothers took some outwitting. The days when we walked home Bruce wanted to race us and he belted us over the head with his father's newspaper to make us run faster. 'Gunyam muggul,' we yelled. Olga and I climbed a tree and hid till he went past. Bruce grew up to play Big League for Newtown – he should have been able to play, he could run fast.

'You look like an orangutan,' Olga said one day, puffing, as she climbed up the tree after me. 'I can just imagine you with a tail.'

I told her about Uncle Ernie Ord and my totem, the willy wagtail. I told her how he could cure people by magic. Not long after this one of the Koori kids in the school (there were ten or twelve of us among a few hundred whites) came to me in the playground and said she'd heard I knew a man called Ernie Ord. I said I did. She said, did I know he died not long ago? I stared at her. 'Come on, I'll show you where he is,' she said. After school she took me to the cemetery and showed me his grave. The soil was raised up and fresh, it was a recent burial.

The girl went away and I sat down next to the grave and I stayed there a long time, until it got dark. Remembering Uncle Ernie, what a good mother he was, what a big jovial fellow, and then feeling sorry that in the ways of our people moving around I hadn't seen him for so long.

On Saturday we took a tom-axe to the river and cut some willow branches with knots in them, for hockey sticks. I was standing next to Mervyn Kenny, one of the kids Aunt Amy and Uncle Pent looked after. I called him Pug Mug, because of his nose. As we cut and trimmed I asked him where his parents were. He didn't really want to talk about it. I realised that all these kids had lost their parents. Pug Mug had two sisters called Margaret and Joyce, then there were Leila and Neil Walker. Someone had christened Neil 'nyunna', or 'Nyunna Foot Fat Fart'.

While we were there the Hogan girls came up with their cousin Reggie Gordon and we cut some for them. We climbed back up, ran through the steers' paddock and crossed the road to our place. In front of the house was a big paddock that used to be a market garden. We found a tennis-ball and played hockey with our willow branches. At first the ground was rough and rutted from the plough but we soon flattened it for a good field. Kids from all around heard us yahooing and came to join the game – the Townsends, Mona, Neil and Sammy, then the Freeburns – Harry, Mona, Cynthia and Kevin. Just when we'd got the teams reorganised the Olive kids turned up with their willow sticks, Olga and her brothers Reggie, Bruce (Burly), Jimmy, Keith and Dollar.

We played hard, hockey one hockey two hockey three, and then you'd hear the voices calling, floating up:

'Hey Rangi, Dollar, this way!'

'Go Burly, go go go!'

'Nyunna, nyunna here.'

'Here foot.'

'Here fart, over this way.'

'Ru – beee!' This was Aunt Amy's voice, calling me to do messages for her at the corner store. When I reached the paddock gate I saw a little boy pedalling like mad on a small two-wheel bike. When he noticed me he screeched to a stop.

'I know who you are,' he said.

I was taken by surprise. 'How do you know who I am?' I said. 'I've never seen you before.'

'You're my tita,' he said, holding out a packet of lollies in his grubby little hand.

'What's your name?'

'George,' he answered, and pedalled away.

Then the memories came flooding back. This was our little brother Mum had before she left us in Coraki. This was the baby wrapped up in a blanket and taken in the taxi.

I stood and watched the boy ride up to the Webbs' place. He had sandy brown hair, like mine, and a plump face. He had hazel green eyes like Eddie Webb.

When I came back from the shop, I joined in the hockey game again. The little kids sat on the edge of the field with a man who lived nearby called Old Roy. He knew Dad from when they were mates timber-getting in the Taloome scrub near Mount Lindsay. He sat and watched us, and sometimes in a pause in the game I saw him take one of the little kids on his knee and then he sang in the lingo, Old Roy, sitting at the edge and singing about Mount Lindsay.

In school we recited a poem about a dingo, 'The Warrigal':

'The warrigal's lair is pent in bare

black rocks at the gorge's mouth –'

And when we looked out the windows we saw Clancy with his thumbnail dipped in tar, and Andy crossing for the cattle, and the Man from Snowy River galloping up the rise. Through the same windows we saw the Lady of Shalott, we saw the solitary reaper, the deserted village, the swains and bowers and the golden sheaves, and behind that the boys' toilets and the woodwork room.

During the breaks I usually sat with my nose in a book. I was obsessed with learning and I had this idea that if I read my history and geography books over and over again I could train my memory. I sat there repeating the words to myself until I knew it, and when I took my tests in the auditorium I wrote the answers to the questions exactly as they were in the books.

When they marked the exams, the teachers thought I was cheating. I had to do the whole test again, under strict supervision. Finally they admitted I hadn't cheated but had really trained my memory. Tiger McGee shook his head at me and grinned.

By Christmas we were finished the koalas and kangaroos and we parcelled them up and sent them away to some underprivileged children.

That summer we swam at the Bamboos again and at weekends we got out the bikes and doubled each other out to Mrs Williams' place where there was a big swimming-hole. I made friends with Mrs Williams' daughter Betty, who was taller and darker than me, and had a thick black plait. We swam across the deep hole with the little kids on our backs. I carried Betty's sister Margaret, who grew up to be the second Aboriginal school teacher to graduate. Some days we sat on the bank fantasising about having our own kids, and some days we talked about going to the city and having a good time when we grew up, little knowing we'd meet in Sydney one day and dress up and go to dances.

One morning Uncle Pent came out onto the verandah and said, 'I think that's your Dad.' I looked up and there they were climbing down from the bus, Dad with Gwen and Rita. We were going to Cabbage Tree Island for Christmas – this was where most of our people lived, including some of Dad's brothers and sisters. Uncle Sam was coming over from Bonalbo to meet us there. All I knew was that the island was in the Richmond River, near the mouth. I said goodbye to Uncle Pent and Aunty Amy and all the kids. Pug Mug stood in the corner looking unhappy.

We crossed the road to the Greyhound stop and the bus was to take us to Lismore then back through Ballina and on to the wharf for Cabbage Tree. It wasn't long before Gwen and Rita had gone to sleep. I looked across their heads at Dad and said, 'I met my brother. His name's George.'

Dad nodded. 'I've seen him a few times,' he said.

'He lives at the Webbs'.'

'I know.'

'Is Eddie Webb his father?'

Dad shifted in his seat, pretending to rearrange Rita on his lap. 'Well, he lives with them.'

'Do you know where our mother is?'

'I think she's still in Sydney.'

'Is Eddie Webb with her?'

'Probably. Ruby –' he moved Rita again and seemed to be hugging her tight. He didn't finish his sentence. We looked out the window at the trees flashing past and after a while Dad started to talk to me quietly about school, and other ordinary things. When we got to the wharf for Cabbage Tree, I couldn't see anyone around. Dad looked across the channel, cupped his hands round his mouth and called, 'Hey – bring – the – booo – ooat – o – ver.' He did this twice, his voice disappearing over the water. We waited. In a while we saw a rowboat coming towards us. The island was about six hundred metres away.

When we climbed out on the other side, I saw the island was a mission. There was a small schoolhouse, the (in those days white) manager's house, a hall and about fifteen houses, each one opening onto the water and with its own boat moored. Uncle Bob and Aunty Winnie lived right over the other side. Behind their place was a back channel about fifty metres across to the mainland, where there was a caravan owned by an old Indian lady named Mrs Singh. She sold lollies and ice cream, and there was a boat tied up so kids could go over from the island.

Dad took us to some of the other houses to visit his sisters, Aunty Kate and Aunty Phyllis. Aunty Phyllis lived with the Marlowe family. She had dimples and a missing finger, and long black wavy hair. She was a good knitter – especially cable stitch. She was nineteen years old and took a liking to me, so I was invited to go up the back channels the next day with them to get bananas.

It was the second time I'd been in a boat. This one had Phyllis, three of the Marlowes and me in, and that felt like a lot of people. Aunt Phyllis put a tin dipper in my lap. We rowed across to the mainland and then up along one of the irrigation channels that ran between the farms. They moored the boat and we climbed out and went into the plantation. This was a banana raid. Not only that, but there were rockmelon and watermelon growing between the rows of bananas, so we collected a pile of them too. By the time we loaded ourselves and the fruit into the boat, the rim was only a few inches above the water, and now I knew why I'd been invited along. I was the bailer! The nearer we came to the island the deeper we sank into the channel. I bailed and they laughed, but my knees were shaking when we got out and I didn't want to go raiding fruit again.

A few days later Uncle Sam turned up, and then Grandfather Sam came over, stepping off the boat tall and rangy, and hugging his two big sons. He was the sweetheart of the women and the envy of the men because he was so good at cricket. A match was organised for Boxing Day but in the meantime everyone settled in for a talk and a drink. It was the first time this mob had been together in years – Grandfather Sam and five of his kids. Grandfather was a widower; my grandmother Mabel Anderson had died when I was little.

I'd never seen Dad drunk before. I was happy he was with all his family again, but he was embarrassed to be so sozzled. He looked at me from under his eyebrows and called me aside. Then he put his arm around my shoulders and leaned down unsteadily to look at me.

'Tell your little sisters Santy won't be coming this year,' he said. He looked out at the island, the cabbage tree palms and the houses and the upturned boats in the heat.

'Tell them we're too far –' and he hesitated and sat down on a stump.

'– from the North Pole,' I prompted.

'– and that – reindeers can't swim.' He shook his head sadly. I could hardly keep a straight face.

'The kids know reindeers can fly,' I said.

He looked up at me grinning and shaking his head, the sun on his face.

'Just say he can't come this year.' He opened his hands to the sides. Uncle Bob was passing by and put a fresh bottle in Dad's hand. The party around us was getting rowdy, there were kids shouting and leaping on to each other in the water, and the grown-ups were walking into each other's arms and hugging and cracking jokes.

Dad reached into his pocket and said, 'Here's some money, take the others over to Mrs Singh and buy some lollies.' I had to laugh, he was so goggle-eyed and so were Grandfather and Uncle Sam and Uncle Bob.

On Boxing Day everything was packed up and all the people went out in boats across to the other side and headed towards the beach. We were running along the sand dunes and stuffing ourselves with pig face, a salty fruit which grew in the sand. The older ones had fires going and were cooking boilers of pippies that you could smell for miles. The men played cricket on the sand and kept an eye on the kids swimming. The beach wasn't patrolled so we had to be careful.

When I looked up from our game I saw Dad way off in the water. He'd been swept out in a rip and one of the older men who was a strong swimmer brought him back in. Dad stood there shaking and dripping, a skinny man, straight up and down like a drink of water. Later he got big like a side of beef, not flabby but a big solid fella.

A few days later I watched a cricket game between Grandfather and his three sons. It was a hot day and they were playing hard, concentrated. Grandfather, who was in his sixties then, played for the Richmond Tweed side and they called him the Bungawalbyn crack. He could out-bowl, out-bat anyone; he could flip the bails to make like he'd caught people out. He had a way of catching the ball and bringing it to crack the stumps all in one smooth motion of the arm, like sleight-of-hand.

My father and uncles had no chance of an even game and finally they threw the bat in. They knew he'd beaten them, they had the huffs with him and refused to play any more. He stood there on the sand with the sun going down behind him and calling, 'Come on goodfullas, come and play your Dad cricket. Come on, goodfulla.' Years later I remember him, a tall thin figure, the way he said those words and his voice calling and drifting across the sand. There was a grin on his face and the sun falling behind him like a giant ball in slow motion. 'Come on, goodfulla.'

The next year Ethel Hogan was captain of the hockey team and I was captain of the vigoro. By now we were best friends. She was vice-captain of the vigoro and I was vice-captain of the hockey. We travelled to Lismore and to Grafton and on the bus we warmed ourselves up with the war cry:

'Mum, Mummelgum, Mummelgum, gum gum
Kanga, Hopiji, Cherriworri, Whipori
Try and beat Casino High, Yah!'

The names are all towns. Mummelgum's not far away from Bonalbo, and sometimes when we set up the chant I'd stop and look out the window and think of all those small towns and wish I was back in Bonalbo. At Casino High there were only about twelve Koori kids, the rest – a few hundred – were white. We were doing okay though; we were doing all right. We were class captain and sports captain, we ran the fastest, wrote the longest stories, and Beatrice Hogan was dux of fifth year. Lismore and Grafton didn't like to see us arriving with our hockey sticks.

Tiger McGee told us about the old sailor who stopped the wedding guest with his glittering eye and we chanted:

'Water, water, everywhere,
And all the boards did shrink
Water, water, everywhere,
Nor any drop to drink.'

But the poem I liked best was about a churchyard in England (Gray's 'Elegy') and for some reason I memorised this part:

'Full many a gem of purest ray serene
The dark unfathom'd caves of ocean bear:
Full many a flower is born to blush unseen,
And waste its sweetness on the desert air.'

In class I always said this part the loudest and Tiger McGee always gave me a strange look.

At lunchtime I went to the Assembly Hall and messed around on a German-made piano called a Wurlitzer. I started with 'Twinkle Twinkle' and progressed to 'Believe Me, If All Those Endearing Young Charms'. Tiger McGee came in one day and showed me how to do the bass, then he told me the correct fingering for the scales. We started up a class band, clarinet, violin, saxophone and piano. I learnt to read music enough to follow easy tunes.

One weekend I was on the track leading down to the Bamboos. The water was shallow at first then it deepened. Across the other side of the swimming-hole was a huge tree that had been uprooted in the floods years before, we used it to dive off. Leila and Neil and Ethel were there, Ethel's friend Cynthia, and Harry were diving off the trunk. When we started a game of tag I decided to dive off, swim right under the trunk (about ten feet across), come up the other side and hide out in the willows. I did this a few times and then I came face to face with an eel.

I turned around and back-pedalled so fast you'd think the devil was chasing me, I never swam under that tree trunk again.

Harry had climbed up the steep part of the bank and gone home to get something. He came back with cardboard boxes and we opened them out and took a section each. We climbed up to the top, sat on the cardboard, gave ourselves a shove and slid right down into the water.

When we'd had enough of that, we girls went up the bank to the trees, which grew big bean pods. We called them saccalene beans. We collected armfuls of them and waited for the boys to come looking for us and then we bombarded them.

In October the fifth year students started coming in to practise for the Debutantes' Ball, and the man who was organising them asked me to play waltzes for them. The night of the Ball came and I went with Olga Olive and the Hogan girls. It was being held in the Casino Memorial Hall. When we arrived there were balloons and flowers and streamers everywhere and a red carpet ran from the stage down the centre of the hall for all the debutantes to walk on after they were presented to the Lord Mayor. I watched and they danced and everything went well, but then I was sent for by the organiser to go up on the stage.

I had no idea what was going on. I waited in the wings

while he was talking over the mic, and he suddenly said, 'I'd like to thank our little pianist Ruby Anderson for playing for our practice sessions,' and he called me out on to the stage. People began to applaud. I walked out with my head down, said thank you and started to leave. The organiser grabbed my arm and made me walk right down the red carpet. I got about a third of the way and then I ran for it.

At the end of my second year Dad came to pick me up at school. He told me I had a stepbrother, he and Mum Joyce had a new baby called Dennis. The baby was blond and blue-eyed, so now we had a real mix. I told him about the flower in the desert air, the hockey games, playing waltzes for the debutantes, how I ran down the red carpet, how I met the eel, how I trained my memory.

He took me up to the headmaster's office and told me to wait on the bench outside. I heard Dad asking him about my progress, and then Mr Rubenach's voice saying he wanted me to go on to third year and do my Intermediate Certificate. Dad said he didn't know about that. Mr Rubenach said I should then go on to teachers' college, the reasons being I was a class captain and school prefect and had come first in my class again.

I sat on the bench, my head buzzing. Every teacher I'd ever seen was white. I tried to imagine black kids being taught by black teachers, then I tried to imagine white kids with black teachers.

'Why not?' Mr Rubenach was saying. 'She's made very good progress, and there's no reason to think she won't continue. The Aborigines' Protection Board would put her through College –'

'No thanks,' my father said in a dry voice, 'if she wants to go to teachers' college she'll get there under her own steam and not through the help of the Aborigines' Protection Board.'

They said some more in quiet voices and then Dad came out and took my arm. He was a very proud man. He looked like a big detective – he always wore a hat and a large gaberdine overcoat. He shook the headmaster's hand and told me to do the same.

Out on the street, he asked if I'd heard what they said. 'Most of it.'

'I don't know about third year. You decide about that. But I'm not having any protection board put you through college. All the protection they've done so far is take people from their land and split up families.'

He marched ahead of me to the bus stop, but in a while his mood changed. He was a man who rarely smiled but when he did his whole face lit up, and now he was hugging me and saying he was proud I'd done so well.

The Kooris in Casino were a very go-ahead lot of people. They had their own football teams and used to hold dances and balls. They also organised buses and trucks to take the whole Aboriginal population of Casino away at Christmas time to Yamba.

Uncle Pent and Aunty Amy were the main ones who organised the holiday, and they asked Dad if I could go with them that year. He agreed. That afternoon he got the bus to Bonalbo to spend Christmas there, and I started packing for Yamba.

There was a truck loaded with camping gear and food, and a bus for all the people. When we got to Yamba the adults pitched the sleeping tents in a huge circle and in the centre a big tent for a galley, with rows of tables and stools. About a hundred metres away was the beach and a huge cliff face jutting out into the sea.

Every morning you could hear a woman further up the beach, singing in the lingo. The boys got up early before the tide went out and came back with fish they'd caught stranded between the rocks. There were bream and schnapper and all sorts, which made for good eating. At night around campfires the boys played guitars and we sang. It was all very romantic. I had a bad crush on a boy called Reggie Gordon who called me Ando and acted off-hand.

Early one morning I was walking along the beach and again I heard the woman singing, chanting on high notes, calling out. It was someone from the Maclean mob at Yamba, they said. In a while I could see her, quite an old woman, very black, standing on the top of the cliff.

I walked along listening to my feet squeaking in the sand and the woman singing above me. A fisherman who'd come from the mission near our camp walked past me and I asked him what the woman was doing. He said she was calling the porpoises in, she did it every day during the holidays. The porpoises circled the beach all day while the people were swimming, and headed out to sea when everyone was gone. He told me there'd never been a shark attack on that beach.

I looked up at the woman again. I didn't know whether to believe the old man or not, but the porpoises circled the beach every day we were there.

On the third day we were playing French cricket, a game of tipping one another under the hand and running away. When it was my turn to run I collided with a boy called Hunk and went over on my ankle. I came down hard in a heap on the sand. My leg was badly sprained and I missed out on the games for the rest of the holiday. People had to help me everywhere I went – to the galley, to the loo; to the beach where I sat in envy of the fun going on – swimming, tug-o-wars, cricket.

I turned fifteen in January the year I would have gone on to do my Intermediate Certificate, but Dad had a lot of worry on his mind raising up us kids and I thought, what the heck, he'd been supporting me all this time and it was only fair I get a job and help out. So I went back to Bonalbo.

I went to work house-cleaning for old Mr Furlonger, the solicitor. He had a grown-up daughter who won a prize for writing a children's book called *The Bunyip Hole*.

I also worked for the butcher, Jim McQueen, cleaning his house and cooking the evening meal for his sons.

Each month on cattle sale days I worked at the hotel as a chambermaid, and helped the cook when the kitchen was busy. I peeled spuds while Mrs Watts made steak-and-kidney pies and caramel-meringue tarts. One morning while I was helping the publican's sister hang washing, one of the house cows calved in the yard. The sister was a city person and nearly had fits. 'I'll never eat butter or milk again,' she said, dropping the peg bag as she ran towards the verandah.

Thirty-seven years and nine kids later, and after I'd been living in the city for a long time, I came back to Bonalbo to visit and stayed at that pub. It stands exactly as it was then, and on the verandah is the same wooden seat with its wrought-iron legs and old-timers sitting in the sun, their dogs between their legs.

Mr and Mrs Peter Bull needed someone to look after their two little girls. They owned a small farm about three miles out of town. Mrs Bull was a nursing sister and Mr Bull worked on the sawmill in town; they went in every day in the sulky. I was to be like a housemaid and clean house, bath the kids and put the vegetables on for tea. The farmhouse was on a hill overlooking Gorge Creek and I had my own room.

From the verandah I could see the Grays' farmhouse and barns and their cows grazing. All these farms were dairies, and I watched the truck calling at each farm to pick up the big cream cans to be taken to the Norco factory in town to make butter. I stood there in the afternoon facing the creek and wishing I could go home to Uncle Sam and Aunt Nell's – three miles seemed a long way then.

I stood very still and watched the sky starting to bruise with a storm blowing up. The colour of everything changed, and a few drops of rain hit the tin roof and then a giant crack of lightning struck a dead tree. I'd never seen that before, it was a mass of flames and it burned for days.

I took the pony down to the creek to water him each afternoon. One time when he stooped down to drink, a wild cat jumped out of the bushes and startled him, and I got thrown. There were a lot of carpet snakes sunning themselves on the banks.

After a while I was allowed to borrow the pony to ride home at weekends. I arrived just on dusk and Uncle Sam was on the back steps calling out, 'Hey Mother, here comes our little heifer who works for the Bulls.' He was such a torment. He helped me unsaddle the pony and he was still passing cakes out the door and blaming it on the fairies.

Sometimes when I rode home there was a storm blowing up and the hit song at the time, 'Ghost Riders in the Sky', crossed my mind as I watched the clouds roll overhead. I rode like mad to get home before the storm broke. It was three miles and I could scare myself silly. I looked down in the creek and saw heaps of carpet snakes and that scared me more and the song kept going through my mind:

'An old cowpoke went riding out
One dark and windy day
Upon a ridge he rested

As he went along his way
When all at once a mighty herd
Of red-eyed cows he saw
A-coming up a ragged cloud
And up a crowded draw'

'Yippi hi – oh yippi hi ay,
Ghost riders in the sky –'

Then the lightning would strike and thunder would boom and I'd ride like the devil was after me and wouldn't stop until I hit our back gate, then I'd let out a sigh of relief and say to myself, 'SILLY GIRL', for being scared of a storm, but I suffered with an overworked imagination, and then some. I had to make the trip back after the weekend was over, and I'd be wishing like hell that no storm would be blowing, and try to change my thoughts to more pleasant things.

I got my first proposal when I was fifteen years old. It wasn't from Reggie Gordon, the boy who'd serenaded me at Yamba, but from Mervyn Kenny, the boy I called Pug Mug, one of the children who lived at the Pentlands. He often wrote to me from Casino when I was living at the Bulls.

When the Casino teams came to play football in Bonalbo at weekends, we met at the games. Just before I left there to go to Sydney with Dad, Mervyn proposed to me in a letter. I was flattered but I was only fifteen and had a lot of living to do yet.

4

The Bodiless Woman

Redfern

Hundreds of smoking chimney stacks; rows of houses squeezed together; a neon sign showing a man in a little aeroplane and some musical notes and then the words lighting up, 'I like Aeroplane Jelly'. We ran from one carriage to the next, looking out the windows. We seemed to be travelling miles and miles to get to Sydney, and didn't realise we were already on the outskirts.

Dad and Mum Joyce had a one-bedroom flat at 22 Great Buckingham Street in Redfern. Gwen and I shared a three-quarter bed on the balcony and at the other end was a kitchenette. The main room had a fold-out table, the big bed, double bunks for the boys, and the wardrobe where Dad kept his money.

I went to work as an apprentice machinist at Brachs' clothing factory in Elizabeth Street. It was a long room with a bench running down the middle and about twenty-five women sitting at their machines on either side of the bench, facing each other. The owners were

Jewish people and their daughter Topsy Brachs, who was a model, was sent to show me my job.

I'd never seen an electric sewing machine before, I was used to Aunt Nell's treadle. This monster roared as soon as I touched the foot pedal and took off across the cloth like a steam train. All that morning I was terrified of it, and at lunchtime Mrs Brachs came and told me that as well as learning to be a machinist I was to be the messenger girl, to make a list and go and collect the morning teas and lunches in a big cardboard box. In the afternoon I calmed down about the power machine and watched how to put a pair of trousers together.

Mum Joyce took great care of Dad. He'd been on his own for years, working the bulldozer at the Warragamba Dam, but now he had a home and family again. He never knew what it was like to come home from work without a hot meal and the table set up. He had a chest of drawers, his shirts were pressed neatly and packed away with his socks and underwear. He had captained a cricket team at Tempe for a number of years and his cricketing whites were kept immaculate in the wardrobe.

We kept asking Dad where our mother lived, and if we could go to see her. I wanted to see what she looked like. He told us she lived in Waterloo, but we'd never been to Waterloo, how far was it? 'She didn't want you kids, so stay away,' he said. He wasn't having any more of this conversation. I went on machining trousers and wondering about her and whether she had other kids and trying not to think about it.

Gwen was enrolled at Bourke Street High School. The kids who went with her were Owen Ramjan and Peter Maroon. Owen was a Fijian kid who lived in the same flats as ours and Peter lived up the street. They were always together like our gang. One day Gwen came in crying and said, 'Dad, Peter Maroon said I got TB, arrrgh, arggh, sob.' Dad said, 'You wait till I see him, I'll kick his gunyam, the little bugger. Saying you've got tuberculosis.'

A few days later Dad ran into Peter down the back lane. 'Why did you say Gwen's got TB, Peter?' and the kid was terrified because Dad was going to kick his bum and he stuttered and stammered, 'I didn't mean it that way Mr Anderson, I meant she's got "two beauts"' – and pointed to his breasts. Dad burst out laughing and came up the stairs in stitches.

On Saturday morning I went to Paddy's market and got a heap of corn cobs and a piece of silverside. While it was cooking Dad fished out some corn – cob after cob – and stood there eating and grinning. 'Don't you eat all my corn,' I said, 'before it's even ready.' He couldn't help himself, he said, it reminded him so much of Bonalbo and the corn cookouts. 'Have you ever tasted anything like it?' His eyes lit up as he reached for another one. 'So sweet, and so salty.'

After lunch Gwen and I went to the matinee at the Empire Picture Theatre in Cleveland Street. A figure in a scarlet cloak and a black mask rode around saving people from trouble, he was the Scarlet Horseman.

In *The Perils of Pauline* the heroine was on the railway track and the baddies almost won out.

Back at home we gave our signal, a three-note whistle, and the key would be thrown down from the balcony.

A few months later, it was after Gwen and I had been talking about our mother (I'd told her about the Evelyn photo, 'You are my Sunshine'; 'Tell me what she looked like,' Gwen said, 'try and remember exactly.'), I was dreaming that Gwen was climbing over the balcony. I woke up suddenly and she had one leg over and was really climbing out. I grabbed at her, screaming with fright, 'Gwennie what are you *doing?*' before I realised she was still asleep. Dad called out, 'What's the matter, Ruby?' and I dragged Gwen back and woke her up. Dad came in and said you must never yell at a sleepwalker, but wake them gently.

'Gently,' I said, 'I thought she'd fall and kill herself!'

'Then try not to be too frightened yourself,' he said, 'it makes it worse.'

I decided to have my page-boy haircut changed, so I went down Botany Road and had a perm. The shop smelled of chemicals and singed hair. Outside I walked along looking at the reflection of my new head in every shop window. I felt different because I felt like a grown woman.

Coming down the street was a part of Casino I thought I'd never see again, Betty Williams, with her thick black plait.

'Betty,' I yelled, planting a kiss on her cheek and wrapping my arms around her neck. She stepped back and looked at me.

'Jesus, Ruby, I thought you were a moggi.'

'It's me.'

'Yeah, I see that.'

'How does it look?'

'I'll get used to it.'

We walked arm in arm down the street till we came to the house where she lived with a Maltese family. In her room was a dressmaker's dummy and a sewing machine. She opened her cupboard and showed me her new clothes, a black taffeta half-circle skirt and a dolman sleeve sweater.

'On Friday,' she said, 'we'll go down to Sussex Street to the Ironworkers Union and dance the night away.' She swept me up and waltzed me round the dummy and out into the hall.

When I got home Dad covered his mouth and shook his head. Everyone was trying not to laugh. 'Look at you! What a fright!' Gwen said, hopping round me.

Dad bought me my first pair of high heels for my birthday. They had cross-over straps and platform soles. I bought a black taffeta half-circle skirt and a dolman sleeve sweater to go with it. That Friday I went in to get dressed but my new clothes were gone. I rushed to the window and saw Gwen dressed up and tottering round the corner. 'Gwennie,' I screamed, 'come back with my things!' but she'd disappeared. I was so mad I could've throttled her. When Dad came home I told him, and Gwennie got a slap and didn't speak to me for days.

That night Betty came by to take me to the dance. She looked at my clothes and grinned.

'Hello Mr Anderson,' she said to Dad.

'Hello Betty, how's the family in Casino?'

While they were talking I went to the bathroom and put on my Mariposa lipstick, and Three Flowers talcum down my front.

It wasn't pay-day yet, so I asked Dad if we could borrow a pound. He pointed to his handbag in the wardrobe and said, 'Take what you want, and make sure you put it back on pay-day.' On the street Betty took my arm and said, 'Well Andy, our first Sydney dance.'

'Well Willy, we smell good enough to eat.'

We paid a shilling for the train ride to Sussex Street, and inside we stood on the edge and watched. Most of the dancers were Kooris and there were some gubbs. After what seemed a long time, two young blokes, Kooris, came over and started to talk.

'You two related?' the tall one said, looking at our skirts.

Willy grinned. 'Sisters,' she said.

The first night we only danced twice, but every Friday after that we danced all night. Willy was a qualified tailoress. Whenever she made clothes for herself, she made me the same.

In the summer Gwennie and some of the kids from the flats played cricket in the back lane. A few doors down was an SP bookie, and when Dad went down to place a few bets he'd bowl for the kids. 'Hey Mister Anderson, come on, it's your turn!' When I saw him showing Gwen the way to googly bowl, I thought of Grandfather Sam calling out, 'Go-oodfulla, come on goodfulla!'

Counting kids, there were nineteen people in the flats who shared the bathroom and laundry. We had a certain day to do our washing. When Mum was sick, Dad went down to the laundry with an old towel wrapped around his waist, and boiled the clothes up in the copper and wrung them out. He wasn't going to let the neighbours see him hanging them out because he reckoned that was women's work, so that was left to Gwen and me.

At this time Dad worked at Henderson Federal Springs where he stayed for ten years. His job was near a furnace, rolling eyes in springs. Cars drove in to have their springs changed and the workmen made money on Dad. They'd bet the customers that Dad could lift the blacksmith's anvil, and he would do it to oblige.

Near the end of his time at this job, he had a coronary, and he died of a heart attack at the age of forty-four. He was a man who worked too hard, had a lot of stress, and who lifted the anvil for white men to win bets.

But at this time we thought he would live forever. He worked without a shirt on because of the heat and ended up two-toned, the top half of his body burned black and the lower half tan. When he came in from work one day looking serious I said, 'Look at you, your face would stop a train.'

'Mine might stop a train my dear,' he said, 'but yours would make one run off the line,' and then we were laughing.

At weekends he lay down on our bed on the balcony in his shorts to try and get the same colour all over.

'Why haven't you got any grey hair, Dad?' I asked.

'I always rinse my hair in cold water,' he said.

'You look so handsome.'

'I know.'

We punched and tormented him, we danced around him singing 'Brylcreme, a little dab'll do ya!'

And although we were happy with Dad, I knew we'd eventually run into our mother, and I knew he didn't want us to see her. All the time I wondered where she was, whether she was in the next street, how many kids she had now. So there was always some tension in the air.

On Saturdays we went shopping on Botany Road for the weekend vegetables and groceries. It was an outing we looked forward to, browsing through the shops, and there were a lot of Kooris there, it was our area. One Saturday, loaded up with lettuce and potatoes, and Dad saying hello to this person and that, we saw a woman with two little girls coming towards us. She burst out crying and ran up to Gwen and me. Dad pushed us behind him and was suddenly shouting at her.

'You stay away from my kids,' he yelled, 'you didn't want them when they were little, just clear off.'

We hardly knew what was happening. He reached round behind him and took our hands and herded us away.

Back at the flat, numb with shock, Gwen and I sat on our chairs. I stared at Dad and he stared at the wall. Little Mum Joyce sat down at the table and put her hand on Dad's arm.

'Henry, you shouldn't stop the girls from seeing Evelyn. She's their mother.'

Dad shook his head. His teeth were set.

At the trouser factory, sitting at my machine, I kept thinking about the two little girls. They were our sisters, and maybe we'd never know them. I found out later that she had another boy, and the girls were named Dorothy and Margaret, the boy was Robert, and counting George, the little boy on the bike at Casino, there were four children she'd had to Eddie Webb.

Much later I became friends with my mother, but it was hard work because she was distant at first, having cut off from us to bring up her new family. My father never forgave her because he'd idolised her when she was young, and couldn't believe she would go off suddenly, in the night like that with another man, while he (Dad) was away working in the bush. But because Mum Joyce had a softer attitude, Dad and my mother finally treated each other as friends, and visited and ate meals together.

My sisters never were able to really forgive Mum, and the things they needed from her later she couldn't give, because her priority had to be her new family. But somehow I wanted to be friends with her, and one night years later at one of our Aboriginal Balls, I was tanked up, I saw her across the room looking dressed up and very beautiful as she was then, and being drunk and not caring what I said I went to her table and sat myself down and raised my glass to her, and I said, 'I thank you for every breath I take.'

Straightaway she put her head in her hands and burst into tears. I thought she'd misunderstood me.

'Look, I love you,' I said. And she went on crying, whether it was finally a softness she felt, or guilt, I don't know, but later again in her old age we spent a lot of time together and talked and it's true I look very similar to her though my nature is more like my father's.

But in those early days Dad took a hard line, and I didn't see Mum again for months. We went on with our lives at Great Buckingham Street. On Sundays Dad took us to watch the Redfern All Blacks at the oval. We sat on the hill among all the other Kooris, and Sunday night we went to Miss Ackland's church in Redfern Street. She was an AIM missionary and taught Sunday School too. At Christmas Gwen and I sang at church parties for the kids.

Friday and Saturday nights in Redfern everyone met at the picture theatre in Lawson Street. Those days, you hardly saw Kooris in pubs, because liquor was prohibited. People who did go to pubs had to show a Dog Licence ('Citizen's Rights') and if a white person was caught supplying liquor to blacks he was given six months without the option of a fine. Aboriginals were all right to join the services and fight for the country that we had no say in, but you couldn't breast a bar with your mates for a beer. The Dog Licence was a product of the Aborigines' Protection Board. And now I understood why Dad was so against the idea of the Board funding me to go to teachers' college. The main function of the Aborigines' Protection Board was to discriminate against Aborigines.

Palms Milk Bar in Botany Road was a place for all the Koori teenagers. There'd be heaps of kids there. He had pinball machines and made the best milkshakes in Sydney, or so we thought. Many a love affair started at the Palms Milk Bar.

Some Sundays in summer the Aboriginal population of Redfern hired buses to go on picnics to the National Park, loaded up with cameras and swimming gear. You could catch the bus in front of the Lawson Picture Theatre.

The All Blacks held dances and Presentation Balls in Redfern Town Hall. Gwen was Belle of the Ball once, when she was a telephonist, in a borrowed dress. I still have the photo of the ball. I nicked it from her a long time ago.

From my work at Brachs' I saved some money and just before the Easter Show I bought a blue dress and a white hat, handbag and shoes. Mum Joyce and Dad were going up to Walcha, where Mum had come from. Dad gave us strict instructions not to go to the show. 'You girls don't know your way around yet, and you might get lost, so stay home!'

After they left, Gwen said, 'Come on, let's sneak out, we'll find our way all right.'

72

She waited, I said nothing.

'Look, the trams go all the way out there, we can catch one down on Cleveland Street.'

'Okay,' I said, 'let's get ready.' We didn't have curlers, so I set her hair up in rags. Her head was all bits of black and white, like a kind of butterfly.

The Showground was bigger than anything we could have imagined. I was thinking you could fit Bonalbo show ring inside this one three times and still have room left. Spruikers shouted outside the boxing tents where there were paintings of the boxers on posters. There was a picture of a Koori boxer called Elly Bennett, then Tommy Burns (gubb), and Freddie Dawson (African American). I was reading the name of another Koori, Jack Hassan, and nudging Gwen to look at his picture, when I saw the real Jack Hassan a few yards away laughing at me pointing at his picture. There was a smell of sawdust and sweat and horses, and someone ran up and down outside the tents ringing a little bell.

I noticed a Koori bloke following us around and smiling at us, so I elbowed Gwen and every time we saw him after that, we hid. We went to the horse pavilion and I thought of Uncle Willy's Arabs and Chiefy Pie and the Bonalbo Show. We saw the chooks and the cows and then a huge stuffed crocodile from Queensland, its jaws propped open with a stick.

All this time Gwen had been eating. She started with hot chips at the boxing tents, then there were hot dogs at the horse pavilion, toffee apples at the cows, and she was halfway through her third fairy floss when we came to the tent of the Bodiless Woman. We paid our two shillings and they let us in through the flap. There were no other people there. Near the back of the tent was a small box with a white cushion and a sword on it. On this sat the head of a blonde woman.

I thought the head mightn't be real so I went closer. The head blinked, then the mouth opened and she said, 'Hello girls, where do you come from?'

After I got my breath I said, 'From the bush.' The head smiled. I couldn't see how her body could have fitted into the little box under the cushion, but I didn't dare ask where the body was.

'Good crowd outside?' she said.

I could feel Gwen breathing behind me.

'Pretty good,' I said. I looked around. Gwen was standing stock still with the fairy floss in her hand and her eyes wide open.

Then the crowd started to file in and I took Gwen's hand and led her outside.

'Wonder how they did that,' she said.

I didn't have a clue but I told her I heard they definitely did it with mirrors.

We tried out the ferris wheel, the octopus, the dodgems and the ghost train, and finally it got dark.

Back home Gwen developed a temperature and soon she was sick. I fed her with aspros but she got worse. Dad and Mum came back that night and when Dad found out we'd sneaked to the Show, I knew we were in for a lecture as soon as Gwen got well. One afternoon I came home from work to find a telegram had come for me. ARRIVING SYDNEY WED MEET ME AT TRAIN, it said, LOVE MERVYN. I nearly fell over. I hadn't told Dad that he'd been writing to me ever since I left home in Bonalbo, and that he'd proposed to me. I knew he was coming to Sydney sometime to try out for the railway, they had to come down from the bush to pass their exams here. But I had the huffs with him and didn't meet the train, because Olga Olive had written me a letter saying, 'Guess who I saw at the El Granda picture show on Saturday, Mervyn and Ethel Hogan.'

A few days later I walked in from work to find Mervyn sitting up having tea with Dad and yarning away. He said to Dad, 'Could I take Ruby down to the Tivoli to see a show?'

'Yes, but don't keep her out late. Work tomorrow,' Dad said.

I didn't like the way my life was being arranged for me, so I butted in and said I was doing some sewing at Betty's and with that I took off out the door.

When I came home Dad said, 'Gee you were real ignorant with Mervyn, you hardly spoke to him, you're real stubborn you are.' I was thinking, 'Let him take Ethel out.' I was very jealous.

In the factory there was another Aboriginal woman whose name was Sophie McKenzie and one afternoon as we were coming out of work, she was met outside by a young bloke and introduced him to me, saying, 'This is my nephew Sam Griffin.' I was surprised and muttered a hurried hello. I'd seen him before, then I remembered, he was the bloke who was following us around at the Showground. I couldn't wait to get home and tell Gwen. I thought he was nice looking and dressed well as he smiled at me in recognition.

A few days later I put my head out the window and there he was going past in the laneway, looking up at the flat. I found out from Sophie that his Aunty Alma lived down the back of our street in the laneway and was a good friend of Little Mum Joyce.

Sam came to visit with his Aunt Alma Griffin and then we began to go out on dates. He came to pick me up and we went to the movies or into the city. Then we went to the zoo and the Manly Fun Pier. I stood there fascinated by the big sharks and stingrays in the aquarium. On Saturdays we took Dennis to the matinee at the Empire Picture Theatre. There was that Scarlet Horseman again!

A few months after I'd been dating Sam, I was on my way to Dante's dry cleaning shop when I saw my mother further up the street. She was on her own, and loaded up with shopping in string bags. I stopped and watched her. She was a solid-built tall woman, and she had waist-length black hair tied back in a ribbon. Everything matched, she was stylishly dressed. It was the first time I'd had a real chance to look at her. I realised I didn't know anything about her. How old was she? What street did she live in? How did she feel about me, a child she had when she was fifteen? Sixteen? And then the other kids. And then how we hadn't seen her for nine years. And here she was on the street, walking towards me. What would I say to her?

'Hullo my girl,' she said. She never did call me Ruby, later. It was always 'my girl'.

'Hullo Mum.' I felt wary. I didn't think I could hug her yet.

'I can't stay long.' She explained she had to get home with the groceries, cook tea for the kids. Then she took out a piece of paper from her handbag and wrote down her address.

'Will you come and see me? Come over and have dinner. And bring Gwennie.'

I stood there outside Dante's shop with her address fluttering in my hand.

I decided not to tell anyone, and a week later I went across Redfern Park and into Beaumont Street, which was a lane with a row of little houses. It was late in the afternoon.

We sat and talked for a while, and then she said, 'I've got something to tell you, you want to stay away from Sam Griffin, he's no good.'

I was angry straightaway.

'You don't have to worry about me now, you never cared before,' I said, and with that she boxed my ears and punched me up. I got up to leave and went out the front, and she decked me again. She hit me so hard it stunned me, and my head ached for days. At home I couldn't lift my head off the pillow properly, to get up for work.

I went over in my mind what had happened. The point where she hit me was just after I'd said 'you never cared before', and this was what had made her angry, and I knew she cared, or she wouldn't have come up to us crying in the street that first time, but I was hurt and she was hurt, and she'd hit me and now I had concussion.

Dad came in to ask why I wasn't up for work, so I told him what had happened. He then summoned Mum to Albion Street Children's Court on a charge of assault. The judge asked Gwen and me if she'd sent us Christmas and birthday presents and we said 'no'. He asked if I was supporting myself and paying board and I said 'yes'. Mum was bound down to keep the peace and leave us alone.

I didn't see her again till three years later, after my third child was born and I was back in Sydney.

After I was finished my apprenticeship at Brachs, which took twelve months, I could do the complete trousers including the hip pockets, the zipper, buttonhole and buttons, and the band. I was a lead bander for the whole factory. At the Christmas break-up party, the workers were all given chocolates and stockings, and the women presented me with a white lace underwear set, for being a good messenger. Dad was very proud of me.

I left Brachs and the trouser factory with Sam's Aunt Sophie, and we took up the shirt trade at Joe Dadah's place around the corner in Cleveland Street. I picked this up quickly. They were making shirts for the Korean War, and I earned one and six a dozen for making up and putting on the epaulettes.

I wasn't paying any attention to my work. I'd doodle on the material with a pencil, Old Joe Dadah caught me and said, 'You finish up on Friday.' I got a shock. I said, 'I'll show him I can work,' and I made that damn machine fly, for the rest of the week I never looked up from my sewing, I was determined to prove myself. Friday came and I was dreading I'd be losing my job.

Old Joe came up and said, 'I've watched you all week. You can work when you want to. I'm giving you a raise instead of sacking you.' I let out a breath. But I still felt weird and like doodling in my mind. I didn't want to do anything.

Gwen had left high school and was training to be a telephonist. I laughed at Dad, saying, 'We get trunk lines for breakfast, dinner and tea.' Gwen had to practise the area codes, and went about the flat reciting to herself out loud. 'Shut up Gwennie, give it a rest,' I said, and she'd recite louder, and I'd take off to some place quiet.

Mum Joyce had just come home from hospital with a new baby boy, who she named Kevin Samuel. Where Dennis was blond and blue-eyed, Kevin was dark and very rowdy. I liked playing with the babies but around this time Sam and I became inseparable. He was well-dressed and kind of charming, I didn't know what it was but something made me really like him and I couldn't understand why my mother had said, 'He's no good'. What did she know? Did she know him?

Soon after Mum Joyce brought Kevin home, I was throwing up every morning. I realised I was pregnant but I didn't know the facts of life. I told Sam and he was okay about it. I couldn't lie to Dad but I didn't want to bring any shame on him, so I told him I was going to Coonabarabran to stay with Sam's mother until I had the baby.

Dad was very upset and didn't want me to go. He said, 'If everything doesn't turn out right you come straight back Ruby, you understand now, you come back.'

5

My Belongin Place

Coonabarabran, Coolah Valley, Bonalbo, Woodenbong
The train left at eight and we travelled all night. Lunch
next day was at Binnaway where we changed from steam
train to a two-carriage rail motor, which took us to
Coona by early afternoon. There were a lot of Kooris
on the train, going home for Easter. Sam knew most of
them. Old Sonny Golden looked at me and said to Sam,
'You better watch her when you get up there, or you'll
end up losing her.' I ignored them and looked out the
window. I remember thinking, I'm sixteen years and two
months old.

Sam had told me the story of his family while we were
on the train. His father was also called Sam Griffin. He
had died young, at about thirty. So Ruby, Sam's mother,
was left with two young kids, Sam and Bill. When Bill
was about two, he'd been burnt to death in a fire at Burra
Be Dee mission. If our baby was a boy, Sam said, he
would like to call him Bill after this brother.

Then Ruby had married Harold Leslie, who was a
rabbit trapper, and had six more kids – Brucey (B.T.),

Alfie, Briany, Brenda, Joanie and Georgie, the youngest a toddler. We'd be living with them in a tin hut on the Gunnedah Hill – what the whites called a shanty town; what we called the tin huts. Sam had written to his mother telling her I was pregnant and she wrote back saying we'd be welcome. I thought it was strange Sam's parents were named Sam and Ruby, like us.

Sam's mother's house was three good-sized rooms, made of a structure of pine rails, with scantlin (timber off-cuts) and opened out kerosene tins for walls. There was an open fire with a camp oven hanging over it. Newspapers and *Women's Weeklies* were pasted on the inside walls to stop draughts. It was pretty good I thought, comfortable.

There were five families on the Gunnedah Hill, all living in huts near an old well, which was our water supply. When it went dry we carted water from the Castlereagh River on yokes with buckets, about half a mile away.

The women cut ti-tree branches to make brooms, to keep the dirt floors clean. Some of them dried their clothes on bushes and some had lines. Their washing was always white.

The other families wanted to know who was the girl Sam had brought home. I went with him to the well, and passing one of the huts I saw a woman out front sweeping with a ti-tree broom.

Sam introduced her as Nerida Chatfield. I didn't know then but this woman was to become my best friend and a loyal mate for the next thirty-eight years. We had many adventures together later on, but this day we drank tea and looked out the hut door at the pine trees. Then Sam and I went on to get the water.

When we got back the old fellow, Harold, Sam's stepfather, was getting ready to go out into the bush. At first I didn't know what he was doing. He was packing about a hundred rabbit traps onto the handlebars and in a tray on the back of his pushbike. He took a billy, a bit of tarpaulin wrapped up with his blanket inside it, a groundsheet and some food. Loaded up like this he went bush for a week at a time trapping rabbits, and this was how he supported his family.

The rabbiting truck went out every day to pick up each night's catch and bring them fresh to the freezing works. At weekends Harold came in with the truck.

There was an albino Koori woman who lived near the tap. She was referred to as 'the old blonde' – her hair was platinum, and she had rough freckled skin. She had pink eyes and wore dark glasses in the day but at night she could see very well. Originally she'd come from the mission at Moree. When I went for walks I talked to her. She had travelled around with the sideshows for a long time.

On hot days I went to the local swimming-hole with Sam's brother B.T. Leslie, his friend Philomena, and her cousin Cyril Bailey (Donk). Willow Vale was down the back of the market garden and on hot weekends half the town would be there to cool off.

Donk and B.T. had their trousers tied up with rope, they were so poor. They called out 'Hey Ruby, watch this swallow dive,' and threw themselves off the high bank, arms outstretched. Wherever I went, I always had these kids following me.

One morning I asked Sam's mother how I'd know when it was time to go to hospital. She herself had seven kids. Sam was the oldest, at seventeen, and George the baby in the sandpit was seven months.

'You'll get pains,' she said, 'across your back or in your stomach, and they'll go away and come again and it'll get harder and keep on like that till you have your baby.' This was my only piece of information about birth, and I hung onto it. I'd grown up with animals giving birth all around me, I'd seen cows calving, but somehow I never connected. And this was quite common, young women, girls, not knowing what would happen. And being given one sentence, that's it.

I soon found out. Three o'clock in the morning I was doubled up with pain. In those days there was nothing like a labour pain, no wonder they called it labour. Sam went to get Morrie Hunt the taxi driver, he was a good bloke, the Kooris borrowed money off him till payday and even booked up runs in his taxi, so he was like a bank too. He drove me to Coona Hospital. The maternity ward was over the back close to the mortuary, and as you walked to it there was a grapevine on a trellis.

I asked the sister if I could have a shower, as there was no bath in the hut. The labour ward consisted of two beds and two cribs and a screen for privacy.

The pains got worse all day, and one sister came and told me to walk around, but not to go out of the room.

It was a sixteen-hour labour and the baby came out like a skinned rabbit, six pound one ounce. To make you pass the afterbirth, they pressed on your stomach. I was glad when it was all over, I was overjoyed with my little son. Then my stomach was wrapped tightly like a corset with a towel, and pinned three times for support, then a nappy was folded into a long strip to hold the big pads in place. This was October 1951.

There were no drugs to kill the pain, and I ended up punching the sister in the arm. It felt like my body was being torn into pieces. I swore I'd never do it again, but I did, eight times.

I'd had my baby right before visiting time, and I was sitting up in bed waiting for Sam, but he didn't turn up. Because I had no visitors and was unmarried it made me embarrassed, so when the other women had visitors, I would turn to the wall and cover my head and cry to myself. The only person who befriended me, and hand-crocheted me a carrying coat and booty set, was Nerida Chatfield who had a large family herself.

Sam's mother came the following day, she'd left her babies with a friend. I was glad to see her coming in, her hair smoke-dried from bending over the fire. Later her hair turned silver grey except where it was scorched ginger at the front. She sat with me and said Sam would be in later. He'd gone to work on the sawmill at Coolah Valley. When he came in we decided to call the baby William after his brother who'd died, and Henry after my dad. Sam was proud to be a father, but all the same

85

straining under the responsibility, even then, and it was left up to me to look after Billy.

Three weeks later I came home, and took my baby to visit Nerida, thanking her for the things she'd made. Later she and her family moved on to Burra Be Dee mission. It was seven miles out, and each pension and endowment day the mission truck would pull into town, and that was the only time I saw her to pass the time of day, and have a chat. Her husband used to drink heavily, and rattle tunes out on the mouth organ, and spent the rest of the time fighting with her. I hardly saw her without black eyes and bruises. She took it for as long as she could, then got a transfer to Wreck Bay, to get away. My existence wasn't much better, and I had my share of black eyes and bruises later.

Sam's job at Coolah Valley meant he only came home at weekends. He bought me a pink and black silk dress, and on Saturday all the Kooris from over the hill went to town to shop. The streets of Coona were very busy then, we all sat on the tree guards in the middle of the street and passed the time away, and did our shopping. Sam was talking up a storm with the young men he'd grown up with. One of them remarked that I was a good sort and I could see Sam's expression change.

On the way home I was pushing the pram with young Bill in it, and on the bush track, which led over to the hill, he said, 'Have you been running around on me, while I'm at work?'

'What are you talking about Sam? I don't know any one of those blokes, they're your friends.'

With that he knocked me to the ground and started to throttle me, the only way I could make him let go was to kick him in the groin. Bill was crying in the pram.

I said, 'You're a mad jealous mongrel, I won't put up with this kind of treatment, if you ever do that again I'll leave you.'

I thought I was a goner, then he was babbling how sorry he was and that it wouldn't happen again, then we went home.

This left me shaken up, and I was always on my guard, I knew his mood could change quickly, and I had no-one to help me.

The old people treated me well. Ruby showed me how to look after Billy, and Harold called me daughter.

Ruby and I took chaff bags and went to chop wood. She reckoned she could get me a job on the sawmill, I was so good at swinging the kelly. We also set traps together and went to collect our rabbits.

One night I heard someone at the door, three distinct knocks. I could see the moonlight filtering through the cracks in the door, and no figure there. I went outside. No-one. The blue cattle dog was asleep under a tree.

'Daughter? Who was that?'

'No-one.'

'I heard three knocks.'

'I did too. But I've looked. There's no-one.'

'We'll get bad news tomorrow.'

Next day when I came in with the firewood the

police were there. They told Harold his father had died in the night.

Later on he took me back to Coolah Valley to stay in the mill huts. These sawmills had both married and single quarters for the workers. We slept on blankets on the floor. I had an open fire with a camp oven and a billycan. I cooked for three Koori blokes – Tom Fuller, John Cain, and John Anderson (no relation) – and for Sam. They all worked at the mill.

Baby Bill slept in my old suitcase on a pillow, with the lid propped open with a stick so he wouldn't smother, he was okay. Further out in the bush men were log-cutting with axes, and the snigger would use two big draught horses to snigg the logs with big chains that were fitted to the harness on the horses and tied around the logs, which were then dragged to a ramp to be loaded on to trucks for the run to the sawmill.

While they were working, I straightened up the hut, then took Bill out. I didn't have a pram as we'd come in a jeep, so I carried him around. Coolah Valley was a windy place, I could hear the windmill which was the pump to the bore – *tunk*, *tunk*, it put me to sleep at night and in the day *cre-eak tunk, cre-eak tunk*. All around us was grazing land and homesteads and properties, and the smell of cattle and sheep. In the distance I saw something on the ground, like a grey blanket, a horse seemed to be walking on the blanket, and now the grey lifted up and started screeching and then I could see the pink underbellies of galahs, and the noise all around me, hundreds of them, a flock of pink covering the sky. I held Bill up to look. I was on my own nearly all the time. There were other women there in the married quarters – white women – but they kept to themselves.

Sam used to get jealous of the boys (who were very kind to me) and belt me up, so the boys told him to leave me alone or else. He soon got the message. We had some money saved up, and I was lonely for my people, so I asked him to take me home to Bonalbo.

The boss of the sawmill took us into town in his jeep. On the way he braked suddenly and there in front of us was a goanna the size of a crocodile. It was on all fours – a dark grey colour. Goannas can adapt to the colour of the soil where they live – sometimes you see one a rust red, with a white underbelly, and sand goannas are the same colour as sand. This one was the biggest I'd ever seen. We waited for it to cross the road, so we could move on.

At this time I was three months pregnant again and we travelled the long journey home by train to Casino.

We wondered how we'd get to Bonalbo, the buses didn't run on a Sunday. We sat in the park near the Rink Picture Show, on the same bench where I used to meet Grandfather Sam. We could hear people barracking at the football oval over the river. It was getting late and we wondered where we could spend the night.

Then suddenly in the crowd coming across the foot bridge from the game, was a voice calling, 'Ruby, Ruby!' It was Midge, the cousin I'd grown up with in Bonalbo, and a man with her. 'Where have you been? I sent you an invitation, I got married two days ago, this is Doug. Where have you been?' She poked her hand under my eyes to show me her wedding ring. 'Is this your baby? Oh look, your Dad and Mum Joyce are at home, they came up for the wedding.' She took Bill from me and nursed him all the way home. We sat together in the football bus and the men sat behind us. While Midge talked, I looked at one familiar head after another on the bus, kids that I'd grown up with. When we pulled in to Bonalbo I thought, *my belongin place.*

Dad and Mum Joyce were surprised to see us. It was the first time Dad had seen his only grandchild. 'He's a lovely little fellow, Ruby.' He had Bill on his lap, and while he was having a cup of tea and some cake, Bill took the cake right out of his hand and started to chew on it with a big grin on his face. Dad got panicky then. 'Can he eat yet? He might choke, Ruby.'

'He's six months old Dad, he's got teeth.'

Next morning I heard Dad up early, moving around in the kitchen. I left Sam sleeping and went to talk to Dad. No-one else was awake. 'How's Gwennie, how's the boys?'

'They're all right. How are you?' I looked at my baby, one year younger than his youngest.

'You all right? Are you managing all right? What's Sam doing?'

'There's work on the sawmill in Woodenbong, he's going up there. I'm gonna stay with Midge and Doug.'

I didn't want to tell him I was pregnant again.

'How's Sam treating you? Is he knocking you around?' he said. I looked at his back, at the tall body that wanted to provide me with the world.

'He's all right, we manage,' I said. Dad looked at me, was I lying? He couldn't tell. I smiled and started to feed Bill.

Dad and Mum Joyce left to go back to Sydney, and I saw them off on the bus. Midge and Doug had said I could stay with them until the baby was born. Sam went to work on the mill at Woodenbong and came home at weekends.

My first daughter, who I named Pearl Louise, was born in December 1952 at Bonalbo Hospital. Cousin Doug rode on his motorbike to fetch the ambulance. He had a job at the hospital, laying pipes under the rooms, and said later I made such a racket that I nearly screamed the place down.

The hospital was a ten-roomed house on a hill, with verandahs all around. Gum trees almost came in at the windows. Pearl was born with about two inches of black hair on her head, and the nurses were white girls I had gone to school with. It was so hot they just put a nappy on Pearl, then laid her on a pillow and carried her round the wards to show everyone. At night a possum came in and took my fruit.

When I came home I moved into the old house at Dyrabba Street where we were raised. Uncle Willy and Cousin John Hinnett were the only ones left there, and I looked after house for them.

Sam came in on the Greyhound bus and spent his time resting up for the next week's work. Sometimes we took Billy and went to the pictures on Saturday night. Other times he'd go have a few beers at the hotel.

'Here, hold Billy while I make his bottle, Sam.'

'Okay,' he said, but soon handed him back to me. I don't know why, but he wasn't able to be very responsible. If Billy cried a lot it would annoy him. 'Can't you keep him quiet?' he'd say.

'He's got to cry, Sam, every baby does.'

Sometimes we sat up in bed and talked, and we could talk about everything. But because these people were my people, he kept quiet with them. He was a loner, and came from quiet people, whereas my people were more outgoing. He would never have caused a row when he was sober.

I was taken up with Bill and Pearl and happy to be a mother and cook for the old boys. By this time I was eighteen years old. Uncle Willy was away droving or working on farms. Cousin John rode his bike to the Bonalbo sawmill each day. He had Japanese swords in his room, and Japanese money. The jewels had been taken out of the swords. The boys had never been married.

One weekend Sam came home drunk and was rowing with Uncle Willy for nothing. Uncle Willy told him to behave himself as the old people wouldn't put up with his drunken goings-on. That night when I finally was able to get him into bed, I dreamed that Sam was grabbing at his throat and saying, 'Get them away, get them away from me!'

I realised I was awake. I said, 'What's wrong with you?' and he said a ghost had him by the throat and was choking him. I jumped out of bed and turned the light on, I had this eerie feeling all over me, I could tell that the old people's spirits were there. Sam was still gasping for breath.

'Uncle Willy warned you, not to be rowing and going on, you wouldn't take any notice,' I said. And with that Sam got dressed and packed his bags and left for Woodenbong and never came back to the old house again.

I knew the house was full of spirits. When we were kids we used to hear the gate click shut, and footsteps on the verandah and down the hall. We weren't frightened, it was our home and they looked after us.

After Sam was chased out of the house by the spirits I stayed on for a while, and then he took us to live with him in a hut on the sawmill in Woodenbong. There were other Aboriginal families living in the huts, and I became close friends with Iris McBride who was about the same age as me. She visited and helped me bath Pearl and Bill and after it rained we went out with a billycan and collected mushrooms in the paddocks nearby. They were sweet and fresh.

Sometimes we went to the movies and here we were separated from the whites. Other Kooris came in from Mulli Mulli (hills hills) mission on a bus on Saturday nights. Iris helped me with the kids as Sam often took off for Brisbane on a Greyhound coach on weekends.

I was a naive trusting person and didn't think why he might be going to Brisbane. Once he brought me back a white taffeta dress.

I earned money by cleaning and washing for the whites in town. Iris knew everyone and helped me get these jobs. She minded the kids while I worked. Sam was a Scrooge with his money, kept it mostly to himself.

Bill was about two years old and Pearl was one, and toddling round the hut.

Sometimes I wished for a stove so I could bake something, but I had a billy, pannikins to drink from, a meat safe, and a dish for catching water from the guttering on the tank. Later we acquired a mattress.

The McBride family had big vegetable gardens so I had plenty of corn on the cob, pumpkin and potatoes given to me. All we needed was some meat. I managed to have a hotpot of stew bubbling on the open fire in the hut.

Later I found out there was another woman named Merle who had a child to Sam, who was born a month after my Bill. At this time all I knew was 'maintenance charge', and that was enough. I walked back to the hut and stared at the wall for a while. The wall was nothing to look at. In a while I heard Pearl's voice, aaerooo-aah, from Iris's place. Ruby, I said, GET UP. Look at our names, flowers and jewels.

You can imagine how I felt. I had no money and two children to look after. GET UP. Everything outside seemed very glary. Bits of glass in the ground seemed to sting my eyes and the smell of the burning sawdust at the mill made my throat ache.

Iris asked what I was going to do. I don't know, I said. I don't know. The house-cleaning paid a pound for a day's work, not enough to live on. In later years I met women who worked as sniggers and log-cutters at Gwabegar, but this mill was all blokes, and it wasn't in my mind because I had the job of being a parent. And really I was too stunned to think. I asked Iris if she'd stay with me for company for a few days, and we talked it out until it was easier to bear.

Two days later I went into town for bread and I ran into Uncle Ernie's brother, Cyril Ord, who we called Uncle Nulla. He was in his working clothes, with sawdust on him, and had just come in from the mill. He knew the gungys had taken Sam. 'It's no good you being in the hut by yourself,' he said. He tipped his hat back on his head and looked up at the mill, the fire they burned all the time, the heat haze and the silence. The town seemed very quiet. Then he turned to me and said he had a room for me out on the mission. I had to get special permission from the manager, then I packed my bags and the two kids and moved out to Mulli Mulli.

And I settled in with Uncle Nulla and his family and they looked after me. I got rations for myself and the children from the manager, and milk from the dairy. And every day I told myself I had to put the worry of Sam to the back of my mind.

Uncle Nulla was a good man, and jovial. He ran dances at weekends in the old school hall. The lighting was a hurricane lamp and the music was guitars and the accordian, which some of the boys played quite well. I was feeling pretty flat. I sat there and watched.

On Sunday after church the young folk played rounders (berutchin – it was called), which was the boys keeping the ball away from the girls. 'They should all keep their balls away,' I thought.

I walked around in the bush a bit. The mission was another place like Bonalbo, wild cherries in the creek, and lilly pilly. It was near the Taloome scrub, where my father had worked timber-getting in the early days. The scrub is supposed to be full of yowies. There's a creek there called Yowie Creek. I don't know whether this is a myth but the old people used to count heads when we were playing berutchin, and said they could see hairy men playing with us. We couldn't see them.

But the Taloome scrub is a lonely eerie place in the night. And there're moggis there, ghosts. You can feel that. An Anderson on Grandfather's side from Beaudesert way, who is a cleverman, was said to have seven little women who came to see to his needs. The Taloome scrub is near Mount Lindsay, the place Uncle Roy used to sing about. The tribe from that country is called Githabul.

I don't know how long I was at Mulli Mulli before Bill became sick and was taking fit after fit. I was terrified. Uncle Nulla took us to a little town about eight miles away called Urbenville. The nurse put Bill in bed and rang the doctor, who said he'd see him in the morning.

But my mother's instinct told me he'd die before morning if the doctor didn't see him. I don't know if the doctor would have roused up and come if it had been a white child sick, but I wondered. So Uncle Nulla said we will take him to Kyogle about thirty miles away to the big hospital.

Uncle Nulla said that because Bill was so sick the hospital would keep me there and that when I wanted to get home again to tell the bus driver that Nulla Ord would pay at the other end.

The specialist examined Bill and isolated him in a room and told me he had meningitis, which is a spinal disease, and that he wasn't expected to live. I sat and prayed beside his bed and wouldn't leave him for a week straight. 'Dear Lord, don't let my baby son die, he's only little and I love him, and need him, please don't let him die.' I repeated this till I had exhausted myself and slept, then when I woke I started again.

From the window where I was sitting I saw Grandfather Sam going past on the road to the mission at Stoney Gully. I ran out to get him, and we sat on a bench in the hospital grounds and talked. He asked me what I was doing. I said I had two children, and my oldest was sick with meningitis and not expected to live. Grandfather put his arms around me and rocked me. After a while he went away again. He was still droving.

The next day the doctor came in and said that Bill

would live. I was so grateful I burst out crying right there. Then they told me they'd have to keep him for a while, but I could go home. I was worried about Pearl, so I agreed to go. I got on the bus and told the driver Uncle Nulla's message and that was okay.

They kept Bill in hospital over a month and then sent me a telegram to meet the bus as they were sending him home. The hospital had asked a woman passenger if she would nurse him on her lap till the bus reached Woodenbong. I ran the three miles to town and when the bus pulled in all I could see was the top of his beanie hat and two big brown eyes through the window. I swooped him into my arms. The houses at the mission had been fumigated because meningitis is contagious and deadly.

Not long after I saw in the paper that they'd found Grandfather dead in a drover's shack. He was thought to be seventy-nine, and was buried at Coraki. I sent the clipping from the *Northern Star* to my father in Sydney, and sometimes when I was walking with the kids in the bush I heard a voice saying, 'Goodfulla, come on goodfulla.' Later I would find out that Grandfather was a great cricketer and a man to be proud of, but at the time I had no idea what people really meant when I was introduced and they said, 'Oh, you're an Anderson.'

Not long after that I had a visitor – Sam. I couldn't speak to him at all, so he told Uncle Nulla that Dad had seen him on the street in Sydney, and asked where I was. Then Dad had given Sam train fares so we could go to Great Buckingham Street, where he could help me.

So we left Woodenbong and headed for Sydney. It was a twenty-one-hour trip in the mail train, stopping at every station. I looked out the window, I attended to the kids, I didn't speak to Sam.

6

Bush Tucker

Sydney, Toowoomba, Sydney, Coonabarabran
'What're you gonna do about this fella, he's got a child with another woman –'

'That's in the past, Dad.'

'Ruby, I've seen him down Botany Road –'

'You just don't like him,' I yelled. For some reason I had to defend Sam. I was still angry with him, but I wanted to make it work. I wanted the kids to have a father.

Dad got a place for us to stay with his friends in Waterloo. It was where the Housing Commission flats in Pitt Street now stand. I couldn't hold a grudge for long, and Sam swore he'd never do it again. We had a room of our own with a double bed and a single bed for Bill and Pearl.

Sam found work but used to go out on the town every weekend. I thought he was out with his mates until I got suspicious and followed him one Saturday and caught him with another woman in the lane.

I packed the children and caught a taxi to Dad's at Great Buckingham Street. I apologised to him for not believing him before. I had had enough of Sam, and by ten o'clock that night we were on a train going to Uncle Sam and Aunt Nell. Dad had given me money and bought sandwiches and fruit for the trip. He told me Aunt Nell was very sick in hospital in Toowoomba.

Uncle Sam was there to meet me. We were to stay in the ex-army barracks with them. It was the first time I'd seen sister Rita since I left home five years ago, and she was now in high school. The first time I saw Aunt Nell she was so thin in the face and arms I cried. The skin was hanging off her. I found out from the doctors she didn't have long to live. She had a tumour in her stomach, which they used to drain each day. We had always joked about her large stomach, and in the hospital they still joked. She was so glad to see me again, and I sat beside her bed thinking about the days in Bonalbo when she stood at the fence talking to Marty Askew, with the pegs in her apron pocket, and the warm fresh smell of cakes and horses. I looked at her stomach now, a mound under the hospital blanket, and I was just thinking how cruel life was, when she said that what happened to her was God's will, and she'd always said the same.

The next day I went to see cousin Midge and Doug. I was sitting at the table with them and the two kids when a man with startling blue eyes walked into the room. They introduced him as their boarder, Gordon Campbell. He drove trucks. He was very tall and tanned.

★

I was three months pregnant (a parting gift from Sam) and was wondering what would become of me and the kids, when suddenly Sam was there, I don't know how he found out where I was, and threatening to have the children taken away from me. I told him to get lost, and that the children were in my maiden name of Anderson, we would see a solicitor together and get him to straighten things out.

The solicitor told Sam that he had no claim on the children as we were not married and he did not have a leg to stand on. So I told him to get lost again and that was the last I saw of him for a while, he must have taken off to Sydney. Good riddance, I thought.

In the meantime I cared for Uncle Sam, sister Rita and Aunt Nell's sister, Aunt Flo. I did Aunt Nell's laundry for her and went to see her each day. She showed me the drain holes in her stomach. I told her about Sam.

Midge, Doug and their boarder called over two or three times a week. I liked Gordon's blue eyes but I couldn't even think about men. Sam was dying inside me, Aunt Nell was dying in the hospital, and I was pregnant with my third child and nineteen years old and when Gordon asked me out to the pictures I just shook my head. But Midge pushed me out and said she would babysit. I felt like I went because I'd been told to, but Gordon was a good bloke.

I could see after a while that he liked me. He came over and took us for rides in his truck. I couldn't string him along so I told him I was pregnant. He said I was very honest for telling him but it didn't matter.

I wrote and told Dad I was pregnant again and he wanted me to come back to Sydney. Did I want Gordon to come with me? He picked up the kids and nursed them. Said he wanted to look after me. He was kind. And a hard worker.

When I told him I was going back to Sydney he left his job, we said goodbye to everyone, and we left the next morning.

I had already told Dad about Gordon and he accepted him straightaway, and got him a job at Henderson Springs. We moved into a flat up the street from Dad and Mum Joyce. Mum's baby was nine months older than mine. We sat these boys together and looked at them. Beautiful black babies. Then Pearl got up and took her first steps, waving her arms like a bird flapping its wings.

At this time I was due to go into hospital with my third child. I was about twenty years old. On the day of the pre-natal visit, while the doctors were examining me, I started to get contractions. They took me on the lift up to the labour ward and in a while I could feel the niggly cramps. My second daughter, who I called Dianne Joyce, was born in April 1954, at Crown Street Women's Hospital. Her first name came from the song 'I'm in heaven when I see you smile/Smile for me, Diane', and her second name after Mum Joyce. It was a relatively easy birth. Dad and Gordon had come home from work and were walking round and round in the flat – I don't know who was more nervous.

I was sent afterwards to a rest home called Cannonbury which overlooked the harbour. I stayed there for two weeks, and one day while I was hanging nighties on the line I saw a woman who looked familiar. I studied her closer and let out a yell, 'Matty!' She turned around and hugged me. It was Matilda Brown, a girl I'd gone to high school with in Casino. I used to swap my lunch for her baked bean sandwiches. We sat and talked about home, and the next day she was gone.

I celebrated my homecoming at Dad's place. Beside my dinner plate were wrapped presents. I opened them up: clothes for Dianne, bootees, a rattle. The family was around me. This was what it was supposed to be like.

A week later I was woken up by the presence of a spirit very strong beside me in bed. I couldn't rest and Gordon said, 'What's up, can't you sleep?' I told him something was wrong with someone. In a while I realised the spirit was Aunt Nell. I could feel her near me all night.

Next morning Dad called in and told me that she'd died in the night. The grief fell out of me in great sobs. She was the only mother we knew. I saw her again in the hospital, her face thin and her stomach so big, and the drain holes in her skin and her cheerful voice. I said to myself, She's not in pain now, and I realised Dad was talking to me. He said he would have to go and bring Rita back, so she could get work. I watched him out the gate. I couldn't travel because I had a new baby.

When Rita arrived she took up the machinery trade like I had. Gwen was still working as a telephonist. In the afternoons I took the kids down to visit her. One time I was coming back to the flat to pick up some clothes for the kids, and when I pushed my door it was unlocked. Gordon wouldn't be home. It had to be a burglar.

I caught sight of someone behind the door and I turned and ran to Dad's place. 'There's someone behind my door, come quick!' and when Dad went in it was Sam Griffin drunk. 'Don't come snooping around any more or I'll put the gungys on you, Sam.' Then Dad gave him a talking to and frogmarched him down to the station.

Not long afterwards Dad had a heart attack. He was in St Vincents Hospital on his back for two months while the doctors dissolved a clot in his heart valve. Dad was the best friend I had, and I tried to imagine what I'd do if we lost him, and my mind was black, panicking. I sat with Mum Joyce at Dad's bed and prayed. In between I thought about Dad and the photograph, 'You are my Sunshine, love Evelyn', about Dad lifting the anvil, then his worry about me, the way I'd chosen Sam who he said was no good right from the beginning. I decided not to grind my teeth over all that, and went back to praying.

Dad made it through that heart attack, and was told to take it easy. He couldn't not work, and Henderson's sent home a small machine with the metal for making small springs. Sometimes in the night he would sit up and roll the springs. He was very conscious that the kids were young and he had to provide for them.

In the mornings he walked up the street to where I lived. I got to expect him at a certain time, and one day

I watched out the window how he walked a way then stopped and rested, how he would stop to rest before he climbed the stairs.

When Dianne was four months old I was pregnant to Gordon and in May 1955 my second son was born at South Sydney Hospital in Newtown. I named him Gordon Allan after his father. He was the largest baby I bore, weighing one ounce off ten pounds, and very blond when he was a few months old. His navel protruded when he cried. There was an old trick then of putting a penny on the navel and taping it flat, which we did, and we called this boy Nobby, the name he's still called today. I had two dark kids and two fair ones and all my time was looking after them and I was happy enough.

Gordon liked messing around with cars. At this time we had a box-shaped Plymouth and one day Sam's brother Bruce Leslie came and asked me if we could drive him home to Coonabarabran. I wanted to see old Ruby and Harold again, and Gordon wanted to take the car for a long run so we packed the kids and set off.

Just as we arrived on the Gunnedah Hill the car broke down. We stayed with Ruby and Harold while we waited for the cog for the gear to arrive. All our money was used up, so Gordon found work in the bush. I was glad to see Ruby again. Her hair was greyer but still ginger at the front from the fire. She played with her grandchildren, my three oldest, and nursed Nobby while I went out for firewood or water. I walked past Nerida's place and wondered how she was doing down at Wreck Bay.

Ruby accepted Gordon all right but Harold didn't take to him because he was a gubb. I was hoping Gordon would turn up with some pay because all we had was the car and the clothes we stood up in. Then he came in and said there was a job burning off at a property four miles out on the Purlewaugh Road. The cog arrived and we fixed the car. Ruby gave me pots and pans and a billycan, and with the money the boss had advanced us on the burning off contract, we went and bought some food. Now for the first time I was going to live in and off the bush. Hard physical gutbusting work and stealing sheep and flocks of galahs overhead and clear hot days and keeping the fires stoked all night.

We slept in the car. There was Gordon and me and the four children, and when it rained we locked ourselves in the car till it stopped. I helped him in the night stoking fires.

The kids played around the camp all day. There was a creek where I washed clothes and bathed the kids, and we had a forty-four-gallon drum of drinking water, which the boss provided. When we needed tucker Gordon minded the kids while I hitched to town and got a taxi back with the groceries.

I must have known I'd be living in the bush one day because I watched how people got by and took note. So a bush shopping list was already in my head, something like this:

tea
butter, block cheese
sugar

jam

coarse salt

potatoes, onions, carrots

split peas

lentils

Pick-Me-Up sauce

pepper and curry powder

Golden Syrup (Cocky's Joy)

lemon-flavoured Sal Vital

plain flour for thickening

self-raising for ashes damper or fried scones

a large tin of Sunshine milk

Lactogen

dripping

cordials (to cover up the taste of kero in the drum
water)

matches

bottles of coffee and chicory

That was what we lived on. I had a meat safe hung in
a tree. Bill Williams who owned the property gave us
a sheep a week, which was part of the contract. I kept
the groceries in half a four-gallon drum nailed to a tree,
and the butter and cheese in the meat safe with wetted
hessian on the sides to keep it cool.

What I remember – a mass of black or white cockatoos
in a dead tree. The shrieking if you disturbed them.

At night possums came after the food. We lay quietly
in the car and watched them scurry up the tree and try

to reach into the drum for food. One possum fell and hit the ground all the time and kept going back and falling again. We couldn't keep quiet any longer and our laughing scared him away.

In the day I watched the children carefully because the property was alive with snakes. Gordon killed them and chased us with them for fun. He could crack their heads off like a whip. One morning I saw a king brown snake crawling down its hole. It was four inches in diameter and I almost froze, not with fear but a fearful respect for the hand of nature. It was the biggest snake I'd ever seen. Gordon grabbed its tail and started to pull it out. I stood well back but there seemed to be yards of it, and when he did kill it, it measured nine feet. He tied it to the back of the tractor and drove off to show the boss.

In the afternoon I decided to make a chocolate cake. We were burning off, so there were plenty of ashes. I lined a Christmas cake tin with brown paper and made up the mixture and poured it in, put the lid on. Sat the tin on hot earth and scooped ashes all over it. Waited. Done. When the cake was cool I made icing and spread that over – 'Come and get it!'

When I made damper I rolled it in flour and put it straight into the ashes. So when you took it out, it was covered in ash and dust. You flick this off with a tea towel or a switch off a pine tree. Then to keep it fresh you wrap it in a damp tea towel. There was no need to try and keep the chocolate cake fresh – blink and it's gone.

When Nobby was six months old I decided to go to Sydney and get my furniture out of storage and have it sent up by train. When I walked into the flat Dad said, 'Here's my baby,' and took Nob from my arms. Mum Joyce put the kettle on. I sat her boys on my lap and felt comfortable again. I was stiff from the long train ride.

'So Ruby,' Dad said, 'what are you doin' up there?'

'Burning off.'

'I thought it must be something like that, cause gee you're blue.' (Very black.)

The door opened and Gwen and then Rita came in from work. We hugged and told stories and laughed. The next day was a Saturday and the girls wanted to take me to Luna Park for a treat. Dad said he'd mind Nobby but I had nothing to wear. Dad looked at Rita. 'You've got more things than your sister, she's only battling, you give her that suit, go on, you can get another one. I'll help you pay for it.'

It was a grey flannel suit and fitted like it was made for me. We went off and had fun on all the rides and when we got back Nob was dressed in a new yellow zoot suit. Dad was asleep and Nob lay in his arms wide awake and sucking on a bottle. He was the last of my kids Dad ever saw.

I went to organise the furniture and when that was done I said goodbye and took off again.

Back at camp I became pregnant with my fifth child and it was getting uncomfortable sleeping in the car. So we built a lean-to out of hessian bags and attached it to the car, and I slept there on a fold-up stretcher we'd bought. The kids had the car, and Gordon slept outside with his bedroll on a tarp. I liked the lean-to, and being able to look out at the sky. When I woke up thinking about snakes I made myself watch the stars change their places and thought about my grandfather who had slept out all his life and how when the Cross was up the other way they would change shifts, when they were droving.

When we ran out of meat I went with Gordon to get a killer in the night. We never took the boss's sheep of course, but the properties on either side lost a few big sheep. The next job we had, we had winches and did the whole thing properly, but for now we had a torch and a knife.

The night was overcast but our camp was near the boundary fence and all we had to do was walk across the road and into the next paddock. Sheep are very docile and easy to catch. There were a few scrubby trees but no moon, no shadows. We chose our sheep by torchlight and when we grabbed it the others ran away. We skinned and gutted it on the ground. Then we rolled the guts in the skin and poked it into a hollow log and stopped up the log with rocks. As I was pushing in the last rock I heard a coughing sound. I turned around and saw the outline of something white.

I said to Gordon, 'Look out, we're goners, it's the boss,' and the white figure moved. I could see now it was a big white draught horse. I collapsed onto the ground and nearly had my baby there – I was six months pregnant.

When we stopped laughing we took the carcass across the road to our camp and next morning it was chops for breakfast. 'After all,' I said to Gordon, 'Bob Menzies said, "Nobody should ever starve while there's sheep in the paddocks".'

While we were on this property burning off, Pearl became feverish and had a bad cough for a few days and then she took a fit. I knew she was very sick. It was the middle of the night and we were four miles out. Gordon watched the other children and I wrapped her in a blanket and started off for town. There was no moon. In a while my eyes grew used to the darkness and I wasn't so frightened and went as quickly as I could.

Sometimes a roo crossed the road in front of me, but I was compelled to go on because of my sick child. Sometimes I'd sit down for a spell and then go on again, all the time checking to see that she was all right. I reached the hospital at daybreak and I was exhausted. The nurses rang for the doctor who said that Pearl had bronchitis. After I knew she was out of danger I booked a taxi back to work. There is no traffic on those bush tracks in the day, no-one to hitch a lift with, let alone in the night, because cocky farmers go to bed with the fowls. And get up with them.

Pearl was in hospital for a few weeks. When we went to get her it was about time for the rainy season and the job had cut out so we packed up camp. We got a message through to the Gunnedah Hill and Ruby and Harold Leslie (Sam's mother and stepfather) came out to pick us up and take us to town. They said I'd never make it to hospital if it rained as it was black soil and boggy. Harold had an A-model Ford called 'The Green Door', which we squeezed in for the trip. We stayed with them and altogether I had four children born in Coona and each time Ruby and Harold minded the kids while I was in hospital and acted with every kindness.

This time we were only there a few months while Gordon was away tractor driving in Gunnedah at the wheat harvest. I loved him for being a hardworking man as I was a hardworking woman myself, but he was a worrier and didn't show much affection to the kids. But by this time matters were practical and not romantic, and we adapted.

When Gordon came back we got a job on Stan Brain's property about three miles out on the Timor Road. We were to look after the place, feed the chickens, milk the house cows and Gordon was to do some ploughing.

Harold gave me six rabbit traps, lifting them carefully off the handlebars of his bike. All he said was 'You might need these.' We couldn't stay in the farmhouse because Stan was keeping company with a barmaid and they often spent nights on the farm.

He owned a garage in town. On weekends he came out and watched Gordon breaking horses.

I pitched a tent and made a good camp this time with beds and a table and a cupboard to store things. The river ran by and I washed down there and set the rabbit traps for a change of food. We lived pretty tight when there wasn't sowing or harvesting work and I chopped the heads off a few of Stan Brain's chooks to keep us going. One night Gordon and Barry Collier his mate went and knocked off a sheep as we had nothing to eat and when they came back into camp they were leading it on a rope. It was as big as a donkey, a crossbreed, Border Leicester and Merino. After it was killed they winched it up in a tree on pulleys that I kept especially for the purpose of skinning sheep. It was so heavy it took the two of them to pull it up, and so fat that one leg baked in the camp oven made a large Sunshine Milk tin full of dripping.

A month later they tried to steal a pig but it kicked up such a racket with its squealing it nearly woke the whole town, and they decided we could do without pork for now.

Gordon went to Gunnedah harvesting again and I kept camp – milked the cows, fed the chickens and horses, cooked and washed and watched the kids, and at night I trapped rabbits. One night I'd set the traps and was sitting in front of the open fire, the blue cattle dog dozing near my feet, the kids asleep in the tent, and I was listening for the squeal that would let me know I had a rabbit in the traps, when I looked across the river past Stan Brain's house towards Bare Mountain going dark in the twilight, and saw a green light flickering, going towards the mountain, a green light moving across the sky, but no sound.

In the bush you could hear a plane hours before you saw it and here was this light moving along then disappearing

114

behind the mountain and reappearing on the other side only to disappear from sight. I was on my way to get a rabbit out of the trap, I could hear it squealing, and then my hair stood on end. I said to myself, bugger the rabbit, and went inside the tent. I couldn't sleep for hours – it was as if my mind was a screen and a UFO passed across it back and forth all night.

When it was time to have the baby, Ruby and Harold Leslie came and took me to town in 'The Green Door'. My fifth child was born in August 1956. I named him David James, after Jim Langford's father.

It was a good birth. He had my colouring and blond hair. Sister Cameron was very stern and dignified and good to us.

When I came home I worked on the property but soon it wasn't enough to support us. Harold Leslie had a job hoeing and weeding for a man called Old Joe the Chinaman who had the market garden at the Gunnedah Hill. We'd visited the garden a few times and stayed the weekend with friends of Harold's, Jim Langford and Kassie. There were a lot of Kooris working in the garden and living near the river in huts. Jim Langford asked us to move in with them, because they had plenty of room.

There were big card games on the hill on Saturday. Jim played the squeezebox accordion and Gordon would be half-charged and rattling out tunes on the mouth organ while Kassie spoilt the kids – she had only one of her own, and he was with her mother. On hot days we took the kids to the swimming-hole at the back of the garden.

Every day I walked through the garden. Harold Leslie and Charlie Cain and the other Kooris were weeding and chipping between rows of vegetables. I walked through with David on my hip, watching them work. Another person walked through the garden every day, an old Chinaman called Willy, a friend of Joe's. Because Joe was the owner, Willy wandered where he liked. He got in the way of the workers and stood there mumbling. They said good-naturedly, 'Get fucked Willy', and he said, 'Oh what for you fuckee me,' and the Kooris fell about laughing.

One morning Willy came and took David from my hip and beckoned me to follow him. It was very hot, I was brushing flies from my face and wondering what Willy would do. He took David to the trough where the vegetables were washed and sat him in it to get cool. He asked me the baby's name. Then he started to croon and talk to David – 'Oh Day, you be my baby …' Every day he did this ritual, washing the baby in the trough. One time I heard him say, 'Oh Day, you be my son, one day I buy big market garden and you look after for me.'

The man who owned the garden, Old Joe, had a new house further up the hill. I worked there cleaning when Gordon went away to Yetman to try and get work. I was pregnant again and we were short of money. Joe owned shares in a Greek café in town and because he knew I had children he brought sandwiches home each day and also that day's cooked fish. He said, 'Looby you want marta and lettuce anything you want you take from garden for your kids okay?'

116

Joe's wife Diah was a very tiny woman. She worked in the garden carrying water buckets on yokes. When Joe killed a pig she made a copper of soup and gave it to the Koori workers and their families.

One reason we'd moved in with Jim and Kassie was that Gordon had become best mates with Jim's son Peter. He was a happy bloke who we nicknamed Chub. He also really liked me, and would sing songs to cheer me up when the strain got to me. While Gordon was away working I hung around with Chub and the kids, I did my jobs and took the kids swimming. One morning Donk (Cyril Bailey) came down to the market garden to see Peter and nearly fell over when he saw me with so many kids already. He remembered following me around when I was pregnant with Bill, and how we'd gone swimming then with B.T. Leslie and Philomena. I told him it hadn't worked out with Sam and I was now with Gordon.

Next morning Donk was back and he and Peter went for a swim down the back of the garden. He dived off the bank and ripped his stomach open. Peter called out, 'Get an ambulance, he's ripped his guts open,' and we laid him on the bed and I tried to stop the bleeding by holding a clean nappy over the terrible cut. He was rushed to hospital where they stitched him up.

Donk grew up to become a good man with his fists and in Coonabarabran he was a crowd drawer. Boxing was big out west and people would come from miles around in buses when he was fighting. At one stage the Lord Mayor gave him the keys to the town he was so popular. He travelled with the boxing troup of Bobby Tute and did the shows. He had itchy feet and liked moving around. He was a saucy and straight forward bloke and all the women chased him. Whenever he had a blue to settle the whole town would jump into their cars or any taxi that was vacant and go out to the aerodrome behind the Gunnedah Hill to see the fight, and he always came back the victor. Strangely I met up with him again when I was living in the Blue Mountains. I always liked Donk's company but his story didn't have a happy ending – he had a bout with the bottle and the bottle won, but he had his day.

Gordon didn't come back until I had my sixth child in October 1957. First I had a false labour and was sent home. When I went into labour again I carried my port across the river and walked to the hospital. Kassie watched the other kids for me.

When Gordon came home, he wanted me to call the baby Aileen, and I gave her the second name Rita, after my sister.

In a while I discovered I was sick of Gordon's drinking and irresponsible ways. I had no support except child endowment and what I earned cleaning at Joe's. I asked Gordon to get a job and help me with the kids, and later he found work on Maloufs sawmill with Peter (Chub).

We moved into one of the mill houses across the river in Drummond Street. This was my first house, and I bought ducks and chickens and started a vegetable garden in the backyard. Willy brought seedlings over and taught me about planting and talked in Chinese to his baby. I remember David in Willy's arms, the old man and the baby, the sun on them, and how happy they were. And I was happy with a two-bedroom house, my ducks, my garden. Sometimes I saw Peter watching me. I ignored him because I was with Gordon, and though the association was wearing thin I tried to keep us together for the kids' sake. If he was using me I was using him just as much. My first priority was the kids and it helped to have someone bringing in a wage now and then. A few times I saw Gordon with other women but I'd just had a baby with him, so I ignored that, and I didn't look at Peter, I ran the house and I looked after the animals, the children, the vegetables. Sometimes I wished my friend Nerida hadn't gone to Wreck Bay, or that Iris McBride lived nearby, but I made do with Willy and the kids for friends.

Gordon and Peter earned good money on the sawmill and we lived reasonably well. Gordon was out in the bush each day cutting logs and Peter was a docker on the mill, guiding logs through saws. They came home each night on the log trucks. They looked a weird pair – Gordon tall and Chub short, Gordon kind of quiet and Chub always singing. At night Gordon played his mouth organ while Chub sang the latest hits.

'Bop bopalop bop, bop bam boo
tutti frutti –'

A few months later, Peter severed the top of his thumb and two fingers on the saw. When Gordon and I went to see him he was in terrible pain, and kept calling out, 'I done me hand in, I done me hand in.' I could see he was in agony. We nursed him along until he was well again. He tried to roll cigarettes with his hand and spilled the tobacco on the floor, but he wouldn't give up and soon mastered it. He held a pen between two fingers and tried to write. I watched all this, I thought he had a lot of guts.

When the insurance came through, about £13,000, he bought a five-ton Bedford truck and he and Gordon made a log jinker by welding old railway lines together. Then they worked doing contract log-carting to the mill. But because they no longer worked on the mill we had to leave the house in Drummond Street.

So here we were without a home again. Gordon found out there was work at Yelta on a mill, so we packed everything on the truck and left for the Queensland border. Peter had a blue Smithfield cattle bitch called Peggy Sue. She sat in the front with us and we sang her song, 'Peggy Sue, I love you', and Peter sang Elvis songs and Little Richard's 'Tutti Frutti'. He was a good man. He may have been singing to cheer me up. I really didn't want to leave that house and the people at the market garden and the life there.

7

The Fencing Circus

Texas, Bonalbo, North Star, Nindigully, Thomby Station
We found an empty hut on the riverbank outside Texas.
I set up camp and the two men went to work on the
sawmill at Yetman. When I went across the footbridge
into town for supplies, I was in Queensland and when I
came back to the tent I was in New South Wales.

I fished in the river for yellow belly perch, using
mulligrubs (like a witchetty grub but smaller) or worms
for bait. The grubs and worms I found in moist places
under cow dung. I had a handline wound around a coke
bottle and I cast out into the early morning light. The
perch took the bait quietly and if I was lucky I'd catch two
or three, about ten inches long and good eating. Early
in the morning there were also plenty of ducks. I had a
·22 rifle and when I had shot some I waded into the cold
water and swam out to get them. It was getting towards
winter. Across the river and behind me were herds of
piebald and skewbald horses. There were the times I had
to myself – the men gone to work, the kids still asleep –
and I sat on the bank fishing and thinking about my life.

My mind always turned back to home in Bonalbo, and how content I was there. Sometimes I wished I'd never left. But then I would never have had my adventures, I told myself. Knowing how to sew trousers was one thing, but knowing how to survive in the bush and be able to sleep under the stars, that was another thing.

We stayed at that camp for six months. Bill was eight, Pearl was seven, Dianne was six, Nob was five, Dave four and Aileen three. I'd bought exercise books and textbooks in town and I sat them on the riverbank and taught them to read and write. On days when it rained we sat in the hut and told each other funny stories, and when the rain stopped we took buckets and went out to collect mushrooms. Texas mushrooms are as big as saucers.

Sometimes I felt like a mother and other times it was like I was the kids' big sister, still a kid myself and playing with them for the day, waiting for the real mother to come home and take charge of us all. And the real mother was me, but where had all these children come from so fast to change my life so much. The days when I felt old and responsible I would look at the kids as separate beings, I'd think about the differences between them, and about their personalities. For instance, Billy was an animal lover. Pearl was a mother hen. I would think about what they'd be like when they grew up.

One weekend I asked the men to teach me how to drive the truck. For some reason I could reverse it better than I could go forward, and when I almost backed it into the river they called the lessons off. But I'd picked up the basics and later when I got in the Hudson car I drove it easily.

When there was no more work at the sawmill we packed up and left for Toowoomba, Gordon's old town. The Darling Downs was like a huge painting and we drove through acres and acres of wheat – a rusty colour, then gold, then pale yellow, according to the stage of ripening. It was September and we could smell Toowoomba before we saw it. In the town there were blossoms everywhere.

We stopped for supplies and then pitched the tent beside a creek on the outskirts of town. These days we'd be called fringe dwellers but in those times we were just bushies, and plenty of people lived like that, poor whites as well as blacks. The men left early each day to find work in town. I should have realised this place was Gordon's old stamping ground, and one day he didn't come back.

'He's probably hitting the bottle again with all his cronies,' I said to Peter. We were sitting on drums by the fire. I told him I had some money saved and I didn't want to leave the kids and go looking for Gordon, I wanted to go home to Bonalbo. My adventures were wearing thin, I needed to be settled somewhere. Peter said he'd drive me back.

We pulled into Dyrabba Street and parked the truck in front of the old home. Midge saw me out the window and came running yelling, 'Ruby Ruby!' and taking her glasses off to see me properly. We hugged each other, I introduced Peter and we trooped into the kitchen. The woodbox where I used to sit was still there. I could hear

Aunt Nell's voice calling, 'Father, where are all those cakes gone?', Aunt Nell who was dead, who would never be in the kitchen again but never out of it either. I looked out at the cowyard – Daisy and Hobby were gone. Some chickens pecked about between the legs of Myrtle, Uncle Bill's old horse.

Midge and I talked most of the night. The last time I'd been here was when Pearl was born, and now I had six children, and Midge had three. We talked about men and how hard it was to find one who didn't mind the responsibility, and kept on loving you, and had a sense of humour.

'Peter's got a sense of humour,' she said. I knew what she meant, but I didn't want to think about it at the time.

In the next few days I made myself think about him. He was always there when I needed him, true. I'd been ignoring him for too long. True. He seemed to be more responsible than Gordon was. After a while I decided to live with him, and we moved into a two-roomed place up the street.

Not long after, we landed a job cutting stays for the coal mine at Gorge Creek. The property where we cut the stays was two miles out on a hillside. We borrowed two good axes from Uncle Willy, and Midge minded the kids for me.

This job meant going through the trees marking the ones we would need, then felling them with the axes. Next we had to strip the limbs off and measure each stay which was six feet. We sat opposite each other and sawed through them one by one, hard sweating back-breaking work. Every now and then Peter signalled me to stop and he'd go and piss on his hands. It was an old remedy to stop the blisters becoming infected. When the stays were cut we loaded them onto the truck. I also had blisters on my hands and we slept like the dead at night.

One morning I rubbed olive oil on my hands to keep them soft, and took Bill and Pearl to the school to enrol them. The teachers who taught me would be teaching my kids, and this gave me the strangest feeling. It was like I could always come back to this town and Marty Askew would be in his shop and Jim McQueen at the butchery and the schoolteachers Mr Tyler and Mrs Parker in their doorways.

I applied for a job at the hospital laundry, after getting work references from Marty and Jim to say they'd known me for fifteen years. The hospital was on a hill overlooking the school on the opposite hill. I looked out the laundry window and saw my two children playing in the schoolyard.

With the money we earned between us, we bought new mattresses and pillows and clothing for the kids. Things were going fine, then one Friday night Gordon was at the door. I mentally kicked myself for the way my heart lifted when I saw him, that long frame (like my father), those eyes. He said he'd given up the drink. 'You and the kids are all I've got.' He let out a breath. 'I don't want to be on my own any more.' I invited him in and he sat in the kitchen talking to Peter. They were glad to see each other again, despite whatever it meant about me and what I might decide to do.

I went out into the backyard to think. He did look sober. He was the father of my kids. A part of me still loved him. I must have *wanted* to believe him, because I went inside and heard myself explaining to Peter and beginning to pack. I think now I mustn't have given myself a hard enough time yet and wanted more trouble, more drama. Who can tell. Peter said he understood and waved us goodbye with a low sad look. He hugged Gordon who he always regarded as an older brother, his mate for life.

Gordon had a job to go to on a property at North Star near Goondiwindi. We said our goodbyes to Midge and Doug. What I didn't realise was that I was two or three months pregnant to Peter, too late for feeling sorry for myself. I didn't tell Gordon. I didn't write to tell Peter.

We called in at the homestead where Gordon was told he'd be night ploughing and sowing, then we went on to the outer station house where we were to live. It had big verandahs all around. There was only scattered furniture here – the kids had beds and we slept on the floor. A new hole was being dug for the bush toilet and I had to watch the kids so they didn't fall in.

This place was very lonely because the only time I saw Gordon was at night when he'd finished work. In the day he went out in the boss's jeep and fixed fences and did station hand work. The ploughing had been done so next he harrowed the ground and then started night sowing. He was working fifteen-hour days. When the kids were asleep I went out to the verandah to look for the light of the tractor so I could feel some contact with the world. Sometimes I made a billy of tea and walked down to where the light was, and he'd stop for a while. I sat on the tractor and we yarned about ordinary things – how long he thought the job would last, whether any mail had come for us at the homestead. We never had permanent jobs or houses, so we were always thinking ahead to when this one would pack up and always feeling a bit insecure.

I wrote to Midge every week and sometimes at weekends we went to the pictures in Goondiwindi. We saw mostly westerns – *High Noon* with Gary Cooper, or Roy Rodgers and Gene Autry pictures. As we drove to town we saw crowds of Kooris walking the ten miles in from the mission at Boggabilla. We loaded as many as we could in the car and gave them a lift, you can fit thirteen people in a Hudson if some are kids. I used to think it was a long way to walk just to see a movie.

Not long after the wheat sowing was finished Gordon had a letter from Peter saying he had a big fencing contract and that he was coming to see us. He turned up in a Ford Customline sedan, the truck had been repossessed. The men fell into each other's arms, the kids jumped on Peter, calling, 'Chub, Chub'. He held me briefly, and patted the swelling at my waist. He didn't ask whose baby. Neither had Gordon.

The next day the men decided to paint the cars. When we pulled into Nindigully where the job was, we looked like a travelling circus – Peter's car was red, blue and yellow, and Gordon's was blue and white. I got out of the car, put the kids on the ground and stretched my legs. The fencing circus had arrived.

Nindigully was a bush pub, a petrol bowser and a shop beside a small bridge on the Moonie Creek. Gordon stayed at the pub and sent Peter and me and the kids to set up camp at the property about ten miles away. First we stocked up on tucker and called at the homestead to see the boss who said he'd bring a sheep out later on. We were to do three miles of eight-foot-high boundary fence.

We pitched a tent between two dams, we'd use one for drinking and one for washing in. The kids went off and came back to report they were getting nipped. Yabbies in the dam, good, I liked to have curried yabbies as a change from sheep and damper, though at the moment the idea of yabbies or any other food made me nauseous, I had morning sickness. I kept looking out for Gordon because if he didn't turn up and I had to build a fence while I was pregnant I wasn't going to be too delighted with him. Late in the afternoon the boss came out with the sheep in his ute. He looked at Peter and me (I was standing up pretty straight by then) and he looked along the line of the paddocks where the fence would be and saw his fence and went off happy.

There was no sign of Gordon, so Peter and I had the job of killing the sheep. I put the chops and the lamb's fry in the meat safe, that was tonight's dinner, and I corned the rest in a kerosene tin. The kids collected wood and got a fire going for me. I unpacked the camp oven and made a stew for tea.

Early next morning we drove up to the fence line with a waterbag and some cold cooked meat and bread for lunch. Still no sign of Gordon. Looks like we had to do this job ourselves. Peter tied netting from the old fence to the towbar, and I got in the car and took off at high speed. That ripped the old fence netting and posts right out of the ground. I kept doing this until I had it all down.

Billy and Pearl did the marking – we had to dig holes for straining posts every ten chains. Then came the iron posts which had to be rammed into the ground, then the running through of the plain wire, and last barbed wire through the top. It cut our hands pretty badly.

By eleven o'clock in the Queensland heat I'd ripped the sleeves out of my dress and dipped a towel in the dam and put it on my head and it was held in place with a man's hat. When the heat was too great I told the kids to sit in the shade of some trees, then when the day's work was finished they cooled off in the dam while I cooked tea.

Some days I was too sick with my pregnancy to work and I stayed in the camp. The kids played around outside, the fence was left to Peter. I was lying on the mattress one day when I heard the kids running and screaming, 'Snake, snake, Mum.' I jumped up and went to where the snake was, I could see it in the long grass, its forked tongue going in and out. I grabbed an iron fence post and bent the end by belting it on a log. I approached the snake, the fence post raised, and when I got to within hitting distance, it ran up a tree. The kids started to laugh at the way I was sneaking up on it – it wasn't a snake but a huge goanna.

I had to restore my dignity so I got some meat and string and showed them how to catch yabbies in the dam and later I made a curry. The next afternoon I heard Peggy Sue barking at something and went to look. 'Bunning,' I said to the kids, 'look, its quills are up. Get me a waddy, quick.' Pearl came running with a stick and I hit the porcupine hard on the head. Now to get the quills off this fella, you need a kero tin of boiling water and one tin of cold. You dunk it in the boiling water to loosen the quills, then in the cold. Hold it by the legs on a log, and use a tom-axe to knock the quills off. Cut it open from the neck to the belly. In the neck are two kernels, like gallstones, where the taste of the ants goes. Take these out or else when you cook it the meat will taste of ants. Gut and wash it. The flesh is pale, the colour of pork. You bake it in a camp oven and the skin cooks like a rind, like crackling.

There is another way you can remove the quills, if you don't have kero tins for water, and that is to throw the porcupine into an open fire. It swells up and the quills burn down, but then you have to pull the butts out, and the better method is to dunk it in water.

I cut up potato and pumpkin and baked them beside the porcupine in the camp oven. I made the gravy.

A baked dinner called for bush sweets, so I made a scone mixture and boiled doughboys. The porcupine was a feast and after we had the doughboys with Golden Syrup (Cocky's Joy) poured over them.

Between Peter and me and the kids marking for us we did three miles of fencing in three weeks. I think it was a record. Sometimes we started while it was still dark and worked by the hurricane lamp and the headlights of the car. This was so we could escape the heat of the day and mostly we didn't finish before nightfall.

When we were short of groceries I put the kids and Peggy Sue in the car and headed for Nindigully. I was speeding along the boundary line and some roos were hopping along in front of me. The kids called, 'Look at the roos! Look at the roos!' Peggy Sue jumped clean out of the window and brought one down and by the time I screeched to a stop and reversed she nearly had its leg taken off. She was very protective of the kids and when they yelled out, she'd thought the roos were going to hurt them.

Just as the job finished and we were packing up camp Gordon drove in. 'Where the fucken hell have you been,' I said, 'on a binge again? Thanks for all your help.' I could see he was sick as a dog from the grog, and he was lucky I only tongue-bashed him, I gave it to him though. Serves you right, I thought, I don't have any sympathy for drunks, and I went on packing.

We went from one fencing job to the next – Toobeah, Talwood, Bungunya, Daymar.

On the way to St George we called in to a garage on the outskirts and got yarning to a bloke called Clem Jollie. Our reputation had travelled ahead of us – when he heard we had a contract to fence at Thomby Station he loaned us a tractor, posthole digger, crowbars and spades. Thomby Station was about seventy miles out on the Moonie Highway, so we stocked up on tucker, placed it in the tin bathtub on Gordon's roofracks, and the fencing circus was on its way again.

It was a huge property – the boss had a private airstrip and a store, and the boundary was fifteen miles from the homestead. We followed the boss in his ute to the fence line, Gordon driving the tractor and Peter driving Gordon's car and me with the kids and camping gear in Peter's car. It was rough ground and very bumpy.

This job would last about three months and we were roughing it. We pitched the tent and put the mattresses inside. Gordon was well enough to kill this sheep. The kids and Peter rounded up wood for the fire. The boss had brought drinking water in two forty-four-gallon drums, along with the sheep. The men had bedrolls and slept in the cars or on the ground near the fire, the kids and I slept in the tent.

That night we were woken up by wild pigs. They could smell the guts of the slaughtered sheep and had come into the camp. The kids slept through all the noise. Our cars had spotlights and we could see the tusks on the boars. We kept the ·303 handy, but Peggy Sue chased them into the scrub. They came into camp every time a sheep was killed.

Next day on the fence lines we could see this job was going to be harder than the last one. The ground was covered in gilgais, deep holes which would fill up when it rained and which made the fence go up and down unevenly. Gordon drove the tractor with the posthole digger and Peter and I lifted the poles in and rammed them down with crowbars. I told the kids to play close by and I kept watch for snakes. I killed four or five a day but they weren't poisonous ones.

A week went by and I went with Gordon to the homestead store. We packed the food in the tin bathtub on the roof racks. By the time we got back to camp it was raining and the gilgais filled with water. I stripped the kids' clothes off and bathed them there, then I washed the clothes because the rainwater lathered well and the water in the drums was hard bore water. I spread the clothing on bushes to dry and years later standing over a washing machine in Alexandria I saw an image of my earlier self squatting over a gilgai – how I'd had two completely different lives.

The following day we broke a part of the tractor and the boys had to go in to St George to get it fixed. I expected them back about nightfall, but there was no sign of them. All I had to do to get myself really anxious was to think – I'm alone in the bush with six kids. There are snakes and wild pigs around. I'm fifteen miles from the homestead and seventy miles from town. There's a car here, but I don't know the way to the homestead, there are tracks going off in all directions. If anything goes wrong, that's it.

I sat on a drum all night stoking the fires. In the distance I could hear the shitringers (Queensland stockmen) rounding up cattle, whistling to their work dogs, the crack of the whip. A curlew called out with its eerie sound.

In my people's way curlews are a spirit bird warning of death. The last thing I wanted to think about. Another bird I couldn't recognise called *mew, mew* like a crazed cat till it chilled my bones. In the dark I heard the soft thudding of roos and just before daylight an owl went *hoo-hooo-oo*. I hadn't slept at all but I was glad to see the sun and go about my chores. I convinced myself the boys would turn up by tea time.

The second night was worse. I seemed to hear every noise magnified, every sound in the bush was going through my body. I held my hands over the baby inside me. I could hear the continual hum of a motor and nothing arrived. When daylight broke I hadn't slept again and went about my chores like a zombie. I had this image of myself sitting on a drum with a ·303 listening to wild pigs grubbing in the ground and an endless parade of roos thudding by.

About dusk on the third day the men came into camp. Gordon's car had broken down. 'Never again,' I said, 'if anything goes wrong again, me and the kids are going too. You're not leaving us out here alone.' I didn't tell them about the night noises and how I thought I was going mad. I laughed about it later, but in a hysterical sort of way.

This job lasted three months and it was as hot as Nindigully. My face felt like it was peeling off in layers. Every day I'd leave the fence line early and go back to camp to cook tea. When we ran out of bread I made ashes damper or fried scones, and when the meal was ready I banged on a pot to call the men in. Every day in the heat one of the kids would remember what they'd be having in town – 'Ice cream' they'd say, or 'pineapple juice' and they'd roll on the ground groaning and giggling.

The day came to pack up. We looked along the fence, the heat haze above the wires, and said, 'Well that's done, let's get to town.' The kids were jumping all over me which started Peggy Sue off and all the way to Clem Jollie's place the kids wriggled and slapped each other and sang songs about town and the silly things they'd do. We hadn't been out of the camp for eight weeks, we were all burnt, and with the tractor and two cars piled up we looked a sight in that empty country. 'Goodbye,' I said to the fence, waving an arm out the window.

We picked up our pay and drove into St George, paid Clem Jollie what we owed him, and on to the shops. This town was a mecca of civilisation to me, look, here was a dress shop – I went right in. I needed a new dress. Halfway into the shop I saw myself in the long mirror, close up. Here was a pregnant woman with blistered hands like a man's, her face peeling like flaky pastry and black, she started black, but her arms were BLACK and the hair ginger. I stared at myself for a long time and then I bought a sleeveless cotton dress and went outside.

I hadn't been in town for so long I was lonely for another woman to talk to, so every woman I passed I said hello, hello, just to hear them talk to me.

8

The Oinky Chapter

St George, Queensland

We found a camping spot across the weir in St George on the Balonne River. It was getting close to Christmas and the men went each day trying to get work. They had no luck and our money was all gone. Peter sold the new tyres off his car so we could shop for Christmas dinner. I bought a big hunk of corned beef and cooked it in our biggest billycan over the open fire. While we were sleeping the blue dog knocked over the billycan and ate the meat. We had nothing left in the camp to eat and I didn't know what to do. I was six months pregnant and felt like I'd used up all my energy building the fences, and faced with a new problem my mind went blank. I sat on a drum and stared at the grass for a while.

Then it came to me. There was a farmhouse down the road apiece, with a market garden. I was too ashamed to go myself, so I sent a note with the kids saying what had happened to our meal. In a while Billy, Pearl and Dianne came back with fresh fruit and vegetables and a couple of chooks already cooked. I was so happy I went to thank the good people.

In the afternoon we crossed the weir to go for a swim. Gordon left the car parked on a steep slope and went away drinking with some men further down river. Peter was already in the water and I was getting out of the car when it started to roll straight towards the river with Dianne, David and Aileen the baby still inside. I ran alongside but the car dragged me along with it and just as it hit the water I pulled the back door open, encircled the kids in my arms and surfaced. The car sank in about fifteen feet of water.

I was still gasping for breath and holding on to the kids like I couldn't let them go when I turned around and saw a crowd of people watching me and I couldn't hold back any longer, I started to yell. 'You dirty rotten bastards, me and my kids could've been killed, not one of you tried to help me, what kind of people are you? Standing there and watching (I screamed), how do you sleep with your consciences at night, you bastards.' When I finished they walked away, not looking at each other or at me.

After this two four-wheel-drive jeeps pulled Gordon's car out of the river and left it on the bank to dry. He came back from the bend in the river, sozzled, and I told him what had happened. 'You can't have put the handbrake on properly,' I said, 'we nearly lost the kids.' He looked at me but he was drunk so I left it. He stayed with the car so no-one would pinch parts off it, and Peter and the kids and me went back to the camp.

I tried not to think about Gordon, to get on with the business of living. I didn't have any bait to fish with, so I lifted up some wet logs near the water and found a cricket with wings on it. I stuck the hook through it and cast out. Everything was quiet for a while, then I pulled in a cod fish weighing ten pounds and we feasted well that night.

A week later Gordon still hadn't turned up. I thought about my responsibilities with him and decided that I was too busy with looking after the kids and making ends meet to worry about him, and look after him every time he got on the piss, and I wasn't surprised when weeks went by and he didn't show. So that was the end of Gordon. He'd left without saying a word. The next time I heard of him was eight years later when Neddy told me he was living with Patty, Donk's aunty, still doing bush work and still drinking.

We moved to the other side of the weir where there was more room for camping. We met a drover called Mac McDermott who had a lean-to attached to his big truck, and we liked him straightaway. We pitched our tent near Mac and I went fishing again, this time with a ground line for yellowbelly perch. The main floodgates had been closed and I was standing in mud and silt, listening for movement in the water. The kids were playing about thirty yards away – David had a milk tin on a long piece of string. Then Bill called out, 'Mum! David's in the water.'

I couldn't see him. I started to run towards them but my legs got tangled in the line and I went down belly first into the mud. When I got up and ran along the bank

I could see Bill holding with one hand on to David's long hair and with the other to the reeds on the bank. They were bobbing like two corks and the other kids were screaming. I pulled them both out and gave David a good slap. He would have drowned only for Bill, who could see I wasn't going to make it to them on time, and had jumped in and held his brother afloat. David never went near the water after that.

I felt like I was living tribal but with no tribe around me, no close-knit family. The food-gathering, the laws and songs were broken up, and my generation at this time wandered around as if we were tribal but in fact living worse than the poorest of poor whites, and in the case of women living hard because it seemed like the men loved you for a while and then more kids came along and the men drank and gambled and disappeared. One day they'd had enough and they just didn't come back. It happened with Gordon and later it happened with Peter, and my women friends all have similar stories. Neddy and I have talked about it often as we get older, and how it's not always different for our daughters and their kids, but those stories are for later.

Now to speak about the camping ground and Mac McDermott. We teamed up with him for the purpose of food-getting and fun. Mac McDermott was thirty-nine years old, five foot ten, hair greying, always wore a Stetson hat and riding boots. He had been droving for years but all he had left of his droving outfit was his truck. He'd sold off all his saddles and horses to survive when he was broke.

He had a cattle dog called Blue, the best trained dog I've seen. At night we shared a fire and Mac said, 'You watch this. Blue, you're a bad dog, go hide your face, I don't want to see you.' Blue would slink away and glance back, waiting for Mac to call him back. 'Go on, go away,' Mac yelled and he went further away. Mac said, 'You try and call him back, see if he comes.' We called and pleaded but he never budged and then Mac whistled and he came running straight back and sat at his feet. When Mac and Peter were roo shooting at night – because the riverbank was a place where there were drinking parties and they'd get rowdy – Mac would say, 'Blue, go look around,' and the dog would circle the camp all night. None of the drunks came near our camp.

Mac and Peter had taken up roo shooting to earn some money and I in turn used to earn £10 a hundred for pegging the skins to dry, a job I didn't like. The skins were kept in a big freezing works but they were stinking by the time we got them to peg out. The men were paid threepence a pound for the carcasses, and I was told that the people who exported it were getting eleven shillings a pound.

The men went out spotlighting each night. Our camp soon looked like a menagerie – the men brought home baby roos whose mothers had been shot. I nailed a chaff bag to a tree and got the knife and slashed a hole in the middle and we kept the joeys there till they were big enough to let go.

One evening Mac said, 'I forgot to tell you, I caught a piglet. It's on the seat of the truck, it might be dead.

I forgot all about it.' The kids opened the door and there it was, badly dehydrated. They filled a big bowl with water and laid the pig in. Soon it was grunting and squealing with pleasure. The kids fed it with a titi bottle and it thrived and they christened it Oinky.

We were on the riverbank for many months. On washdays I put everything in the big round tub, put a packet of Rinso or Persil in, and got the kids to help me down to the river. While I washed the clothes the kids swam and sometimes they washed Oinky and used nearly all my Rinso to get him clean and beautiful then he'd roll right back in the mud, then follow us back to camp and sleep under the bed in the tent all day.

There were some sleeper offcuts lying around and we used them to build a pen for Oinky. He needed somewhere safe, where people couldn't steal him. In the day he followed the kids around butting them and squealing if they wouldn't give him any bread when they were eating. He grew quite big with the loving attention the kids gave him and eventually became a member of the family. On endowment days I drove to town in the Ford Customline to do the shopping. Bill sat in the front with Peggy Sue, Peter's dog sitting up beside him. The other kids were in the back with Oinky who sat at the window and paid a lot of attention, like Peggy Sue did, to the outside world. The car had no low gear so I clutch-started it from the camp but then sometimes on the way to town it would stall. Fortunately there were workmen on this road and when they saw a red, blue and yellow car, with fins, and a black woman getting out, and a Smithfield cattle dog and a pig looking at them from the windows of the car, and six or seven faces of children, they were only too pleased to help by giving a push.

In town I had to do a lot of talking and finally I convinced the manager of the grocery store to keep my endowment book and let me get groceries ahead of the next pay, which I'd then sign over to him.

One evening when we got back Mac had set lines in the river for yellowbelly perch and cod. He put little bells on the lines and in the night we heard them ring and went to get our fish. Next day he shot an emu and brought the steaks back to camp. It was very dark red meat with sinews running through it like blade steak. When there was no work Mac went into the bush with his ·303 and came back with a couple of killers (sheep) and when I asked how he was able to get them in the night time he said, 'Well I drive around until I see sheep in a paddock and wait till it's dark, then I call out *baa, baa-aaa*. When the sheep answers back I fire towards the sound, and I always get a couple of sheep.' He was a crafty old drover, an ex-army man and a crack shot. His gun didn't have a telescopic sight, but we joked about his telepathic scope.

The kids wanted a hole put in a piece of piping to make an axle for a billycart, but we had no drill, so Mac stood the steel pipe up against a gum tree, up with the rifle and shot a hole clean through it. The kids were delighted – they put a bolt through and screwed the nut in place and they had a billycart.

Mac used to love his grog too, and could recite poetry. I used to think what next, a drover who stands in front of the open fire and gives forth with 'The Man from Snowy River' and 'My Country' by Dorothea Mackellar. The kids sat listening in quiet wonder at Mackless their friend and billycart maker.

Dianne had invented a game with words one day which led to Mac being called Mackless. We were in the car going to town and some roos passing by made her say, 'Kangarooster!' and the other kids started to turn words around for fun. 'Hoppergrass!' Dianne said. Bill looked at her. 'Emu?' he said. 'E-me!' said Dianne. Back at camp they looked at Mac and Dianne said, 'Mackless!' and we called him that for the rest of our time together.

Oinky grew into a beautiful big pig. We'd built pens for keeping wild pig which we fed on our scraps till the rank game taste had gone from their flesh, and these ones we ate. But Oinky was a pig apart – he'd grown up with the kids and thought he was one of them. He didn't associate with the wild pigs but ran around free and at night the kids locked him up.

At this time Peter made friends with the people, poor whites and Kooris, who lived in the camping area across the river. Often there were ringbarking outfits there, waiting to be picked up for work. At night they had card schools, they played mostly poker and a game called pups, and the gambling would go on till the early hours. Men and women played, they sat on the ground or on rugs or sometimes four-gallon drums under a bower shed made of poles with branches and leaves for a roof. Peter became a mad gambler, and the kids and me went to the card schools with him and slept in the car while we waited.

One night when we got back Oinky was out of his pen and I shone the hurricane lamp on him and I could see something was wrong with his ears. I called him over and then I nearly cried – the dogs had ripped his ears almost off, they were just hanging. I asked Peter to cut them off because they'd get infected, but he wouldn't.

The next day Oinky's ears were fly-blown. I could see he was in agony, so I got the kids to hold him down while I cut his ears off and then caked the holes with wet mud. In a few days the mud had dried and his wounds were healed, but he was deaf. Otherwise he was okay, and he still followed the kids everywhere and joined in the games.

A month or so later I had taken the kids to town and when we came back Oinky was gone. I asked Peter where he was, and he told me he'd sold him to a butcher to pay off a gambling debt. I couldn't believe it. 'You had no right to sell Oinky,' I yelled, 'he was the kids' pet,' and I swore and yelled some more but it was too late to save Oinky. The kids hardly spoke to Peter for a week. Everyone was quiet.

Once we had got over the loss of our pig, we moved to the camping area across the river, about half a mile out. Here there were showers and washing tubs and coppers, and quarter-acre plots where you could pitch a tent or build a hut out of scantlings. We were lucky to get one that was already built, and this was where we stayed. Peter was close to his gambling school, I had the kids enrolled in school, and Peter found work on the local council.

I started to get labour pains. Peter heated water over the fire and filled up the tin bath so I could have a tub before I went to hospital. I don't know what I would have done without Peter – he was always there to help me out and always singing songs and making jokes, and even though I was still mad at him for selling Oinky he was good around the camp and good to me. When my time came I was in St George Hospital and had a relatively easy birth. My fourth daughter who I named Ellen Linda was born in April 1960. Peter picked the first name, Ellen was his mother's name, and I called her the second name Linda after the song, 'Please forgive me, Linda darling'. A few days afterwards I noticed cotton wool around her ankle and asked the nurse what it was for. She said it was to stop the baby rubbing her feet together, but it wasn't so. Ellen had gastroenteritis and nearly died. Her eyes were sunken back into her head and I was ready to go home but I had to stay because she was so sick. I found out what the cotton wool was for – they were giving her drips to put fluid into her body. I went crook at them for not telling me and as soon as she was well enough I took her home to the camping area and she soon picked up.

One night I was woken up by someone trying to take her out of my arms. I sat up but there was no-one there, then I could feel the presence of a spirit. I waited quietly but I couldn't tell who it was, and I stayed awake half the night. Next morning a truck pulled into the camp with a lot of men on the back, a ringbarking outfit from Moree. Among them was Sam Griffin, looking sharply dressed even in his work clothes, I recognised him straightaway. He saw us and came over.

'I'm sorry to hear about your Dad,' he said.

'What about Dad?'

'Didn't you know, your father passed away about two months ago. The family's been trying to get in touch with you.'

I collapsed onto a chair. Now I knew who the spirit was, trying to take the baby out of my arms last night. No wonder I couldn't sleep. I gave way to great sobs and Peter and Sam stood by helplessly watching me. They both knew how Dad had been mother and father to me, and he'd *always* been there when I needed him, and now there was no more always, no Dad. It was very hard for me to believe.

The truck Sam was on had just called to the camp to pick up more workers, and they went on their way. He didn't go to say hello to the kids, who were playing nearby, I don't know if he even looked at them. But I only registered this underneath the emotion about Dad.

I was so stunned by his death that I got in touch with Mum Joyce straightaway. It seemed all the telegrams and police messages had come when I was working on Thomby Station. We didn't come into town till the job finished, and no-one knew we were on a fence line seventy miles out of St George. Peter left his job and sold the car to get extra money. We gave Peggy Sue to Mac, because his dog Blue had been hit by a car and killed not long before. It was hard saying goodbye to the old drover and our dog. We got the bloke who bought the car to drive us to Mungindi, the nearest railway, and we were on our way to Sydney.

9

A Stranger in My Camp

Alexandria, the Gunnedah Hill

It was May 1960 when we arrived at Phillip Street, Alexandria, where Mum Joyce was living with Rita and Dennis and Kevin. She fell into my arms at the door and then we sat down and had a good cry. She was lost without Dad – they'd been together for eighteen years.

'I want you to have these things belonging to your father,' she said. It was his cricketing cap, I put my face into it and could still smell the Brylcreme, and every time I wanted to remember him, I'd smell his cap, his personality was so strong in it, it was just like he was there and not gone.

The other thing was his cricket trophy which read BEST ALL-ROUNDER: H. ANDERSON and the date was 1951-52, the years that Billy and Pearl were born. There was also a hat-trick ball mounted on a trophy, Rita got that.

We settled in but with thirteen people in a two-bedroom terrace the tempers flared and Peter didn't like living in a mob scene. I spent a lot of time with Mum Joyce and it was like we were locked into our own world of grief for Dad, and Peter wasn't part of it. He decided to go and stay with his sister in Redfern.

I didn't like to stay with Mum Joyce and not help out, so I applied for welfare support. I'd get a cheque each fortnight but it wasn't enough. I thought if I could put the kids in the Church of England homes and go back to machining I'd manage better. I think I must have decided this in the numbness of shock over Dad's death.

The big head of the homes was a floor manager at Mark Fays in the city. I'd made enquiries and had an appointment to see him. I went up in the lift, my heart sinking as the lift rose, wondering how long it would be before I could afford to get the kids out again. I told him I was a qualified machinist and wanted to place my kids in the homes till I got settled. I'd give him the endowment and what I could afford out of my wages. He asked all sorts of personal questions and I told him everything. He said he'd give me a date, and that someone would come and pick the kids up.

The kids and I were sleeping on the floor on mattresses, Dennis and Kevin who were ten and eleven were sleeping with Mum Joyce in her bed and Rita was on the divan downstairs. At night my mind was in a turmoil and I came slowly to the realisation of what I was doing. The people would be picking the kids up in a few days and I couldn't bear it.

A wind was howling and blowing up the stairs, it was so strong it blew the bolt off the door. In my anguish I tossed and turned and was weeping as though my heart would break. Then I could sense my father's spirit, he was there, I could feel him patting my arm, comforting me. I fell into a deep sleep.

A few days later Peter was there with his sister's car loaded up with fruit and vegetables from the market. 'Go and get dressed up, I'm taking you somewhere,' he said. I was shocked but in a strange way pleased he'd come back. I put my best dress on and he took me to Newtown and pulled up in front of a jeweller's store. What is going on? I thought. Why's he being so secretive?

Next thing he pointed to the wedding rings and said to pick one. 'You and me are getting married today –' He had a big grin on his face. I didn't know what to do, I was dumbfounded. I picked one with orange blossoms on, and we had to go to Marrickville to the Schools of Arts to have the words said over us. The JP who married us introduced herself as Mary Louise Hills, and we asked the janitor and his wife to be our witnesses.

On the way home, to celebrate, Chub took out on hire purchase a black-and-white television set and we took it home for the kids to watch. Mum Joyce and the boys moved to Wilson Street and sister Rita moved away with her boyfriend Podge, and left us the house. I didn't have to put my children in the homes after all. Peter was working and I landed a job cleaning in a printing place in Henderson Road, where I live now, twenty-seven years later. My work started at five in the afternoon and finished at nine. Sam's sister, Brenda Leslie, came to live with us and she and Peter fed the kids at night.

We had just settled in and got the kids started at the school around the corner, Alexandria Public, when a letter came from Chub's father, old Jim Langford, saying he was sick and needed Peter at home. I wasn't sure what this meant. Peter was his youngest son, and maybe he just wanted him around. I knew from things Jim had half-said that he didn't think Peter should take on a woman with so many kids to other men, and though the baby, Ellie, was Peter's and mine, Jim didn't seem to take this into account, or the fact that Peter might have decided he wanted to help me bring up the kids.

I couldn't say any of this to Peter, and maybe the old man was really sick, at any rate we were soon on the road again. Brenda Leslie came with us, also her boyfriend Reggie Morris, who was Mum Joyce's nephew. We didn't own any furniture at this time. Chub took the TV back to the hire purchase place, and we packed our clothes into suitcases. We travelled all night and into the following afternoon in the Holden ute, Chub driving with me, Ellie the baby and Aileen in the front, and Brenda and Reggie in the back with Billy, Pearl, Dianne, Nobby and David. On the road, those flat roads going west through paddock after paddock of sheep and wheat, I thought Coona was like a magnet to me, always drawing me back. I was always in the thick of the city or at the edges of country towns in missions and camps, there was no in between.

We were tomato picking a few days later, the smell of ripening tomatoes all around us and the green viney smell of the bushes, and then we were apple picking and I was like a permanent Eve, eating the apple and having babies and walking around the orchard in a daze of good smells and backache. Brenda and Reggie had gone to live on the Gunnedah Hill with her mother (my first 'mother-in-law') Ruby Leslie, and we camped with Jim and Kassie in the workers' hut near a creek on the farm five miles out on the Barradine Road. Old Jim was picking tomatoes and apples along with us, he didn't look too sick to me and I realised he had wanted Peter home, and this was the way he'd gone about it. There was no point saying anything, we had work, the kids were happy and healthy, but I see from this distance now, it was another example of me being moved about by other people's needs and I would not have minded being settled.

When the work finished, Jim and Kassie moved back to old Joe's market garden and Peter and I pitched our tent on the Gunnedah Hill down from the Leslies. It was no trouble in fine weather but it leaked pretty bad in the rain. We looked around for work but things had gone very quiet, and then Peter told me he was going back to Sydney to look for a job. I didn't know then that it would be the last time I'd see him for years.

I was alone with seven kids and one on the way and no money for food. My camp was near the aerodrome, only used by light planes, and other people camped round about. Drunks would see my fire and come over but didn't bother me – if they got rowdy I'd say, 'Please go further

153

away, my kids are asleep,' and they would. But I was scared and I slept with a butcher's knife under my pillow.

Harold Leslie gave me a camp dog, a cattle dog cross. She had a litter of six pups and when they grew up I had seven watch dogs. I had to have a plan to live so I applied for the dole at the police station, and because I had no word from Peter I took out a maintenance order against him for non-support, then the battle began.

I'd put my endowment book in at Billy Woo's store and have it used up months in advance. I earned money scrubbing out his shop and when that ran out I gave him my wedding ring to hold for £6 worth of tucker. There go the orange blossoms, I thought. As far as I know the ring is still there.

Then I bought a dozen flour bags off Colin Neate the baker and some twine and a bag needle and opened the bags out and sewed a big fly for the leaky tent and put bits of tin round the side to stop the wind. When the dole came through we got a voucher each fortnight for groceries, value depending on how many were in the family, and another voucher for meat. This took care of the food, then to get it back to the hill I'd wrap it in my coat and carry it, or book a taxi. My next concern was to gather some things for the hospital, nighties, baby's clothes. That had me stumped for a while.

Back in the tent at night Billy had the kids on their knees praying. 'Please Lord bless mummy to have all the things she needs, for our new baby brother or sister.' It made me proud to see their little heads bowed by the light of the lamp without a globe and the wind somehow not blowing it out and the kids' voices curving round the tent walls.

One night we could hear a big storm coming up and the kids were praying again, 'Please Lord don't let the storm blow down our tent, it's the only home we have,' and the wind howled and it knocked down pine trees and blew roofs off houses in the town and it blew all around the tent and never touched it. The light didn't even blow out and I felt kind of powerful then, that God was on my side if he existed, or at least the kids had the power to stop Mother Nature from destroying her own.

And all the clothing I needed came from nowhere, people gave things to me. Pauline Harvey came over with her father's station wagon loaded up, she had a double bed and mattress and a big cane pram, which she said was hers when she was a baby, and boxes of baby clothes and nighties, also a side of sheep and boxes of eggs and vegetables. I'd lived on her father's property before, and used to make skirts and blouses for her. So I ended up with everything I needed for hospital and then some.

A young bloke who said his name was Robert, not the full quid but harmless, came sometimes to help me carry water and cut wood. He wouldn't accept money for the work, so I gave him tea and damper with syrup. At weekends he rounded up the kids to go to the Dep (town dump) and they rummaged for toys.

One day he was digging trenches around my tent, drains to let the water get away when it rained. He kept going back and forward to the bush. I thought he had the runs, and didn't take any notice till he started to fall over.

I rushed to see what was wrong and I could smell metho on his breath. 'Robbie, who gave you the goom?' He pointed to the bush and said, 'Montie Chattie,' and passed out. I picked up the biggest waddy I could find and ran at the bushes. Montie took to his heels and ran like blazes.

I was still finding it hard to make ends meet. One morning I wrote to the Smitho's head office in Sydney and they sent some of the head catholics in Coona over to check me out and these people then brought boxes of clothing and food. I managed to buy another tent and I paid two young fellas from the mission to pitch it for me. The first storm we had arms and legs everywhere, in the space of two seconds FLOP the tent caved in on us and the scramble was on, me and the kids fighting to get out from under all this tarpaulin and laughing and grabbing each other's legs and falling over again. But after the fun I was wild and I went down to the mission, about two hundred yards, to see if I could find the helpful young men. But they'd shot through and later a few of the old fellows came and pitched it properly for me, pegged it down tight and put drain holes so the water could run away. Pauline came to inspect my new place and after a while she was teasing me about the new baby's name and threatening not to speak to me unless I called the baby after her. I mentioned that I had four girls and three boys, maybe the new one would be a boy to even it up, but Pauline put her nose in the air and said very sternly, 'This one will be a girl.'

Every day I went down to the mission and got through the fence to their tap and carried my drums of water back to camp. On the way sometimes I met old Ruby coming down from the shanties and one day she told me Brenda had had her baby, a girl called Regina. This child was first cousins with Billy, Pearl and Dianne. Ruby and I sat our water drums down and rested, halfway back up the hill, and talked about who was related to who around the place, which was half or step, which was full, and so on. It took us quite a while, and when we had that sorted out we carried on our way. I was two weeks from my time and I went in to visit Brenda and Regina and felt lonely in advance that I'd have no man there to be glad of my new baby and I kicked the foot of the bed (without thinking) and Brenda said, 'Ow!'

When I went into labour Jackie Milligan took me into Coona Hospital in his taxi and my eighth child was born a girl and I named her Pauline Ann. It was January 1962 –hot, fine, and this was the fourth child I'd had in this hospital and it was Doc Frazer attending me.

Back at the camp I sent the kids to the Dep for drums to sit on, I was tired of having no lounge room furniture. When I was well enough for walking I went to the Dep myself and obtained my laundry – a copper for boiling the clothes. At this time I also improved my method for carrying water – I had a forty-four-gallon drum near the tent for my tank, and I'd been filling it by carrying eight gallons at a time from the mission tap, four gallons in a kero tin in each hand. Now I made myself a yoke with wires, I put a towel on my neck then the yoke and this was easier on the stomach muscles. I couldn't take it too easy because I had to cut up big trees and drag logs home for the fire. Billy was now eleven and Pearl ten, and they helped with the lighter work.

My tents started to look like a home. In one I had two double beds and one single for Bill and a cot in the corner for Pauline. In the other I had a table and four chairs I bought when I received some welfare money, and a kitchen cabinet for food and crockery. My toilet consisted of three pine trees growing in a triangle, which I nailed hessian around, a seat pan the council collected once a week, and an umbrella on a limb in case it rained.

Once a month a welfare officer came to see me, to check on the kids, and he was surprised, he said, to see everything spotless and the kids off to school each day on the mission bus. By this time Pauline was five or six months old and when she was bathed and fed I laid her outside the tent under the shade of a tree to sleep, with a mosquito net over her. I was arranging the net one morning so it didn't drape on her face when I heard a 'Hello' behind me. It was the welfare officer again. I offered him a drum to sit on and stoked the fire to make tea. I wondered what it was about this time, he looked serious.

'I want you to get in touch with the Aboriginal Protection Board,' he said, 'because I'm gonna recommend you for housing land in town. It becomes freehold in ten years, what d'you think?'

'I'll be pleased if you'll do that,' I said, and straightaway while he was talking I had fantasies about getting a roof over the kids' heads and having taps, and floors. Full of excitement and plans I wrote the letter but not long after a reply came that I was refused, because I was a woman who had eight kids and no husband to support me and was only surviving on welfare and endowment payments and what I could earn washing and ironing in town.

Pauline took sick with gastroenteritis, flies everywhere and on the hill sandflies. I took her to Doc Frazer and he said she was okay, and then in the middle of the night I noticed she was dehydrating, her eyes were sinking inwards, so I wrapped her in a rug and left the kids asleep in the tent and carried her to town, about two miles, and at the hospital the sister called Doc Frazer and he came straightaway and said quietly, 'It's a good thing you're an observant mother.' He admitted her to hospital where they kept her for two weeks to make her well. Doc Frazer gave me a lift back to the hill as I told him I'd left the others asleep in the tent.

About a month later one of the kids from the mission caught up with me carrying my water back to camp, and said Doc Frazer wanted to see me. I went in to his surgery and sat down, not sure what it could be about. He said, 'I've had a private investigator track your husband down. He's with a sideshow next to Cadbury's chocolate factory in Tasmania. You go and tell the police this information, Ruby, and we'll see what they can do to get some maintenance out of him.' I thanked him and when I was walking to the police station I realised he must have paid the private eye out of his own money, I felt pretty grateful about that.

The police told me I'd have to pay to have him extradited back to face maintenance charges, so I said, 'Look, let him rot in hell,' and walked back to my camp.

At night when the kids were asleep I started to write, and that made me feel happy. I entered a NADOQ (National Aborigines Day Observance Quest) writing competition. The subject was what you would like to become, and I wrote about doctoring. A while later I received notification that I'd won the quest. My prize was one guinea, and I was very happy to have it though the prize for this quest today is an all-expenses-paid trip overseas. There you go.

On a hot morning I was washing clothes in the big tub and glanced up to see a tall man going by on the road up to the Leslies'. I thought it was Sam, he waved, and I waved back. A few days later I went up to Brenda's to borrow some camphorated oil and she introduced me to the tall man, whose name was Lance Marriot. He patted me on the head and called me Shorty. I slapped his hand away and stormed out, saying, 'Don't manhandle me,' forgetting the camphorated oil I'd come for.

Later in the afternoon he came down to the tent and apologised to me. He reached in his pocket and took out the camphorated oil, and I made tea and we yarned.

He soon had me laughing and got my axe and offered to cut me a heap of wood, and I was grateful for the help.

We became good friends and in the night he brought his guitar down and sat by the fire and played. The kids from the mission heard him and came through the fence and over to our fire one by one appearing out of the shadows and one by one they'd go home to bed, and when all mine were asleep, we'd sit and drink tea and yarn half the night away.

He came from fruit-picking country at Wentworth, near Mildura, from a family of seven, one girl and six boys. He'd lost his mother and his youngest brother through cancer. His mother was an up and coming tennis player in her day and she was part Aboriginal, and his father was a Pom from Shropshire who was a head chef at Heidelberg Repatriation Hospital in Melbourne for many years, and before that in the merchant navy.

Lance said he was married (to a Koori) and separated, he'd left home as a boy when his mother died and hitchhiked around doing bush work. I looked at him while he stared at the fire and talked. He had a Koori nose, broad shoulders and a long thin body like a runner. Dark eyes, dark hair, big bony knuckles from street fighting. He told funny stories, he liked to laugh.

I didn't know then I would live with this bloke for eight years and have a son with him. All I saw was a stranger in my camp, someone who'd helped by cutting me some wood, a laughing sort of man at a fire surrounded by kids and singing:

'I fell in love with a Mexican girl –
night time would find me in Rosa's cantina
the music would play and Fillina would whirl.
Black as the night were the eyes of Fillina,
wicked and evil while casting a spell –'

And Lance sang this song looking past the kids at me, he serenaded me and I was in love again.

I was happy living on the Gunnedah Hill. They nicknamed me the bush lawyer – anyone on the mission needing forms filled in for endowment and pensions came to me. I was renowned for winning one guinea on the subject of doctoring and now I was the local writer.

But later on I became sick from all the gut-busting and heavy lifting I had to do and I developed a hernia. Every time I coughed my navel popped out and eventually Doc Frazer told me I needed an operation, but I'd have to go to Sydney to get it done.

Lance and I were living together now, that serenading with the guitar had done the trick. When I told him what the doctor had said, we discussed it and decided to move to Sydney. Lance had been doing bush work and we had some money saved.

The day we were to leave I called my seven camp dogs to me and stood there with them for some time. There was no-one who would feed them and I couldn't leave them to starve, and just as I was deciding what would have to be done, Nerida Chatfield, my old friend from the days I'd lived here with Sam, turned up, having come from Wreck Bay to the mission to visit her relatives. She flung her arms around me and hugged all the kids. I introduced her to Lance and then told her about my operation and the dogs. Lance looked at the dogs, then at me, then mimed firing a gun and I nodded. Without a word he went off to the Leslies' place to borrow the rifle, and while he took the dogs over in the bush and put them to sleep and dug holes and buried them, Nerida was helping me dress the kids and cut sandwiches for the trip. I would spread margarine and hear a rifle shot, do up buttons on a dress, hear a rifle shot, spread Vegemite, a rifle shot. It was pretty hard.

I gave my tents to Brenda and Reggie and they bought my camping gear off me – beds and cabinets, chairs and table, the camp oven (which I thought of as a friend, my old faithful). I stood looking sadly at the only home I'd had for my kids, and wondered if I'd ever improve on it, then Jacky Milligan and Morrie Hunt arrived with their taxis to take us to the station.

When I bought the tickets we were still short, and the train was waiting for us. I yelled to Jacky and he backed up. I gave him my endowment book, signed, and got the rest of the money off him, and I gave him my address to post it down to me. Saved again by the taxi-banker. I hugged Nerida hard and told her where we'd be in Sydney, we herded the eight kids on to the train, and we were on our way to Sydney again.

10

Corroboree/Phaedra

Redfern, Surry Hills

Mum Joyce and my stepbrothers lived over a coffee shop in Regent Street, Redfern. They only had two rooms, so we slept on mattresses in the kitchen. Lance found work and I went into Rachel Foster Hospital for my hernia operation. Mum Joyce watched the kids while Lance worked, and he took over at night.

I was eight days in hospital, and one afternoon an elegant woman in a yellow suit and black gloves, bag and shoes walked into the ward. It took me a while to realise it was my mother come to visit me. She asked where I'd been all the time. I said I'd been moving around, working in the bush. I didn't know how much to say, there was no point worrying her, but I would've liked to tell someone close what was happening. In the end I talked mostly about the kids. I was very thirsty and she gave me ice to suck on.

I came home still weak and hoping to rest but the kids all had the measles. Between cooking and washing and caring for my little brood I hardly slept for a week, but there was nothing to be done about it.

At this time Aunt Phyllis was leaving the three-bedroom place she had, and asked us if we'd take it over. With thirteen of us in a two-bedroom place we jumped at the chance, and Aunt Phyllis took us to meet the owner, Mrs Kearney.

When we first moved into Ann Street, Surry Hills, we survived on my endowment and any casual work Lance could get, but it only covered food. I took the kids to the Smith Family to get outfitted and with eight of them we took up two fitting rooms. They got to know us well and we'd go home loaded up with brown paper parcels and cardboard boxes of tinned food. One morning they approached me at home and asked if they could take photos of the kids for their Christmas appeal. Somewhere in their files is a picture of me with a beehive hairstyle sitting on the front step of Ann Street nursing Pauline, who was two, and Ellen (four) sitting beside us.

Lance was working on the Water Board and I got a job around the corner at Silknit House making trousers for Reuben F. Scarf. I asked my cousin and his wife to stay and they saw the kids off to Cleveland Street School each day. Things were looking up. We bought a Ford Mainline ute and went to Paddys each Saturday for food, then we took the kids swimming at Coogee.

Nerida and her new man Booker Trindle turned up. Booker was a mate of Lance's from the days after Lance's mother had died and he was on the road. They'd worked together in the bush. I remembered Booker from the

Clifton one night where Lance had introduced him as his brother. I shook his hand. He was very handsome and dressed in a suit. I was taken in but they were only conning me up. Now Booker and Neddy were living in Redfern.

Our favourite Koori watering hole was the Rockers. Its real name was the Macquarie, it was down in Woolloomooloo on the docks. They had big jazz bands and we got dolled up and went down sometimes to listen to the bands and have a few beers.

Lance and Booker wouldn't let Neddy and me go down there by ourselves, that was where the sailors drank and they were frightened they might lose us two good-looking sorts. We decided to give them a piece of their own medicine.

We sneaked down there one night and we were having a great time when who should walk through the doors of the pub but Lance and his sidekick Booker. 'There you are, you two,' they said, and, 'We've been looking for you everywhere.' We said we'd only just gotten there, which was a lie, we'd been there for a couple of hours and we were having a great time, but they frogmarched us out and told us to get home.

We said, 'We'll get a taxi,' and they said, 'Start walkin'.' Big men, and they made us walk all the way to Surry Hills. Blokes were driving past and whistling at us, and they'd tell them to piss off, and say to us, 'Keep walkin'.' I thought we'd never make it and we were buggered when we did get home. Well we never did that again, I mean sneak away by ourselves, it was a lesson well-learned for Neddy and me.

Not that they could put anything over us two, we were too cunning. They'd have to wake up early to catch us out.

'Look here,' Neddy said one day, 'there's a photo of you and the kids in the paper.' She handed me a copy of the *Mirror* and there we were, smiling for the Smithos.

Booker came in late that night, hair and clothes everywhere, he must've been on a binge for a week. Lance grabbed him by the arm. 'What the hell are you doin'? Look at you, why don't you look after yourself,' he said. 'Use my razor, come on, get in here and have a bath, here's a clean shirt, come on Booker, straighten yourself up.' The times Booker came in and didn't take any notice of Lance, Lance thumped him. They were like that, like brothers.

The kids were going to Sunday School round the corner in Commonwealth Street. The place was run by Central City Mission and was also a soup kitchen for the needy. They gave the kids bread and pies and cakes to bring home when we had no food. The Brown Sisters came to our rescue, they were called Our Lady of the Poor and wore brown habits.

I'd heard about the Aboriginal Progressive Association and I decided to go to the meetings. Charlie Perkins was there, and the Bostocks, Eadie and Lester, also Bertie Groves, Charlie and Peggy Leon, Joyce Mercy, Ray Peckham, Helen Hambly, Allan Woods and Isobel McAllum whose father was Bill Ferguson, a member of the Aborigines' Protection Board. We elected Charlie Perkins spokesman – he was still at university – and we met at the Pan Hellenic Club rooms in Elizabeth Street. Charlie organised that because he played soccer for the club. I was elected editor for our newspaper *Churringa* (meaning message stick). Ever since school and the long stories I'd wanted to do some writing, so I was happy.

It was about 1964 when we formed our first Sydney APA. We heard some dancers were coming down from Mornington Island to perform a corroboree at the Elizabethan Theatre in Newtown. At the next meeting we decided to apply for concessions. I'd never seen a corroboree or been in a big theatre before. Our seats were upstairs overlooking the stage.

When the lights went out we could see the glow of a fire on centre stage, with bodies huddled around it, and we could hear a didgeridoo in the background and clapping sticks and then the chanting. In a while the whole stage was aglow with the light from the fire, and the corroboree began.

A narrator talked over a microphone, explaining the action as the dancers performed. After each performance we clapped and clapped. Something inside me understood everything that was going on. I had tears in my eyes and I could feel the others in the group were entranced like me.

One story in particular made me sad. It was about a tribal family – man, woman and child. It told how another man came and took the woman away, and left the baby to die. The father searched and hunted until he found the man and speared him. His wife threw herself over a cliff and died. The final scene showed the father burying his child, and it was the most moving part of the corroboree. It showed him digging the earth up with his hands and placing the bark-covered body into the ground, and, as he was covering it with earth he'd smite himself across the chest and wail for the loss of his child and cover more soil over the body then smite himself again and this went on until he had it completely covered. I was crying by then.

Afterwards, we asked permission to visit them backstage. It was strange because they were dressed in khaki overalls and they were so tall, big rangy warriors all over six feet. Only one of them could speak English, a bit pidgin and they were wary as they looked at us, until the one who could speak explained that we were part of them, and then they gave us big toothy grins and we were shaking hands all round. I can remember almost every detail from that night.

I went to a meeting of the APA on National Aborigines' Day in Martin Place. The Governor General and several other dignitaries (black and white) were going to speak. I wore a fur stole over my dress. I put my stilettos on and did my hair up. At Martin Place I met up with the others and found a seat. The Police Band sat behind us. A man on the dais was singing in the lingo and I listened closer. It was Bundjalung language, words and sounds I hadn't heard for a long time. It was an eerie feeling in among the skyscrapers.

I looked harder and I recognised the singer, it was Uncle Jim Morgan. When the singing stopped a hand tapped me on the shoulder and a voice said, 'Hello Mrs Campbell.' Someone from the time I was with Gordon, I thought, turning around. Coona. It was Max Gruggan, the policeman who used to pull Gordon out of the pub and send him home to Charlie Harvey's property. 'I didn't hardly recognise you, all done up,' he said. We swapped notes – he'd transferred to Penrith in the meantime. I couldn't concentrate much because I was thinking about Uncle Jim Morgan and the singing.

In a while I went and found Uncle Jim. I hadn't seen him since I was at school in Bonalbo and he was glad to see me too, like meeting someone from your own town in another country. He had to go soon after and so I put word out about him.

Some time later my cousin Margaret in Wollongong sent me two paper clippings – one about Grandfather Sam and one about Uncle Jim. JAMES MORGAN LIVED IN TWO WORLDS, it read. He had collapsed and died shortly before he was to address a large crowd in Casino for National Aborigines' Day. 'A full-blood Aborigine, Mr Morgan was known as "the last of the Dyrabba tribe".' Dyrabba? That was the name of our street in Bonalbo. 'He was born on the site of Casino racecourse ... He was a fluent speaker of Bunjalong [spelt that way] and had a working knowledge of the twelve dialects in the Bunjalong area which extends from Ipswich to Grafton ... He was also an expert on folklore of this area. He made many recordings for the Richmond River Historical Society …'

This meant I could find out some more about my history. I decided to write to the RRHS for the tapes.

His funeral was to be held at the chapel at Box Ridge, he was to be buried at Coraki cemetery. Home ground.

I came home after an APA meeting one night about nine or ten and Lance was standing on the balcony calling out, 'Why don't you stay home and look after the kids instead of running around to meetings,' and so I had to give up my political work before I'd edited the first issue of *Churringa*.

Just over the road from where Mum Joyce lived in Regent Street was the Empress Hotel, the main meeting place for city Kooris at weekends. For the Kooris coming to the city it was a place where you could find out where all your relatives lived. It was also where you could find out things you weren't supposed to know. I was a trusting person and didn't even suspect, but I found out Lance was sleeping with my good mate, so the next time I saw her at the Empress, I belted the hell out of her and they carted her away in an ambulance.

Lance tried to stop me, he punched me in the mouth and broke my false teeth, but I still wouldn't stop. The boys at the hotel defended me, they knew what Lance had done, and they held him back while I meted out justice. 'Leave her alone,' they said to Lance, 'if she's gonna do that, let her do it.'

When I finished with my friend and she was taken away I reached out for my coat, someone was holding it

171

for me. It was a cream and tangerine reversible coat and it had blood all over it. The two broken parts of my top plate were in the pocket. I turned the coat to the other side so the blood didn't show, and I lurched out into the street and hailed a taxi.

I felt very bad. It was the first time I'd hit back at anybody in my life, I wasn't brought up to be violent. And I'd hit a woman, and she was my friend. 'George Street,' I said to the cabbie, without thinking.

When he let me down I walked along the street in a daze and turned into the Regent Picture Theatre, not looking to see what was on, and bought a ticket. The word 'Phaedra' came up on the screen, followed by the names of the actors, Melina Mercouri and Anthony Perkins. The story was set in Greece, and concerned a young man having an affair with his father's mistress, a story about betrayal.

I found out later it was the first movie shown in Australia with explicit sexual scenes. I sat watching the same movie over and over, lost in my own thoughts, and stunned at the close-ups of giant bodies and their sexual desire, doorieing everywhere. I was seeing it in my mind, and when I looked up, seeing it on the screen.

I didn't forgive my friend for about four years and I don't think I ever trusted Lance again. But time heals, I forgave and forgot, and we were together for the next seven years.

Lance was practically never home now he was working, and he teamed up with Donk. They went pub crawling nearly every weekend. I became a loner and only went out with Aunt Phyllis for a few beers at the weekend. Around this time there was a bad scare in Surry Hills. This bloke they called The Slasher hid in trees at night and jumped on men, slashing their private parts. I think he slashed about three or four. Lance worked night shift one week and day shift the next and I wouldn't open the door to anyone till he threw his bag up on the balcony and I knew then it was him and let him in.

We hardly went out together any more, Lance and I, we seemed to be drifting apart. I was getting dressed up for Aunt Phyllis' birthday and he said, 'Where are you going?'

'I'm not staying home while you're out running around, I'm going to Aunt Phyllis' birthday party,' I said.

He said nothing, only hurried out to go and pick up Donk.

Over at Aunt Phyllis' place in Lewis Street, Redfern, I kicked my shoes off and was dancing around with my people, getting drunk and enjoying myself, and I forgot the time. I heard a taxi pull up outside and in the light I could see Lance's long frame and I panicked, I thought he was going to give me a hiding for being late, and I grabbed my shoes and ran out the back and up Redfern hill to the station and caught a cab home to Surry Hills. I wasn't long home before he came in and demanded to know why I'd run out.

'I thought you were going to belt me one for being late.'

'NO,' he said, 'I came to be with you and brought

more beer for the party. I've been neglecting you. But you must've been with another bloke, to run off like that.'

'NO, they were only all my people, my relations –' and with that we started fighting and made such a racket the neighbours phoned the police. When they knocked on the door Lance ran through the house, jumping up and knocking all the lights out in each room as he ran, out and over the fence he went like in the movies, gangster style.

11

Salt-of-the-earth Women

Katoomba

In August 1964 our landlady Mrs Kearney turned up and said she had a three-bedroom house in the Blue Mountains, which would be ideal for our family to grow up in. It had about three acres of land with apples and pears and plums growing, and the rent was eight pounds a week. We hired a truck and sent our furniture to the train depot, and we travelled by utility. The house was in Lett Street between Leura and Katoomba. It had verandahs, a fuel stove, an open fire and lots of trees.

We soon settled in and dug gardens and planted potatoes and pumpkins. We grew tomatoes and covered them with hessian against the frost. Lance got a job on the Main Roads, and we bought six pullets and a rooster and built a fowlhouse. The kids disappeared straight into the bush and made cubbies and climbed trees, they were so happy, all I could hear were little squeals coming in from the orchard or the bush. There were times when I sat with my hands flat on the table and looked out the back and thought, right, now maybe we're settled. I thanked God for Mrs Kearney.

From our front verandah you could see the trains coming up the mountains at night, like a giant caterpillar all lit up. The kids went to school each day with rosy cheeks and at weekends we went for long hikes to Bridal Veil Falls. Past the Falls was a swimming-pool and a picnic area with change rooms like Fred Flintstone's house, built of rocks. We went to the Three Sisters and looked at the tourists.

The kids took the billycart out collecting wood for the fire and exploring. They had two dogs, Rinny, a part alsatian, and Tiger, a cattle dog. In the house I made good work of the orchard – apple turnovers, pies, plum jam.

Nob and Dave liked the bush and were always off somewhere. Earthmovers were working down the end of the street, and I went with the kids to pick up stumps for the fire. These two boys knew all that part of the bush, the tracks and the creeks and the animals they were likely to find. They came back at mealtimes and then went off again. They'd made a rope swing on a tree and I heard them calling 'Oooooo-ee!' as they swung out over the hill. Waratahs grew there, and wild jonquil and daffodils. In winter there was the smell of woodsmoke everywhere.

At the Health Food Store I'd buy a twenty-five-pound bag of flour and a fifty-pound bag of rolled oats, and bring them home in a taxi. I also bought whole cases of macaroni for twenty-three shillings, two-pound tins of tomato paste and half-gallon tins of olive oil. I made hot porridge for the kids in winter. Katoomba was three thousand feet above sea level and it snowed the first winter we were there. None of us had ever seen snow before. The kids made a snowman in the front garden, with my good scarf round its neck and big black buttons for eyes. But snow cut the power lines and we had no electricity for three weeks and no wood, so we burned tyres to keep warm.

In spring the plum trees outside the girls' bedroom window were coming into blossom. Foxes had taken all the chickens but one, and this one followed Pauline around. It came inside and laid eggs in my clothes' basket. One afternoon I found Pauline asleep outside under a fuschia bush, and the chicken asleep in the crook of her arm. In December blood plums came on the trees, and the girls reached out the window from their beds and pulled them off and ate them.

Not long before Christmas some white women turned up on my verandah, wanting to know if I'd like to become the first Aboriginal member of the Blue Mountains CWA. I asked them to come in. One of them was tall and one was short, they were wearing skirts and twinsets and they looked like salt-of-the-earth type women, which they turned out to be.

The tall one said they'd been down to the school and seen Ellie who was in kindergarten, and they wanted to pay for her to have ballet lessons. Now Ellie was always on her toes, she danced on the table. At this time, my kids had blond hair with their dark skin, and there weren't many Kooris in the mountains. So these women had noticed Ellie, and would she like lessons. I agreed, and they said they'd organise it.

We made some good friends in the mountains. There was a short red-headed bloke named Billy Dawson (Blue) who worked with Lance on the Main Roads. Lance earned extra money bouncing at the stomp dances in a place called The Cellar. Ray Brown and the Whispers and Billy Thorpe and the Aztecs played there. I went to the dances sometimes with my gubb girlfriend Helen Saunders. Her husband was a bouncer too. Blue's wife Margaret often came, and Vic Gardoll from up the street. We met at the Katoomba Hotel (the Family Hotel). But all these people moved back to Sydney later on.

The following week a letter came for me. It was an invitation from the APA to be their rep at the World Conference of Women. It was an all-expenses-paid trip for the weekend to Sydney, a hotel, and the events culminating in a mass rally in Wynyard Park. I showed Lance the letter and he pushed it away.

'You can't go,' he said. 'I've got a job that weekend bouncing for Billy Thorpe and the Aztecs. I can't watch the kids.'

'Couldn't Peter Saunders take over for you, or someone?'

'I've got things to do,' he said. 'I can't be watching the kids.'

I was so frustrated I could hardly speak.

At Christmas the CWA women came again, this time with hampers of food and boxes of toys. 'We saw how many kids you've got, we thought you could do with some help,' the short one said. I thanked them and we sat on the verandah talking. I told them how I'd been involved with the APA, and explained what it was about. Then I told them about the World Conference of Women, and how I could've been the rep. After that we sat there for a while looking at the orchard, and then the kids came in from school.

Lance had sold the Mainline and bought a little Prefect. He went to Sydney most weekends, and one time he brought Donk back with him and said they were going fruit-picking in Victoria. They took Helen's husband, Peter, with them too.

They were gone a long time and Helen had nothing for her kids, so I took her in. We sneaked out at night when the kids were asleep and raided orchards (we'd skint ours). We got food orders from the Salvos in town and had to lug everything home. Later we dug up Lance's potatoes and ate them all. Still no word from these great men.

Helen's kids slept in with mine and she dossed down over the back of me. One night late I was woken up by a hard punch in my face, whack. It was Lance, who'd climbed through the window. Helen jumped up screaming, 'It's me, Lance, it's me.' He started to laugh, because he thought I was in bed with another man. All he could see was Helen's blonde hair on the pillow next to me. With that I hauled off and punched him straight in the face and got up and kicked him in the guts. Helen had to break us up. Her husband was there also, and when we calmed down Lance took them home to their flat.

A few weeks later a letter came for Lance saying his brother was sick, down near the Victorian border. Lance wanted to go see him, because his younger brother had already died of cancer. Donk and Lance had money, so I left the kids with Helen and we took the two youngest, Ellen and Pauline. Lance's home town, Wentworth, was nine hundred miles away. He and Donk had become inseparable, so Donk came too.

Lance's brother, Les, and his wife lived on a fruit block outside Wentworth. I'd never seen fruit blocks before – there were acres and acres of oranges, grapefruit, lemons, fruit everywhere you looked. We wound down the car windows and sniffed in the powerful citrus. In another area nearby there were miles of vineyards. Lots of Koori people do seasonal work on these places, just pack up the old car and go.

Lance took me to the pub and introduced me to people he'd gone to school with and known all his life. I was feeling a little sick and in the afternoon I started to haemorrhage. I realised it was a miscarriage but till then I wasn't sure whether I was pregnant because my cycle had never been regular. That night I was taken to hospital. I would have been about three months pregnant.

In the meantime Lance had lost his wallet and had given his brother the last twenty pounds he had. I discharged myself after four days, still feeling weak, went back to the fruit block and rallied Lance and Donk. We had no money for petrol to go home, so Les filled our car from the bowser on the fruit block and we picked some oranges and grapefruit, and that's what we had for the road. I wanted to get back to the other kids – we'd been gone a week already.

The men propped me up in the back seat with the two kids, and we travelled till we ran out of petrol. Then they pulled people up in cars and hummed petrol from them. 'We've got a sick woman and two kids in the car, we've got a long way to go, we've lost our wallet.' Some people gave us petrol and we battled on till we reached Hay.

I got out of the car with the kids and walked along the main street till I saw some Kooris. 'Where's the St Vincent de Paul?' I said, after we'd told each other where we came from. 'Over in that big store,' they said. Right. I took the kids' hands and went in and asked to see the manager. I explained our situation and he told me to write out a list of food. He gave us vouchers for petrol and enough money to get us home. I was grateful and thanked him, we shook hands.

The girls and I sat in the back of the car gorging up on saveloys and breadrolls and cheese and tomato and tinned meat. We were starving. It was a good thing the old car lasted the distance.

Back in the mountains the kids were okay with Helen, but I ended up in hospital as I'd started to haemorrhage again. They gave me a curette and scraped my uterus out as they'd left rubbish in me at Wentworth.

It was coming on to winter when Lance said he wanted to move back to Sydney. I agreed because my chest didn't cope with the cold air too well. I knew the kids would be disappointed and Ellie would never learn ballet, but I didn't realise how upset the boys would be till they ran away from Newtown and the police brought them home.

We said goodbye to our friends from the CWA and the stomp dances, and packed for Sydney.

12

The Debutante Ball

Redfern, Newtown

We settled in Fitzroy Street, Newtown, where we were to stay two years. I didn't know how well the kids would take to the city – they liked the bush life best. But the place had three bedrooms and was near a big park. It turned out we had troubles in Fitzroy Street but we had friends and there were plenty of good times too. Katoomba had been a healthy life but isolated – not enough Kooris to go around.

Now I met up with my old mob again – my sisters from Mum's second family, Dorothy and Margaret, my best mate Neddy, and a friend from Bonalbo, Gert, who I ran into at the Empress one night. We made new friends as well, Pommy Bob and Bronc the Mad Scot and a man called James Golden who could sing in the lingo. 'Do wana nanarabi,' he chanted, a story about the mating of an emu and a kangaroo. Years later my kids still sing this song.

We didn't find Fitzroy Street straightaway but camped at sister Margaret's place in Redfern where we had two rooms. Margaret had no gas, so I said, 'Come out the back with me.' We walked down the lanes till I found a four-gallon drum and two iron bars. We took them back and cut holes all round the drum with a knife. Then I sat it on bricks in the backyard. We built a wood fire in the drum and put the iron bars on top and we cooked on that. We were up in the night stoking the fire to sterilize baby bottles. This was how sister Margaret learnt to make a fire-bucket.

Lance couldn't get work for a while and I did the rounds of the charities again. Then one night Neddy's boyfriend Booker Trindle came tapping on our window. We sneaked him in, he had half a dozen beers and he and Lance were sipping quietly. The kids were asleep. 'Have yous got any money?' he asked. We whispered no. 'Wait on, I'll be back soon.' He climbed out the window.

About an hour later he came back and handed us ten pounds and said, 'Here, buy some tucker, okay?' We thanked him and he went off in the dark. I found out years later he'd knocked and robbed to get us a feed.

Not long after, sister Dorothy was leaving the place in Fitzroy Street and we took it over. We'd been crowded at Margaret's, fourteen of us in the house, and the kids weren't adapting well to the city. At the new place they ran up and down the stairs playing cops and robbers, then out into the park. You could hear them yelling, 'Look out, here come the gungys!'

I enrolled them at Newtown Primary, and Lance found work with old Vic Gardoll (from the Blue Mountains) at

A. J. Bradshaw Excavations. Vic was a plant operator and worked on the big diggers, Lance was a pick-and-shovel man.

Lance and I had been together for about six years and I was pregnant. He was delighted, it would be his first child. I was happy too, I loved that man and he'd taken on all my children. In a way I felt like I was returning the favour.

Neddy showed up with her two youngest kids Phillip and Ian. They'd come up from the south coast where they were bean picking. She and Booker had broken up, they used to fight just as much as Lance and I did. We talked about Booker for a while, then I asked after her kids. Her eldest daughter Cynthia lived at Dapto, Dawn was in a caravan park at Warilla and Donald was in Victoria, they were all married with kids. Billy and Danny were working with their father in the bush, and Alfie had stayed down near Bega bean picking. Altogether she had ten kids and with my eight it took all afternoon to catch up on the news.

While we were talking, some of the boys were out the back planning to run away to the bush – Nobby and David, Neddy's boys Phillip and Ian, and their friends Danny and Kenny Weldon. They were nine, ten, eleven, twelve. When we realised they were gone I reported it to the police, and they were missing about a week. I was pregnant with my ninth child. Every time I heard a car door slam I ran to the balcony and leaned over to see if it was them. I tossed and turned for days, Neddy sat in the kitchen watching the door. We didn't know what to say to each other. One night I heard a car door click and it was the police. 'Do these things belong to your boys?' They held up a jacket with the lining torn and gym boots with the sole nearly off. David. I burst out crying and Neddy talked to them about where the things were found, whether the boys had been seen. They hadn't.

Some time later, I don't know how long, the boys were caught by the police at Campbelltown. When they came in I was glad to see them but still very frightened, and we'd have to go to court about it. It turned out they'd jumped a train at Newtown near the Police Boys' Club, and got as far as Liverpool. They slept under the bridge where some soldiers who were partying there fed them, then they travelled next day to Campbelltown and stole chocolate heart ice creams from corner shops. Later they broke into the school and found the keys and locked all the rooms. Then they threw the keys away.

Next day they sat on a hill watching while police searched for the keys. They watched the headmaster walking around because he couldn't start classes. After this amusing scene they took a swim in the town's water supply and started to walk into the bush. When they got hungry they went to a farm and asked an old lady for something to eat. She made them sandwiches. While they were eating, she went to another room and phoned the police.

Nerida and Val Weldon and I fronted court for the boys and they were let out in our custody. I said to Lance when we got home, 'Take them upstairs and give them a good belting.' He frogmarched them upstairs and we could hear the yells. Serves them right, we thought, they deserve it. We didn't find out for years that Lance was hitting the beds and telling them to yell like they were getting hit. They kept this secret well.

About this time, Bill made friends with Terry Priest, a white kid who used to visit us. Terry had lost his mother when he was eleven, and lived with his father Jack Priest, who worked for Max Factor in Glebe. The boys would get different kinds of make-up and sell it to Dianne and Pearl for petrol money. Terry had bomb cars he fixed, he said it took him about six years to teach Bill to drive. I wondered where the lessons took place and soon found out they were drag racing at the Brickies, Homebush abbatoirs road, at night. The police gave me this news. The boys spent a night in Minda Remand Centre until Jack and I could go for them the next day. They looked very sheepish, ha, ha, we said.

These two were called the Black and White Minstrels and were inseparable friends. They had a fort built in a park in Newtown somewhere. Bill spent weekends at Terry's and likewise Terry would stay with us. Old Jack Priest was a returned digger and a good man. I shared a few beers with him once or twice and he spoke of Bill's good manners, said he was welcome at his place any time.

I was getting bigger with my pregnancy and not enjoying the heat. Lance came in from work and we were sitting over a cup of tea talking about names for the baby when Terry ran past the kitchen and called, 'Hi Fattie!' Lance immediately jumped up and ran out to grab him. 'Don't you say that sort of thing to Ruby,' he said, and gave Terry a swift kick up the bum.

The following Saturday Bill and Nobby came home from a dance at the Aboriginal Foundation and said they'd been invited to have a holiday at King's School, Parramatta. A man would come and see me about it. A few days later a tall athletic man wearing glasses came to the door and introduced himself as Owen Mortimer, the Deputy Principal of King's School. He said they'd be billeted in the dormitories, they were going to put on a play, go on excursions and play sport. I agreed straightaway.

When the boys came back they described the place. It had big lawns and gardens going down to the river, and displays of trophies for Head of the River. Rowing, I said, they must do rowing for sport. The boys couldn't stop talking. Then Owen Mortimer turned up with a copy of a magazine called Variety. On the cover was a young man with his arms outstretched like an actor and a harlequin cap on. I smiled and handed the magazine back. 'Know who that is?' he said. It was Nobby, I couldn't believe it. When he left I said to the kids, 'He's a good man, it just goes to show you.'

Another time he took the two boys to Coffs Harbour to his brother's banana plantation for a holiday, and they came home with big bunches of bananas in the boot of his car.

'It goes to show you not all people are twisted and bent in the world.'

'Okay, mum,' Nob said, 'he's an angel.'

My ninth child was born in King George V Hospital in October 1966. I had a hard time with this birth. I was twenty days overdue, owing to my stomach muscles being stuffed from all the gut bustin I had to do to survive. When the doctors examined me someone said, 'It's big enough to be in the cot. Induce her tomorrow.'

Next morning they gave me trylene gas to make me groggy. The doctor started to break my waters and the baby turned completely over with the cord around his neck. 'Don't push, don't push,' the doctor said, but it was the stage of labour where you must push, where your whole body is pushing for you, and he knew that, and I knew that, and he held his hand on me to stop the baby coming out.

Then he threw a sheet over me and said, 'They're going to have to give you an emergency operation to save the baby.'

'Okay,' I said.

I was groggy from the gas. I scribbled my name on a consent form and they wheeled me to the lift. 'We're going up to theatre,' someone said, leaning over me. The doctor still holding my baby back. From tiny windows in the theatre a hundred eyes looked down at me. I grabbed the doctor. 'Who are they?' I said.

'Students. We'll send them away if you don't want them to watch.'

'No. They have to learn.'

I had to get over this, I told myself. I looked up and waved to them. They waved back.

I woke up and heard my baby crying in the distance. 'What did I have?'

'You have a beautiful baby boy, nine pound six and a quarter ounces. Born by caesarian section.'

I thought, bit stupid, eight kids normally and ninth by caesarian, and went sound asleep.

I named the baby Lance Jeffery after his father. Because I'd had an operation the kids weren't allowed to visit me unless they were over fourteen. Pearl and Dianne came in wearing lipstick and eye-shadow borrowed from Neddy. Billy walked in proudly, then Lance beaming smiles. Vic Gardoll arrived half-tanked carrying long-stemmed red roses and fruit. I was there for sixteen days after the birth and then I signed myself out.

I stepped out of the taxi and peeped through the French windows of the front room. There was my old friend from Coona, Donk Bailey, showing Lance how to fold a nappy. Lance didn't know any of this, Jeffery was his first baby. The house was clean and organised and the kids off to school except for Bill who worked as an offsider on a Shelley's drink truck.

When the kids came in they made a great fuss of their baby, the first baby in the house for five years. Lance was grinning as he taught them how to fold nappies and I knew I'd have plenty of help with this one. I also knew he'd be my last baby, the nine I had and the extras I was adopting like Terry and Sparrow were enough for any person. But I was happy with my brood. I still wanted to write a book one day but I had a life to live first.

Bill paid board out of his small wage and gave the rest to Pearl to mind for their fares each weekend. They went to dances and concerts at the Aboriginal Foundation in George Street.

The Foundation was also a place where you could go and get clothing, it was like a welfare organisation. Mrs Eileen Lester arranged holidays for underprivileged kids with families of whites. My kids were taken on a few holidays and they liked it, they came home loaded up with toys and clothes. I don't know what happened to the Foundation since, but in those days we had trouble raising funds from the government (gubbment) for any Aboriginal projects.

Neddy's son Alfie had come to stay and was a good friend to Bill. He was about fourteen, a hazel-eyed boy with sandy ginger hair. Some of his brothers and sisters were real dark, Neddy's family were a mixture of colours like mine. The kids called Alfie 'Happy' – when he laughed you had to laugh too. Lance was always falling about laughing when Alfie talked.

He took the younger kids out with the billycart and down the back lanes looking for firewood. We had the bare essentials then but no money left over for things like gas. 'Look aunt, I found this big red garbage bin for you.'

He'd filled it with wood. I thanked him and kept it in the laundry.

That evening Dianne and Pearl pegged the boys' trousers and they went to a dance at the Foundation. Bill and Nobby and Alfie were turning into young men before my eyes, and the girls to women. It was the strangest sensation because I could remember my own days of going out dancing so clearly, and I sat there shaking my head and feeding Jeffo.

Sunday evening they went to a concert and when they came in about eleven I'd just made a pot of tea.

'We saw this really funny guy, Mum, Boomenulla,' Bill said.

'The lovable Boomenulla, he's a great comic,' I said 'and any singers?'

'Allan Saunders –'

I knew Allan too, I'd heard he came second to Slim Dusty in the Australian Amateur Hour on radio once.

'– and then Harry and Candy Williams, they sang country-and-western too.' The kids eyes were shining.

'I'll tell you something,' I said to my three oldest children. 'Your father and I used to go to the School of Arts in Newtown for dances when we were teenagers, and that's where I met Candy Williams, they called him the Candy Man. When I came round to him in the progressive barn dance he'd say, "Hello, Ink," and I'd say "Hello, Charcoal."'

Bill looked at me and said, 'Did you like dancing with Dad? What was he like?'

'He was a good dancer. We won a contest for doing the La Bomba –'

I pulled Bill out of the chair, put his arm around me and showed him the steps. 'Twas all o – ver my jealous – y, da dum, da dum bom bom –'

Next morning Alfie left to hitch back to Bega (where Neddy was) for the bean picking. I made sandwiches and gave him a few bob pocket money.

Several days later I woke up and found the red garbage bin burnt to a crisp in my laundry. The house was timber and would have burnt down in our sleep if the laundry floor hadn't been concrete. I knew I was going to hear bad news. The next Tuesday a telegram came from Neddy: ALFIE KILLED IN SHOOTING ACCIDENT. NERIDA.

I ran around everywhere, trying to get someone who had a car to take me down to Bega to be with her. I felt hopeless because I couldn't find anyone. Lance and I had grown so fond of Alfie and it was hard to believe he'd never reappear again laughing. Why take a kid, I kept thinking. And why him?

When Neddy came back she hit the piss and I had to try and comfort her. In the middle of the night she'd wake up screaming, 'Alfie, Alfie!' and burst out crying. I sat and held her hand. 'Don't cry anymore titi, that won't bring him back,' I said.

'How would you like it if it happened to one of your

kids?' and she'd cry some more. Through her tears I tried to imagine what it would feel like, and couldn't. When she calmed a bit, she said in a low voice, 'You know Rube, at the funeral, we were in the church and they got no freezing works down at Bega, and his body had started to smell. So we had to leave him outside while we went in for the service. I kept thinking of him out there rotting and with the bullet hole in him. Between the minister talking it went so quiet, all you could hear was a few flies and a bird calling and I wanted to wake him up and bring him back to life, I can't bear it that he's dead.' She started to sob, quietly now, crooning as if the pain would never go away. The noise woke Bill and he came in and held her other hand.

A week later, with Neddy cried out almost, I went down to the Empress with her to keep company. We were sitting over our beers when a short little black gin came into the lounge and stood looking around. I knew that face, the hazel eyes. I looked again. Yes, it was Short Stuff, Gertie Williams, my old titi from home with her little poddy belly.

'Hey!' I called, 'come and sit with us, titi.' I could see her face change as she recognised me. 'Ruby,' she said. She came grinning towards us and I introduced her to Neddy.

I first met Gerty Williams when her father and a couple of her sisters came to Bonalbo. They lived in an old farmhouse about three miles out of town and as we were the only Aboriginal family in Bonalbo it was only being neighbourly that we would visit back and forth when they came into town to shop.

'Where's your bagel?' she said.

'Oh, he's at home, Neddy and me just come out for a few drinks.'

We settled in then.

'So titi, how many jarjum you got?'

'Nine,' I said.

Ten,' Neddy said.

I gave Neddy the thumb, always one-upping another woman.

Then Gert said quietly, 'I only had one jarjum but it died at birth. I would've had a son.'

We sat quiet for a while then Neddy said, 'I lost my son a month ago, he was shot at Bega.'

'Gee titi, I'm real sorry,' Gert said.

We talked about Alfie for a while but Neddy was getting upset. Gert turned to me and said, 'Did you ever find your mother?' When we were kids, Gert and me, the thing we had in common was, no mothers. I pointed up towards the Housing Commission flats in Redfern. 'She lives up there,' I said. 'I see her now and then. She told me she's related to your father, Gert.'

We drank our beers and talked about old times for a while, then some of Gert's relations came in and she jumped up, excited. She'd come down on the train from Mulli Mulli, the mission at Woodenbong on the Queensland border. At that time there was a general drift from the missions to the city where people were looking for work. Sometimes they found their friends and went out to do seasonal work, fruit-picking. Gert spoke Bundjalung and Githebul but not much English, and somehow she'd made it to Sydney alone and found out that the Empress was the place to look for her people.

She brought her relations back to our table and they were talking in the lingo. They were asking for jum and gulay. Someone jokingly punched Gert on the arm and she said, 'Ningana' and patted her arm, laughing. I leaned forward. I had the strangest feeling, hearing people talk Bundjalung again. I could smell the smoke from the open fire in our place at Stoney Gully Mission, I saw Mum pick me up and put me down again, I felt her strong arms, she was giving old man Ord his tea and saying, 'Here, nyathung.' I saw her grinning at Dad when he came in the door with some eggs our chooks had laid in the long bladegrass under the railway culvert.

As I listened to Gert and her friends, other words came back to me. It was a language I hadn't heard since I was six. My mother only spoke to me in Bundjalung then, she'd told me that before I could talk I understood it. Dad spoke Bundjalung too, they were the same tribe. When Mum left, Dad and Uncle Ernie Ord talked in the lingo but in Bonalbo where we grew up I didn't hear it at all. Uncle Sam was Bundjalung but never spoke it because he had no-one to talk to who understood it. Aunty Nell and her brothers – I don't know where they were from – maybe Githebul people.

In the old photos Aunty Nell and her sisters were already westernised, they wore Victorian dresses with pinched waists and bodices done up to a high neck and long Gibson-girl sleeves. Mum and Dad were the last generation to speak Bundjalung in our family. Gert's people spoke the lingo fluently and only had broken English.

'Don't kiss me on the cheek, titi,' she said, 'they'll think we're leggos.'

I wrote my address on a coaster and told her to make sure to come and visit, then I kissed her on the cheek again and we left. Back at Fitzroy Street the Smithos had arrived with Anne Deveson and a TV crew. Pauline was nursing Jeffery and the cameraman was off to one side talking to Lance. It took them about an hour to get all the shots they wanted, then I cooked tea. Every night cooking was a big production, with eleven of us and visitors or the kids' friends, often fifteen people.

Our two extras the next night were Gert and her new friend Pommy Bob. She'd asked him to buy her a chicken and some beer. She was always conning blokes up when she was joogy-happy.

Bob was an industrial chemist. He was about thirty and his hair was silver grey. He was dressed in a white shirt, maroon tie and a navy suit. Something in the chemicals had turned his hair grey.

'Sit down here,' I said. 'We're pleased to meet you.'

'Thank you. I'm very interested to see how the real Australians live,' he said. 'I've been here six months now.

I asked someone where I could meet Aboriginal people and they sent me to the Empress.'

'That's where I found him,' Gert said, laying her chook on the table.

We sat around the fire and asked him questions about London, and he asked us about corroborees and tribal life and missions and what was happening to black people now. He had an enquiring mind, Pommy Bob.

He became a regular visitor at our house. On Saturdays he hired out horses in Centennial Park and took the kids riding, then at night he took them to Luna Park. He never arrived empty-handed, there were presents for the kids and beer to quench our thirsts. We bedded him down on the lounge when he stayed for the weekend.

Neddy, the old rogue, was up to her tricks again. She didn't know how good a friend Pommy Bob was to us, and one weekend when he was asleep on the lounge she ratted his pockets and took his wallet. She showed Lance and he made her put it back, 'NO Neddy, he's too good a friend to do that to.'

At Christmas he came in with a mouth organ for Lance, a set of saucepans for me, and a tape recorder for the kids. Bill taped me when I was snoring, and that tape gave them many hours of pleasure. They played it to Gert when she came around, I snored for every visitor.

Neddy had been staying with us for about three months. One morning she asked if I'd go to Melbourne with her.

Her daughter Dawn had a bloke with a station wagon and our agreement was that we'd pay for the petrol going down and she'd pay for it coming back. Neddy had about three months of pension back-pay to pick up at her son's place in Heidelberg. We loaded the wagon with blankets and pillows and I took Pauline and Jeff, who was fifteen months old, and left Gert to look after the elder ones.

I'd never been to Melbourne before. Lance wanted to see his Dad and show him his first grandchild, Jeffery. We arrived at Neddy's son's place. Her husband was there and they started on a few flagons.

Lance's father was pleased to see us and bedded us down. Their little cottage had fruit trees and a veggie plot and chooks. He was a Pommy and had been living with a Scottish woman since Lance's mum had died. They spoilt Pauline and Jeffery, and brought friends home from their club to see the baby. Lance's dad worked as head chef at the Repatriation Hospital in Heidelberg.

Each day the kids collected the eggs for him, and he got dressed in his whites just to cook for me. He and his old lady were always arguing. A few days went by and we didn't hear from Neddy. A week went by and I started to get worried. Our money was running out and I couldn't remember her son's address. Then we remembered the pub where they drank, so we went there and saw a couple of Kooris who knew her. They told us she'd gone back to Sydney.

Now we were stranded and all our money gone. We couldn't get any help from Lance's dad so we went to

Aboriginal Affairs and asked for a rail pass. It took a few days to arrange. We enjoyed the visit with Lance's dad – he was a nice old man – and when we were leaving on the train, the old guy was wiping his eyes and crying as he didn't want us to go.

We had to get back to the other children and Neddy. I thought, wait until I get my hands on that woman, I'll give it to her for leaving us stranded. She was always boasting up about the Spirit of Progress or the Southern Aurora and saying how smooth they were to ride in. But there was a plane strike and they put extra trains on, and it was a goat train and rattled and shook our guts up all the way home.

When we arrived at the front door guess who was there opening it for us and saying, 'I'm sorry titi for leaving you, I got drunk and didn't wake up till I was back in Sydney.' And there was no pension as her son had cashed her cheques and I could have throttled her, but she had a baked dinner ready to pacify me, the bitch, and I said, 'Never again, never again, Neddy,' and I told her about the lovely train trip home and we burst out laughing at that. It took me nearly a week to get over the trip, and later she told me she'd been drinking flagons with her husband and got carried away and I said, 'BULLSHIT, Neddy, BULLSHIT!'

Gert and Neddy and I were the best of mates and known as the Three Musketeers. We went everywhere together. Lance had been reacquainted with his friend Blue, from Katoomba. Blue and Margaret had split up and their kids were in homes. Blue came to stay with us.

He'd bought a Mini Minor but had no licence so Lance drove him around. I had many a row with him, because I blamed him for Lance being away all the time. One night I smashed a bottle over his head, another time I was throwing bottles at the Mini as he and Lance were rounding a corner to get away from the row. Otherwise he was a good friend. He had a beautiful singing voice and had sung on the radio in Katoomba.

One night we had a birthday party for him and he asked me for a kiss, which I did, after all it was his birthday, but Lance got jealous and broke his jaw. The next thing he was in hospital all wired up, and when I took the kids in to visit he muttered through his wired jaw, 'I'm never going to kiss you again.'

He wanted some smokes and I looked in my purse but there wasn't enough money even for a small packet, so he asked the kids to go bumper shooting. They came back with a packet full of butts and he was delighted. He and Lance were still best friends after that.

Not long after he came home we had a flea plague and Blue would kill one, jump up, beat his chest and call out like Tarzan, 'Ahhh ah ahh.'

He and his wife got back together and had three more children. He would never talk about the older ones who were in homes, it hurt too much. They moved away and we lost contact for about twelve years.

After Blue left, Lance became mates with James Golden. James could sing in the lingo. His grandmother was full-blood and he was born in Tipperina Mission, near Narrabri. When he came to visit he sang his tribal song:

'Do wana nanarabi, nanarabi widingay
do wana nanarabi, nanarabi widingay
ima jayna, ima jayna, ooh.'

And the kids learnt it too. He told them the song was about the mating of an emu and a kangaroo. The kangaroo came up and smiled and tapped the emu on the shoulder, but the emu wouldn't respond. The emu's reply was: 'I am not of your meat'.

Later, when Lance left and I was approached by some man or other, I would think to myself (if we had nothing in common): 'do wana nanarabi'.

James had been a drover and he knew tribal songs from other places too. He was a well-travelled man. At this time he worked in the woolsheds at Ultimo. When his wife left, he brought his kids to me to look after while he worked. They stayed a few weeks till he could send them to their grandmother in Coonamble. I paid a fine to stop him from going to gaol and he never forgot, after that he called me his tribal sister.

One Christmas, when we had no gas, he invited us to his place. Neddy and I were standing out on a corner of King Street, Newtown, holding ten chooks and a leg of pickled pork, the hot sun on us, joking about what it would be like at James' place. We got ourselves, the food and the kids to Wattle Street, Ultimo, and looked in the door. Horrible mess. Without a word, Dianne and Pearl started to clean the place up and set the table. Neddy and I began cooking. As fast as I stuffed she was sewing them up and by two o'clock it was on the table, including a big ham baked. It was tough going but we made it, while the men were in the lounge chatting and sipping on a flagon of wine.

Lance had been at the Empress one night and he came in with a man he introduced as Bronc Borland.

'Some Koori blokes were gettin' stuck into him,' Lance said, 'so I stopped them. He's a Scot, you know.'

Bronc began telling stories, mostly far-fetched, but funny. He'd been knocking around with Kooris for years. On Anzac Day we were in the Town Hall Hotel at Newtown having a beer after the march, and there was Bronc Borland all decked out in his kilt. The women in the lounge had him bailed up, and were lifting his kilt to see what he was wearing underneath. We rescued him and I couldn't keep a straight face. He was a bright shade of red. Years later even after Lance and I separated he came to visit often. He took Neddy and me to the Aboriginal balls. He called me his big sister. We called him Bronc the Mad Scot. He told us he had heaps of money, but I think he was an ordinary working person like us, we never took anything he said too seriously.

On a Saturday in July of 1968 the Foundation had its first debutante ball. It was to be in Sydney Town Hall and Pearl (who was sixteen) badly wanted to go. Money was short and Lance was unemployed then, so I went to the Smith Family in Crown Street, Darlinghurst, and asked the welfare worker for a white ball gown. The only one they had was size 18 which was miles too big for her, so no problem, I got out the machine, took the dress to pieces and remade it, adding a bow on the waistline. I was half way through this when I went broke and had to pawn my machine to get a feed for the kids. I finished the rest by hand, just in time for the ball, and I did up Pearl's hair. Charles Perkins brought her a pair of white shoes and gave me a free ticket to the ball.

When I arrived the twenty-five debs, all Aboriginal girls, were being photographed in the foyer. Pearl looked radiant in her remade dress and as the ball began I went inside to watch the girls being presented to the Prime Minister, John Gorton.

Pearl was twenty-second out of twenty-five debs as they formed a circle with their partners, Jimmy Little (the singer) was announcing. A grey-haired man walked up to Pearl and clicked his heels in salute and took her hand. He led her to the middle of the floor and the band struck up and away they waltzed. I couldn't see from my seat very well, so I asked someone, 'Who's that man dancing with Pearl?'

Next day it was in all the newspapers. Pearl had made history being the first Aboriginal ever to dance with the Prime Minister. I was so proud, and later Gorton wrote me a letter.

By October that year Pearl was doing part-time modelling. I went to watch her at the Waratah Festival at Burland Hall in Newtown. Our Aboriginal Advancement Programs were starting up that year, and Pearl was asked to model for a fashion show in the Waratah Festival, at Hyde Park. When we got there, the good guys from 2SM were setting up for their concert. They were sponsoring a fundraising for our first Aboriginal hostel, Kinari, and Pearl and the other models and artists were to perform. It was good to see some black talent in Hyde Park. When it was Pearl's turn to model the radio announcer said, 'We now give you the girl who danced with the Prime Minister, Pearl Anderson, and look at those lovely dark eyes.' Larpa Stewart kicked free footballs into the crowd and they announced the girls would go among the crowd and take donations for the hostel.

A Koori band called The Silver Linings, all dressed in silver suits, started to play and then I saw Pearl and Sue Briant being escorted by two police with cement bags collecting money. Altogether they raised $4,000 in one night.

After the concert, Pearl took me into a huge tent where the newspapers had set up a display of the most outstanding photographs taken during the year. She told me to close my eyes and led me inside. When I opened my eyes I was standing in front of a huge photo of Pearl and the Prime Minister dancing, right next to a photo of Lionel Rose when he won the world championship fighting Harada, from Japan. I was so proud I was crying, and then people were gathering around Pearl, looking at her photo and recognising her, so she took my hand and we ran out to get away from them laughing.

13

Deaths and Weddings

Waterloo

Nobby and some mates were playing in Newtown school playground one afternoon when one of the kids noticed the door of the store room was open. So they went in and helped themselves to cricket bats and basketballs and hockey sticks. They were having a whale of a time playing until someone reported them to the police and they were rounded up along with the equipment and charged with petty theft. Nobby had to go to the Children's Court and he got six months in a boys' home, along with several of his mates.

It was to be the first of many times I went to court for the kids.

In the meantime the lease had run out at 2 Fitzroy Street, so we moved to a house in Enmore with a friend of mine called Thelma Ball, and her family, until we could get situated again. We were there about a month, the whole family in one large room sleeping on the floor. I sat around chatting to Thelma's man, who I knew from Coona – we'd worked on his brother's property. One morning I was out at the clothesline when Thelma started swinging punches at me, jealous as a cat. I ducked a few times but in the end I hit her and she fell on the watermain, which burst and sent water gushing everywhere. She got up and came at me again. She was a big woman, Thelma, twenty stone then and I was half that but I was mad enough to knock her out and she lay there for a while quietly on the footpath while I thought what to do next. Maybe James Golden would take us in at Wattle Street.

The first thing Thelma said when she came to was, 'Get out!' We agreed to that, we hustled the kids together and went to Ultimo. James' house was boarded up. We had to sneak the kids in at night to sleep then be gone early in the morning. This went on all weekend, then on Monday I saw a place advertised in Portland Street, Waterloo. It only had two bedrooms but there wasn't time to look around so we paid $10 key money and went to check it out. We said we'd take it, and the agent asked how many kids we had.

'Four,' I said.

'That's rather a lot for one room.'

'We'll manage,' I said, trying to keep a straight face and I could see Lance was turning around to hide his expression.

We soon settled in, the girls in the front room and three boys in the back, Lance and me on a divan in the lounge.

Billy was seventeen and on a pension because of his epilepsy. Pearl had a job at the Fountain Foods factory, she was sixteen. Dianne was fifteen, she had an exemption from school so she could help me at home. Nob was in Daruk, the boys' home at Windsor. Dave, Aileen, Ellen and Pauline were at school and Jeff (two) at home. We were okay again except for the worry about Nob. Lance worked at Alexandria driving a crane.

When I went out for the post one morning there was a letter from Nobby, written in pencil.

Daruk Training School

Dear Mum,

How are you and the family in the best of health I hope as it leaves me the same way and I am sorry that I caused so much trouble for you and I hope you will find it in your heart to forgive me because I love you so much and I didn't want to hurt you …

He asked after the rest of the family and then:

I hope you will come to see me if you are not busy well I'll say cheers for now goodbye. And I will be a good boy. Mum I love you very much.

The kisses were drawn feathery and overlapping like a cloud.

★

We needed things for the house so we opened a Walton's account and bought a second-hand fridge and washing machine. Lance was often out drinking but I wasn't aware he was running around on me again till Philomena Gundy told me, and when I fronted him with it he belted me in the mouth and busted my false teeth. It happened so suddenly I had no time to defend myself and there was a lot of blood, my lip was cut open and pouring.

The police came and took me to Rachel Foster Hospital. The doctor gave me an anaesthetic and fourteen stitches. When I got home the kids said the police had picked Lance up and put him in gaol, charged with assaulting me. Next thing there was a knock on the door and it was the cops again, this time they wanted to take me to the cells and show him how cut up I was. Naturally I agreed to go, by now I was angry and sore.

They stood me in front of him. I looked through the bars. He didn't say a word. My lip was so swollen it was like another object on its own, attached to my face but not really part of me, part of something he'd done. At the same time, I wondered how Thelma was feeling. I didn't feel too sorry for her, she'd swung the first punch. And I just looked at Lance, stared at him. Finally a cop said, 'Aren't you proud of yourself, doing this to a woman? Big man.' Lance was by now sober and he cried and cried, but I hated him so much then. I'd had enough of bashings and being knocked around generally, it was the beginning of the end for us.

When we went to court on Monday, the judge asked me how long I'd been with him and whether I had any children with him. 'Seven or eight years and I have a little son to him. But I have eight other children too.'

The judge stopped to think. 'What do you want me to do with him?' he said.

'I don't want to see him in gaol, but I don't want him to ever come near me or the kids again. I've had enough of bashings.'

The judge bound him down to keep the peace and stay away from us for three years.

Neddy took me home and nursed me until I'd recovered. My face was swollen for weeks, my mouth was in a mess. Lance circled our place for about a week in his black car and then he was gone.

David was learning to box and in a while he was boxing for South Sydney Police Boys' Club. His best mate there was Sparrow Freeman, a kid with a bird's body and a big heart. He was a good boxer and a crowd drawer at the clubs. The boys were about nine or ten years old at the time. Sparrow came over to Portland Street dressed in his boxing regalia.

One night I went with the kids to see Sparrow and David fight, and they were the only two to win their fights. The crowd showered them with money, and shouldered them and carried them out. I was so proud I had tears in my eyes. My eldest kids were there with some friends and they cheered and clapped so hard the stool tipped under them and they landed on their bums on the floor. It was a good night.

The boys went to Newtown Public School and were often late home. One afternoon I was up on Redfern Hill doing some shopping. There was an old bloke selling hot dogs out front of Redfern Station in a hot dog stand. As I came out of a shop near the station I saw Dave and Sparrow with aprons on just touching the ground, selling hot dogs while the old man relaxed and read a paper on a crate beside them. When they saw me they scattered. Back at home Pearl and Dianne were talking to their boyfriends. They'd decided to have a double wedding and the boys agreed. So they were sitting there making plans, describing their dresses and suits.

When David and Sparrow came in they made out like they were Boy Scouts doing their good deed for the day. 'And in the meantime getting your bellies full of hot dogs,' Dianne said. I looked at them as stern as I could and said something about wopping school. 'We didn't wop,' Dave said, innocence shining from his eyes. I leaned over him. 'Then why did you run when you saw me?' I said. They had no answer to that, and slunk off.

We were never lonely in Portland Street after Lance had left. James Golden came to stay and I bedded him down on the floor. He had a job over on the North Shore at the Mater Misericordiae Hospital, and when he had no fares he walked to work over the bridge and then he got food orders from St Vincent de Paul and carried the box of food home, back over the bridge.

Neddy was staying with me too. At weekends to break the monotony the boys, James and Lester Ritchie, would hit the publican of the George Hotel in Waterloo for some beer and a couple of flagons till payday. When the kids went to sleep we spread a blanket on the floor in the kitchen and put the smokes and beer in the middle and in a while we were calling ourselves after movie stars. James was James Cagney (Little Big Man); Lester Ritchie was Jeff Chandler because his hair was greying at the temples; and Gert was Priscilla Presley because she was knocking around with a bloke named Tony who played the guitar; Neddy was Connie Frances because she sang tear-jerking songs; and I was Shirley Bassey because I could out-drown everyone. I always sang too much when I was drunk.

When we got tired of country-and-western late in the night, James played drums on the empty beer carton and sang quietly, 'Do wana nanarabi' and we joined in 'nanarabi widingay'.

My kids christened Neddy the Road Runner because she was always going around some corner (*beep beep*) to Coona, Bega, Melbourne, Warilla, Dapto.

When Neddy went out and got charged up she'd forget that she told blokes where she lived, so when a knock came on the door she hid and gestured to me from behind the door to say she wasn't there, so I'd say, 'Sorry, Nerida Chatfield doesn't live here.' I used to laugh at her and say, 'Neddy, one of these days you'll get your signals crossed', and before long it was me hiding behind the door and gesturing to her and she'd be saying, 'Sorry, Ruby Langford doesn't live here.'

Gert got great pleasure out of spoiling my kids. We had a row because she didn't like me chastising them. 'Now titi, don't go crook on your biggest son.' Bill had to take tablets to stop his epileptic seizures, and he often didn't take them. I'd had brain wave tests done on him and the doctors said he had no tumour, just scarring of the brain tissue from when they'd put the needle in to draw off fluid when he had meningitis. He would grow out of taking the fits when he was about twenty, but in the mean time he had to keep on with the tablets. I bullied him, Gert bullied me, and we were great mates.

Gert's favourite drink was sweet sherry or port and Neddy and I mostly favoured beer and brandy, lime and sodas. Gert smoked Rothmans, sometimes she'd lose her breathe and say, 'Hit me titi, hit me!' I had to hit her in the chest until she could breathe again. She frightened the hell out of Neddy and me.

About this time Neddy bit some bloke for a smoke down near Central on a rainy night. He bought a chook and they shared it, and she brought him home to visit. His name was Bob McDonald. We noticed he took ages to say anything and later the story came out.

As a child in Gladesville, Bob was climbing through the fence, he'd pinched a loan of his father's ·22 rifle to go rabbit shooting with some other kids. The rifle fired and shot out five inches of his brain, including part of the speech centre. They'd put a plate in his brain. He took fits, and was a very tender-hearted man, always saying 'Dear this, dear that'. He became Neddy's boyfriend and was a friend to us all.

We'd got a copy of the big photo of Pearl dancing with the Prime Minister and had it framed. We hung it on the lounge room wall with two boomerangs at the top. We showed Bob the photo and introduced him to all the kids.

On a Saturday not long after this, Pearl was walking down to the swimming pool. She had a tranny in her hand and a towel over her shoulder, just walking along. Then a loud bang. A car and a van had collided at the intersection and the van mounted the footpath and struck her, slammed her into a brick wall. She went into a coma and I was summoned to Rachel Foster Hospital and I sat with her hour after hour. It was Saturday, 20 December 1969. I could hardly speak. I held her hand and watched her fight for life. Images of her dancing at the ball, running out of the house and waving, modelling at the festival in the park, then the photo exhibition, that huge photo of her and Gorton dancing, the way she took me in secretly, then how we ran out laughing. Pearl the mother hen. I watched her fight for life, thinking if only I could let my strength flow into her and will her to live.

I left the hospital around nine-thirty. The sister told me to get some rest. I went home and sat out the back under the budgie cage on a long seat and the kids and Neddy and Gert were with me, comforting me, when there was a loud knocking and with my heart racing I beat everyone to the door. I knew my daughter was gone before I opened the door to be met by two policemen telling me she'd died half an hour after I left the hospital.

My eldest son Bill was down at the Foundation, so my brother Kevin went to fetch him, and when Bill was told about Pearl's death he hit the door with such force it cracked and split right down. 'Why, Mum? Why her. Why couldn't God take me with my sick brain, not her. Why?' Kevin took him away crying, they went for a long walk and left me to my misery and anguish and sorrow. I vowed I'd never be sure of anything again.

We buried her on Christmas eve and she had a large funeral. I buried her with my father, because I couldn't afford a plot of my own. Nobby was brought back to the house from the boys' home. A fourteen-year-old, handcuffed for his sister's funeral. The officer sat with him in the mourning car and later they took him straight back to the home. He wouldn't let anyone mention her name. He locked Pearl away in the back of his mind.

We had planned to have a wedding and instead there was a death. No-one could take it in. Pearl's fiancé, Greg Vincent, was lost. He followed me around for days. I was sitting on the lounge and he'd be there in a shadow, sitting on the floor, his head near my knee. He didn't say anything. He didn't go more than ten feet from me.

After the funeral Neddy and her boyfriend Bob McDonald (the one she met in the rain) asked me to go with them to get the shopping for Christmas. I hadn't thought about it. After we shopped we went and got blind drunk and ended up at the Cross. From the windows of the El Bongo Club we saw daylight coming. Neddy kissed Bob on one cheek, I kissed him on the other, and with these different shades of lipstick we got him into a taxi and the driver said to him, 'Looks like you've been in among the raspberry jam.'

'Let's go, driver,' Neddy said, 'we gotta get home to cook the turkey.'

'Fuck the turkey,' I said.

In my anguish over losing Pearl I started to drink heavily. I lashed out at everyone and everything, I went to the Big E and got drunk and if anyone said anything that sounded insulting to me I'd be fighting at the drop of a hat, I'd throw them over the bar and punch the piss out of them. People I knew would walk around me, and were too frightened to say anything in case I became violent and punched them.

All of a sudden I woke up to myself, I thought, my father didn't raise me to be a drunken fightin foulmouthed woman, and I gave it up. But I can remember that in my drunken state I'd con up some bloke in the Empress and get him to take me out to Botany cemetery and I'd leave him in the car and climb through the fence and I'd lay on Pearl's grave and go to sleep. That was how I got through it. When I woke up and looked around, the man was still asleep in the car outside the cemetery.

The kids weren't with me when Pearl died. They were on a holiday in Melbourne with the Foundation – David, Aileen, Ellen and Pauline. Mrs Iris Lester had arranged for them to be billeted there. Harold Blair the Aboriginal tenor was looking after all the Koori kids and they rang to see if I wanted the kids brought home. I'd said no, don't spoil their holiday. They were too young to understand properly. Blue and Margaret took Jeff for a few days till it was over. I don't know how I would've managed without friends.

Early in 1970, not long after I buried Pearl, Lisa and Tommy French came to visit and brought two chickens for me to cook up for the new year. I put them in the fridge, then they asked me to go and have a beer to cheer me up. We went to the Warren View in Enmore, and while we were there they introduced me to a bloke named Leslie Potter who was walking with crutches. They told me he was living with Lisa's sister Mary Chatfield, Neddy's sister-in-law. He had taken the full force of a taxi when he pushed Mary out of the way to save her, and had a pin in his hip.

Lisa was always running away from Tommy when he got drunk as he'd get argumentative and start to fight, so as soon as he went to sleep in the pub, she said, 'Come on, let's go down to the Burlington.' I took off with her as I had no money of my own and didn't want to be left behind. We were getting into a taxi and there was Les with his crutches trotting after us and saying, 'I'm coming too,' so away we went, and later on we went home to Portland Street.

I took Les and made a bed on the floor for him as he had nowhere to go. Later Tommy came and took Lisa home, then Les asked if he could board with us. I needed the money so I said okay.

One day he'd been to a doctor about his leg and been given strong painkillers. When I came home from shopping I was wondering why Leslie was falling all over the place then I smelled metho. I found a milk bottle in the sink and it reeked of metho. I jerried what was up and yelled for Bill. I thought, My God he's taking those painkillers too, he'll kill himself, and I searched him and found the bottle half empty. I said to Bill, 'Quick, get an ambulance,' and they took him away to pump his stomach out in hospital. They saved his life.

I didn't know he was an alcoholic and desperately needed help but he signed himself in to dry out and when he recovered he always came back to visit and we became the best of friends. I visited him in hospital where he had several operations on his hip. Today he's made me very proud, he's an alcoholic counsellor and has run Aboriginal hostels for alcoholics in Moree and Darwin. He's still helping our people with drinking and drug problems. He always said that when he gets his insurance we're all going to Spain and we're gonna sit under a cactus and drink tequila and eat oranges.

Neddy went away to Melbourne and when she was gone her boyfriend Bob McDonald called over and asked me out. I said no, but Bill pushed me out the door saying, 'Go on, get out and live a little. I'll watch the kids.'

So we went to the Empress and down to the Clifton. Bob bought a big bottle of gin and put it in my bag. We got so pissed that when I woke up next morning Bob was on the divan beside me. I was embarrassed about this, he was Neddy's boyfriend. Oh well, she would take these little holidays.

When she came back I told her about it. She had a good laugh about my embarrassment and said, 'Okay, he's your boyfriend now. No problem, plenty more fish in the sea.'

My kids called Neddy the claw and me the hammer. When Neddy got drunk she'd scratch people, and I was always hammering them. We shared our fun, we were all in the same boat. No money no land no jobs no hope. So we had to find ways to keep our spirits up and that didn't only mean our spiritual ones but also our liquid ones.

Neddy and I were socialising at the Empress, our pub that we called our 'home away from home'. We didn't know what to expect – in that place there was never a dull moment, us Kooris always found some way to break the monotony. The jukebox was blaring and Lance Carr was stepdancing, and everyone was clapping him and he'd dance more or Batman Silver would be singing at the top of his voice, it was a good place to be until a blue broke out, anyhow it was a meeting place for all us Kooris. Neddy and I were charged up and this gubb bloke flashed his big wallet and said, 'Hey girls, want to come to the dogs with me?' and we looked at him and said, 'Look mate, we've been going to the dogs for years,' and he looked at us real stupid, as we walked by him chuckling.

Bill mostly minded the kids. He was on the invalid pension because of his epilepsy, and he didn't like it that he was getting a pension, he wanted to work. He'd grown up to be a very nice young man. He had a set of drums and played 'Wipeout' and 'Finglebunt'. Max Silver came over and showed him how to play. They kept the kids amused, singing and joking around.

If Jeff did something wrong and I went to hit him, Bill stopped me. He would say to Jeff, 'Come on baby, get dressed and brother will take you out,' and I wouldn't see them all day. He took Jeff riding up and down in the lifts in the Housing Commission flats in Redfern, he brought him home sound asleep with chocolate on his face and his pockets full of yo-yos and lollies.

We went out nearly every weekend but the house was always cleaned and the kids had food and were well looked after, only mother was drinking to forget Pearl's death. Our weekend run was the Empress then the Clifton and then Civic in the city. Then into a taxi and up the Cross to the El Bongo (open till four o'clock) then the Congo Club (open till six) then into a taxi and back to the Palace and the Burlington in the Haymarket. We kept this up for three weeks, I don't know how we lasted the distance. I was untidy and without makeup and Neddy and Gert were the same. The kids hunted us home to get cleaned, saying, 'Shame, shame.'

The Congo Club opened from four to six in the morning. If we didn't have our entrance fee Stan would let us in and we'd pay him when we had it. The beer we were shouted made up for our fares over and over. Neddy and Gert and me. We had our regular friends and we'd sit and drink with them and dance till the early hours. I hardly ever talked about Pearl.

The club had three bouncers, big burly blokes, and one night a fight broke out. Four blokes were giving this fellow a bashing, and I was pretty drunk, and all of a sudden I couldn't see anyone there with me. The place was empty except for the blokes who were belting the other one, and he was unconscious in a pool of blood.

I called out, 'He's had enough, you mugs' and, 'Leave him alone.' One of them looked up at me and said, 'Shut up, you black bitch.'

I looked for something to throw at them, I saw the

beer in front of me, full cans they were, so I up with those cans of beer, I'm pretty good at throwing, and every one hit a mark. They were throwing chairs at me and I was well into it by then, I was catching them in mid-air and throwing them back. I looked around for someone to help me.

The others were upstairs in the women's loo, and the big bouncers had disappeared. Then there were sirens everywhere, and the ambulance came and took the bloke away, I don't know if he was alive or dead, and the police came and closed the joint.

The next night when we went back, Stan said, 'You're either the bravest woman I know or the silliest.' I said, 'Why?' He said the blokes I'd been fighting with were gunnies, underworld men, and I nearly shit. He sat us down and bought all the food and drink we could eat for nothing and fed the jukebox with money. At the end of the night I made a chain of beer can lids and draped them around his neck like I always did.

We were in the Empress one night, Neddy and me and her brother Tommy T. and B.T. Leslie, and we were partying on and when it was shut up time we were going to Neddy's daughter's place in Carey Street, Marrickville. We walked up the hill from the Empress and there was a bus that said St Peter's Station so we jumped on. Neddy's son, Dan, had joined up with us. What we didn't know was the bus terminated at the station.

I was drunk and singing loudly and Danny said, 'Sing it Shirley Bassey' and I was letting it go. We were the only ones on the bus.

Neddy was up front with her arm around the driver, trying to con him up to take us to Carey Street, but he said he couldn't. It started to rain. We got down at the station and B.T. was carrying the beer in a carton and it got wet. The cans tipped out and rolled down the street and we were chasing them along and rounding them up. Up pulled a cab and we rode along singing in the rain.

One morning early after our run of the Cross, we had an Islander girl, Manya, with us. We caught a taxi and she said, 'I know a place that's open now, the Yugoslav Club in Elizabeth Street.'

We'd no sooner sat down and bought a beer, when the police raided the joint. They grabbed Gert, the little one, first. They were hauling her off and she called out, 'Don't take me without my titis,' so they came back and grabbed us.

Neddy, Manya and I were shown into the van. Next we were herded into the charge room at Central Police Station. We were put in a cell with the other women. So drunk we started singing at the top of our voices. The police drivers joined in. Then we turned on a go-go session. Gert was in the corner at the wash-basin crying, 'I've never been in gaol before ahh, ahh,' and I looked at her and Neddy and burst out laughing. 'I haven't either,' I said and we couldn't stop laughing. When the police walked past our cell we wolf-whistled even though we couldn't see them. Manya said, 'My husband will kill me.'

They kept us four hours to sleep it off. When we fronted the magistrate, we'd all given bodgie names – I was Ruby Marriott, Neddy was Mary Ford. Gert gave some name and forgot what it was, so when the name was called we elbowed her.

We were getting our property from the office and the sergeant said, 'You've got a good voice, where do you sing?' I said, 'The Empress Hotel,' and we left feeling ashamed of ourselves for being pinched for drunk. At home Bill said, 'Mum, where've you been? I've been ringing up the hospitals, I thought yous were in an accident.' We told him we'd been in the cells and he burst out laughing. 'Hah, look at the gaol-birds!' We didn't live it down for months.

In February 1970 we were just getting back on our feet after the shock of Pearl's death, when Neddy asked me to go to Wollongong for the weekend. Her daughter had a Housing Commission home in Dapto. I agreed, thinking the break would do me good, so after giving the kids instructions I left them in the care of Dianne and Steve and Billy who were only teenagers but well able to look after the kids, or so I thought.

We arrived at Dapto and she asked me to go further down the coast to Wreck Bay, as she wanted to show me where she'd lived when she left Coonabarabran years ago when her children were little. She took me and showed me where she lived on the mission there, then we visited Huskisson. We went back to Dapto only to find the police waiting for me to tell me that Jeffery had been abducted from a park in Newtown. Then I was frantic.

Neddy's son drove us back to Sydney. It was a Sunday and the traffic was banked up – it took us three hours to travel fifty miles. I listened to the car radio, it was even being broadcast there. They said the police were concerned for a three-year-old boy who was taken from Newtown Park and no trace of him could be found. I felt dead inside. I'd just lost Pearl, now this, my baby was missing. I never stopped praying all the way home that he'd be found unharmed.

When we arrived in Sydney I had them take me to Redfern Police Station. I burst out crying while I was explaining that I was the mother of the missing boy, but then they told me he'd been found and was safe. The police told me to go home and they'd bring him – he was with Dianne at CIB headquarters.

Back at the house, I let into the kids and screamed at them, 'What are you doing to me? All of you couldn't look after one little boy!' I was so furious I screamed and swore badly at them, then we were all crying together. I loved them so much, and the struggle to raise them was beginning to tell on me.

About an hour later, Dianne and Steve arrived with the little fellow in a police car. I was so relieved all I could do was hug him and cry.

After a while I was told the full story. This is what happened on that day. Bill had a car and he took our kids and went over to Georgina Street to pick up my sister Margaret and her kids to go to the beach. On the way back he dropped our kids off at Portland Street and because the car was full he didn't notice young Jeff was still in the back with Margaret's kids. He let them out in Georgina Street. The car was mucking up so he lifted the bonnet to fix it and didn't notice Jeff taking off with the other kids to play in the park across the road. Bill fixed the car and drove home.

When they noticed Jeff was missing they reported it to the police so Bill, feeling bad, went into the Clifton Hotel for a beer. He was just lifting the beer to his lips when he heard Pearl's voice calling 'Bill —', and he looked around towards the door. Her spirit was beckoning him to go with her. She was warning him that something was wrong. Bill said he left his beer and went looking again.

It appears there was this bloke, a new Australian who had no kids of his own, who took Jeff from the park. The man lived only about four doors from my sister's place. When Jeff was found the police took him with Dianne to CIB headquarters. He wouldn't answer the police when they were trying to find out if the bloke had hurt or interfered with him, so they got Dianne to sit him on her lap and she asked him, 'Where did you sleep, baby?' He replied, 'I slept with a ghost, my sister Pearl slept with me.' So there she was, still looking after him, even when she was dead.

★

Not long after this Nob was let out of Daruk and came home on the train. He was wearing his diso suit (discharge suit) and was taller and quieter. He talked about what it was like in the home and we told him our news. He wouldn't hear mention of Pearl's name, he'd taken it very bad. I remembered the picture of him the day of the funeral, stepping out of a police car handcuffed and sitting handcuffed in the church, then being taken away again. I was so glad to have him back and soon he settled in.

Bill and Nobby were very close. I'd see them getting dressed and combing their hair to go out and I'd say, 'Where are you two going, all slicked up?' and they'd say, 'Chasing girls.'

'You'll go bald chasing gins against the wind.'

They laughed as they went out, arms around each other's necks.

Dianne and Steve decided to go ahead with plans for the wedding. Somehow we still thought of it as a double wedding, we couldn't put Pearl out of our minds. When we talked, we tried to make the wedding how she would have liked it too. Greg came in and out, hardly speaking. The date was set for 2 May 1970.

Money was scarce so I rallied all the mates to help with sandwiches and Bob McDonald was out the back with a boiler full of eggs, cooking them on the open fire. We had no gas. Neddy and Gert wrapped Alfoil around sandwiches and packed them in cartons. Mum and my sisters from Beaumont Street made cakes and savouries, Aunty Beryl made angel food cakes. Steve sold raffle tickets to get his suit and Dianne hired her gown. A girlfriend of mine did Dianne's and my hair, and Bob escorted me to the wedding.

The church was just off Elizabeth Street, Waterloo. The minister paid Pauline twenty cents to run up and down to the corner and tell him when Dianne arrived. We walked to the church and our dog Judy followed us. When Judy saw Pauline going in to the church to tell the minister, she ran inside too.

Then Judy wandered in and out among the wedding guests till Dianne appeared at the church door. She waited till Dianne stepped in, then she followed her down the aisle. Judy took up a position near Steve and the ceremony began. When they went into the registry to sign, Steve tried to shoo Judy away but she wouldn't go. Then the minister tried to shoo her and she lurched forward and bit him on the hand. Outside, when Dianne and Steve were getting into the wedding car, Judy put her paws up on Dianne's shoulders and licked her face side to side 'like she was congratulating me', Dianne said later. (All the wedding photos had Judy in them.)

We drove across to the Foundation in George Street for the reception. The women had put up streamers and balloons and vases of flowers all along the tables. After the toasts and a small speech by me, Max Silver and his band Black Lace struck up and we danced for a while.

Bob and I were left to straighten up after the reception, along with a few others. No-one had mentioned Pearl. It was Dianne and Steve's day. But we'd all noticed Judy, the brown and white fox terrier, in every scene.

We joined the wedding party at the Clifton where the Mad Scot Bronc had put his wallet over the bar and the drinks were flowing. The bride and groom were floating on cloud nine. I think, as I remember back, that everyone we came in contact with was floating.

Back at Portland Street I gave Dianne and Steve my room and I slept on the divan. It was a windy night. Next morning at breakfast Steve said to me, 'Did you hear anything last night?' I looked at him. 'Pearl was at the bedroom window,' he said. 'The wind was blowing and the curtain was whooshing. Then I saw her face at the window, smiling and throwing kisses.' Nobody said anything. We kept eating.

A few days later Dianne was passing the girls' bedroom and looked in and caught a glimpse of Pearl's legs, then her feet. In the girls' room there were bars on the window, this house used to be a bookie's joint. A week later I was laying on the bed near the window to have a rest and thought I was dreaming when I saw Pearl's spirit blowing kisses to me through the bars. I was so startled I sat up rubbing my eyes, then she was gone. Blowing kisses as if to say 'Happy Mother's Day', then gone.

Not long after that the house in Portland Street was to be sold. The owner gave me $150 to move quickly, so the kids and I scanned the papers and found a place about half a mile away. Number 13 John Street was a two-storey place with two bedrooms and a balcony. The street ran directly onto Botany Road and the kids went to school around the corner at Waterloo. We couldn't have a dog so I took Judy to have her put down, and it was one of the hardest things I've ever had to do.

I always had a houseful wherever I went. It was a means of survival. My brother Kevin and his wife and brother Dennis stayed with us, they slept in the lounge or dining room and Neddy shared the upstairs bedroom with me and the girls. Dianne was with me too, as Steve had gone to New Zealand with the All Blacks football team for three weeks.

Eight months after Pearl died, I woke up one morning and the boys said, 'Come quick Mum, brother Bill's having a fit.' I rushed into their room and looked after him till the seizure was over and he went into a deep sleep, which always followed a fit. I slipped an old dress over my nightie and went downstairs to have a smoke.

The kids had gone out to play, Neddy was away and Dianne and Steve were at football, so were Kevin and Deirdre. I turned the TV on and was thinking how quiet it was, the house so silent.

Then all of a sudden there he was there in front of me asking for a smoke. I said, 'You okay son?' He answered, yes, and left the room. I turned back to the telly and watched for a while. It was Saturday, *Bandstand* was on. I couldn't get over how silent the house was, when suddenly something said, 'Go out there.' I got up and went to the dining room, then on to the kitchen. I pushed on the door of the bathroom.

That's where I found him, slumped over the bathtub. I guessed what had happened, I screamed, 'Billy!' and pulled him out and gave him mouth to mouth but he was gone, he was blue-lipped, I was too late.

Ten minutes it took for my son to run about eight inches of water into the tub and bend down to wash a pair of trousers. He'd taken a fit and fallen headfirst into the water and drowned. If only the plug wasn't in, I thought. I kept saying, 'Oh my God, not again. Not again.' I was hysterical. He was gone, my Bill.

Nobby came in then, and I told him what had happened. He seemed to be staring straight through me. Not able to believe it. He came into the bathroom with me. Bill had kicked off one of his shoes in the struggle. We stood still for a while. I said, 'Don't leave your brother there.'

He picked up Bill's body and put it on a bed in the dining room. I could hear him crying. He took off Bill's other shoe and covered him with a blanket. He ran out crying and I didn't see him for days.

When the family came home I told them straightaway, before they could get started on the football news. They stood there in twos and threes, shock registering like waves across their faces. Bill? they said in soft voices, as if he couldn't really be gone, they'd just spoken to him this morning about a boat, he was going somewhere in a boat.

I ran out into the street crying and then I turned one way and another like a crazy dog looking for something, it didn't know what, nothing, nothing was there, half-whimpering and half-hysterical I ran up and down the street and turned in circles till one of the neighbours came up and said, 'Ruby, what's WRONG?'

One of the neighbours rang the city Coroner's Office and they sent a car to take Bill to the morgue.

Just then Terry came in and said into the silence, 'Right, where's Bill, we're going out on a boat today, he's late.' I burst out crying. 'Your mate's dead, they just took his body away.'

'Ah Mum, don't joke like that.'

'I'm not joking. Why do you think I'm crying?'

Soon after, Terry left the house in tears too.

I buried him on 27 August. They kept his body for a week, I couldn't rake up a lousy $55 for grave-digging fees among my family and friends. In desperation I rang Bob McDonald and he showed up with a cheque for $100 and we gave it to the funeral directors, with the promise I'd pay the rest when I received Pearl's insurance.

I thought of the specialist we'd been to, the brain wave tests. He had no tumour, yet he was dead at eighteen years of age. Pearl had just turned seventeen. We had to walk past one to bury the other. That day we followed the pall-bearers up the hill, and Bill was put in the ground forty yards up from where my father and my daughter were. It was a sunny day. An ordinary day. Birds flew over and people wandered in and out among the graves, bending to place flowers or pull up a weed. I looked at the row of date palms near the front gate and a low brick fence, then I turned and looked out at the sea. Nothing made any sense.

After Bill died I couldn't hear anything. I stayed in bed for five days and Neddy and Gert looked after me. I saw them come into the room and go out, but I couldn't hear anything. It was like I was in a huge fog. Nobby came and took me out the back to the toilet and waited, and brought me in again. There were no outside noises. Bill's spirit had me locked in. I stayed in bed. People came into the room, I could see their lips move but I couldn't hear the voices. I stopped eating. Gert and Neddy sent for my mother.

I could hear my mother. She told me to go out to the grave and talk to him, and tell him to leave me alone. I knew if I didn't get out of bed it would be the end of me.

Gert came with me down to the bathroom where I'd found Bill dead. We shut the door and turned the light out. I called to my son in the lingo, I told him to leave me alone, 'What about the other kids? I have to look after them too. Do you hear me, Bill?' Then I said over and over the words my mother had told me, 'Nunyars jarjum, ningana, you're making me jung, I have to live for the other jarjums too, so leave me alone, you hear me, Bill? Ningana.'

There was a loud noise. A heap of stones had fallen onto the roof, loud as hail. I knew he'd heard me then, so I went back upstairs. Now I could hear people talking, could hear the sounds of life, children playing and cars out in the streets.

When I could think again my mind went round on rails. Why why why why why. It was a hurt I thought I'd never recover from. Later it seemed to me as if God had looked down and said, 'Here's a woman battling and struggling to raise her family, I'll take a couple to lighten her load.'

14

The Boys in Trouble

Waterloo, Alexandria, Erskineville, Surry Hills
We had to leave John Street because the house was being renovated to be sold. I asked Ray Barrington, one of Bill's friends, to move us – he had a truck.

Brenda Leslie lived in Lawrence Street, Alexandria, and said we could doss at her place until I got another one. I put my furniture in the shed out the back.

In the last few months Bob had proposed to me nine or ten times but he'd been passed on to Thelma. I was keeping company with a bloke named Les Bourke from Victoria, Shepparton I think. We stayed at Brenda's a week then I found a place in Victoria Street, Erskineville. I enrolled the kids in the school around the corner.

I set up house in this three-bedroom place, another battle ground. I had enough money for electricity but before long the gas was cut off. Dianne and Steve and my brother Kevin and his wife Deirdre and their kids were staying with me. We pooled together for rent and food. Steve and Kevin had casual work, but not enough to feed us all.

We had no food as all my money went on rent, so I said to Nerida, 'Go on, titi, you're the only one I can trust, go and see what you can do to get us a feed.' So she got dressed and away she went. We didn't have the price of a smoke even. She was gone for about an hour and a half, and then she was back with a captain. Loaded up with bread and chickens, and lollies for the kids.

I'd gone to bed. She came in and said, 'I've got food downstairs for the kids.' She said she was going to let this bloke have a sleep as he was half-charged. I said okay and went off to sleep.

Next thing she was waking me up and hit me in the chest with $50 and said, 'Put this in your chest.'

'Did you roll him?'

'He's loaded, Ruby. A wallet full.'

'Don't take any more, he might call the cops.'

'Okay. Don't worry, I've got a plan.'

She asked my son-in-law Steve to come upstairs and make out he was her husband. She gave him $10, so he came up the stairs walking heavy, entered the room and said, 'What the hell are you doing in bed with my wife?' The bloke got up, slipped his trousers on, grabbed his shoes and ran down the stairs like the devil was after him. He was running so fast he ran right past his car. We were leaning over the balcony laughing. That would teach one more gin jockey a lesson, *ha ha*.

I decided to have a house-warming party and invited all our friends. James Golden and Lester came and Les Potter and Brenda and Neddy. We were having a good time until Les Bourke got drunk and started making a show of me in front of my friends. I said, 'Look mate, go and have a sleep,' and he wouldn't take any notice of me, so I took him into the from bedroom and knocked him clean out, threw him onto the bed and covered him up for the night.

Next morning my knuckles were swollen and so was his face. I'd broken four knuckles when I hit him. He left not long after to go back to Shepparton. 'Ta ta,' I said. I could barely wave.

It was after I'd lost Pearl and Bill that the two boys, Nobby and David, started getting into trouble. I was forever fronting court for them. I don't think there was a children's court I didn't go to – Albion Street, Yasmar, Newtown. They ended up in Daruk, and later Nob was in Mount Penang and Tamworth Boys' Home. I always fronted for them but it did no good. The two deaths had a bad effect on them. They started truanting, thieving, running amok in general. They went into Daruk for car stealing when Nob was fifteen and Dave fourteen.

Allan Barrett grew up with Nobby and David. They met in the boys' homes. Allan's family was a big one and because the family couldn't keep all of them, some were sent to the homes, and from boys' homes to the bighouse (gaol). Allan's been fighting the world ever since, he's been hitting back ever since. No-one knows what it's like better than he does, to grow up unwanted and unloved.

He grew up like a brother to my kids. I'm the only mother figure he's ever known. He sends flowers and cards on Mother's Day, birthdays and Christmas. He's got a soft spot for kids and we called him the Pied Piper. He spoilt Jeffery as he was growing up, then my grandkids Ronny Boy and Steve and Davy Boy.

The other boy close to ours at the time was Terry Priest, Bill's friend, who now befriended Nobby and David. One day he called in his car to take us out to Daruk to visit the boys. We drove through Windsor and when we arrived we had a picnic in the grounds with David and Allan. Nob wasn't allowed to join us – he was in the gymnasium on punishment for fighting.

I asked Terry to stay with David while we visited Nobby. When we came out they were gone.

Terry had put David in the boot of his car and driven off, leaving me to explain to the manager of the home that my son had been abducted by my adopted son and that I didn't have train fares to Sydney as my handbag was in the car. I was very embarrassed and cursed them all the way back from Windsor.

One afternoon I was sitting on a wooden chair in front of the fire-bucket, cooking a big boiler of curried sausages for my hungry brood, and when I stood up to stir the curry Ellen (not noticing I was using the chair) took it to reach a peach in the tree above where I was cooking. I backed back to sit on the chair and ended on my backside with curried sausages everywhere. I laced her real good, I bet she couldn't sit down for a while.

Neddy and Gert called to see me regularly. Once they came with a flagon of port and said, 'Happy Mother's Day, Titi.' Titi had never drunk port before, but had a go to celebrate. Titi ended up in hospital gasping for breath.

Then on my birthday Nobby ran away from the home and was hiding down the lane. He wouldn't come inside because he thought I'd send him back. I sent the kids to bring him in, I was so happy to see him I'd be the last one to give him up. Except for David I had my kids together again and it felt good.

We had no gas and I could barely pay for the electricity for lights, so I rigged up the fire-bucket again, thinking it was a good thing there were so many four-gallon drums in the back lanes of Erko. Nobby stayed at home and was all right again.

Les Potter came to visit and he and Nobby made fritters over the fire-bucket. They called them 'Les and Nobby's Fritters', the brand name.

Terry and David were gone three months and when the law caught up with them they were in Brisbane. Terry went to Long Bay for two years for abducting Dave, and Dave went back to Daruk for twelve months.

Metropolitan Remand Centre
22/2/71

Dear Ruby and family,
I hope you do not mind me writing to you like this mum
as it stands now I have no one else, I do hope Jeffery and

all the girls are well and you too of course and David too
would you please tell David that I'm very sorry for taking
him away from Daruk … as you know mum I have no
mother but you and your kids made me feel like I was
wanted especially David he's been like a brother to me
and that's how I tried to treat him but it looks like I didn't
do a very good job … I do wish you would come out and
see me any Monday to Saturday …

Love Terry

Early in 1971 we had to move again – this place was being sold too. I wrote to our local MP about my housing situation and reminded him I'd been waiting for a Housing Commission place for eight years. As a last resort I rang Mrs Kearney, the landlady from Ann Street, Surry Hills and then Katoomba, and she only had two rooms and a kitchenette three flights up in Riley Street, Surry Hills, and so I took it. We had to walk down three floors to the bathroom laundry and toilet, but it was home.

One evening Nob came in with seven thousand dollars worth of watches. He and a mate had taken a van for a ride and then discovered the loot. He brought some of the watches in and handed them around. When I went to tuck Jeffery in he was already asleep with watches up both arms. A few weeks later Steve got caught fencing them and went to the Bay for six months. Nob and his mate took off and were caught in Grafton, kept there a week then sent to Tamworth Boys' Home for a year.

I had a lot of sons in gaol or homes and a lot of letters to write that year. Dave and Allo were in Daruk, Terry and Steve in Long Bay and Nob in Tamworth.

Terry sent another letter in May.

Central Industrial Prison
23/5/71

Dear Ruby,
... after we left Daruk we were going real well working on this carnival we made about $300 and we were going to send you some money but we decided to go to Dalby in Queensland and when we got there nothing seemed to go right and we ended up flat broke so we had to borrow a car and come back to Sydney but we only made it as far as Cootamundra where we hit a tree at eighty five miles per hour but I suppose if the tree wasn't there we might be still out, anyway I got two years for my trouble I know I deserve it but I hope you don't give David a bake because I talked him into going ...

Terry

He wasn't allowed to write to David direct so he had written to him on the back of this page, and asked me to take it to him.

Dear David,
... I didn't mean to get you into any trouble but I missed you that much I did not know what to do I think a hell

of a lot of you maybe because you look like Bill but that's why I'm here now ... it was a silly place to put a tree anyhow when you get released I do hope you come and see me if mum lets you and I do hope you write to me and when you get out tell fatso if he lays one finger on you I'll pay him a visit when I am released ... so I'll see you Dave.

Your mate, Terry

James Golden and Neddy had to move from their flat in Leichhardt, so I told them about the empty flat next door to us and they moved in. Later Brenda and her kids moved to the top floor in the same flats as Neddy and James, and before long cousin Gloria Morgan and her man Mitchell moved into the middle flat between the others and everyone was happy. We visited back and forth and later I managed to get the ground floor and we moved down next to the yard.

When Steve came out of the Bay, he and Dianne had their wedding anniversary in the backyard and I cooked and the Redfern All Blacks turned up. I bought them an eighteen-gallon keg as a present. Dianne was pregnant with my first grandchild.

Still so much battling. I robbed Peter to pay Paul and my electricity was turned off. One day a delegation of hippies arrived from up the street and introduced themselves. 'Mrs Langford,' they said, 'we're going to Luna Park and we could take the kids if you like.' They became good friends and took the kids to the parks and the zoo. When they were told we had no power they approached me and asked my permission to pay the bill, I said I was sorry, I couldn't accept their kind offer. But they went and paid it anyway.

I went to their place to thank them and they gave me a painting of an African woman. Underneath it said, 'Portrait of Anne Kelly'. The woman was sitting on a chair with her arm on the chair's arm. She was a modern woman. Her hair was braided. I thanked them for the painting and kept it with me for years. I still remember the look in Anne Kelly's face. When I lived in Green Valley later the doctor offered me four hundred dollars for the painting, but I wouldn't sell it. Some time after that, it got pinched.

We had some good parties at James and Neddy's but those two would end up fighting. I always had to be on call as a peacemaker or referee.

Brenda's kids and mine went to Crown Street Public School. Her son Reggie Boy had been hit by a car and took epileptic fits. Sometimes I sat with her half the night because he took fits in his sleep too. He'd get the wanders for two weeks straight and he was brought home in a police car. When he was six or seven he was always getting lost in the city.

James was going back and forth to the Clock Hotel getting flagon after flagon. When he was partying at his place he'd pay for one flagon and knock the other one off. The publican must have jerried what he was up to because he took a big swig of the next flagon and spat it out, it turned out to be coloured water. I laughed so much I had cramps in my stomach. 'Serves you right for stealing,' I said.

Terry had got my letter and wrote back to say he was missing us.

> *Anyway thank Dianne for writing to David for me and I hope she comes thru the hospital all right. I bet Steve will be worried he'll be pacing up and down like a frog on a hot frypan.*

My first grandchild was born at Crown Street Hospital just down the corner. Dianne had a son and called him Steven Craig. He was born on 20 October 1971, the day they opened the Opera House, and I was overjoyed.

The kids were always playing tricks on me, saying, 'Look Mum, here comes Lance,' and I'd jump and run to see, but he wasn't there. Until one day they shook me awake and said, 'Here's Lance, he's here.' I said, 'Go away and let me sleep.' They shook me again and when I opened my eyes he was there, crying. He'd been back to Coona and Ruby Leslie told him I'd just lost Pearl and Bill and he'd come straightaway. I know he loved my kids and we cried together. He had a new wife and a young child with him. She was quiet, not like me open-mouthed and straight out.

They slept on the floor for a few days and he left crying, pointing to his chest, 'I still have you in my heart.' His wife was crying too and afterwards so was I. But I wouldn't let him see my tears for him, they were hidden in my heart too. He'd come to offer sympathy for my kids – he was that kind of bloke.

In November 1971 Dave came home from Daruk. He handed me a wedding ring he'd found in the street. It was thick gold, eighteen carat.

'Look Mum,' he said, 'I remember what happened to your other wedding ring, you gave it to Billy Woo for £6 worth of tucker. So here's one I've found for you.'

I put it on and it fitted perfectly. I wondered whether someone had just dropped it, or thrown it away because they were sick of their marriage.

Terry wrote to say he was glad David was out.

I really thought David would have written to me but I don't really care any more I think a lot of David I would have done anything for him but now I know don't I mum you've got no friends in gaol – I feel like one of those lost souls in the Siberian desert.

Later the writing cheered up and he said:

When I get out I will go up to Kay's Rent-a-Car and hire a big Galaxy for the weekend and we will ride around like toffs HA HA.

He signed it: *Your loving son and veteran Terry.*

The council was digging up the street out front and the kids made friends with an Islander bloke named Mick Porter. He came from Palm Island, it turned out I knew his uncle at the Empress. He was kind to the kids and I checked him out, he was only missing his people. I invited him to tea a few times and he came with beer and lollies for the kids.

At the Empress there was a bloke I'd known a long time called Mervyn, who was sweet on me then. I saw him watching me from further up the bar. I called out and raised my glass to him and said, 'Eat your heart out' to torment him. I didn't want to settle down, I was having too good a time. There were others who offered tempting promises, but I'd taken my love to town too many times and I was always on the defensive. My son-in-law Steve said, 'When are you going to get married again?' I said, 'When I can get a man who can look after me better than I can do myself.'

One morning I sent a bloke from up the street to the butcher with my pension cheque and he robbed me. I didn't realise till he'd gone. A while later we were in the Empress and Steve asked me, 'Is that the bloke who robbed you?' I tried to make out it wasn't so there'd be no trouble but I couldn't fool Steve, who walked up to him and said, 'You robbed my mother-in-law' and knocked him down and they carried him away on a stretcher. I bet he doesn't rob anyone again in a hurry.

Later that year Steve and Dianne moved to Port Kembla, down to the steelworks where his uncle worked, not long after Dave came home from Daruk. Seeing Dave made me realise again how lonely the other boys would be and longing for news of the rest of the world, so I sat down and wrote letters to Nob in Tamworth and Allan in Daruk and Terry in the Bay.

In February there was a letter from Nob.

Institute for Boys
Tamworth
12/2/72

Dear Mum and family just a few lines to let you know that I am very well and healthy up here. How is the family is David still working ... well mum I hope you will write soon and send me a parcel and tell Dianne and Nana Joyce to write. I can say that we have to be very fast up here to get up the ladder and I hope I will make it to the top ... On Tues night we had bread and milk and Sat night we had spaghetti and meatballs and my work is making scrubbing brushes and some boys cover books I hope I will get kitchen after a while ...

One of the people I met in Riley Street that year was a big black fellow named John King, who came from Melbourne. We became good friends but it wasn't long before I found out he was a very bossy person, and we had a blue. He was trying to run my life and he hit me on the head with a shoe with a thick heel on it. I collapsed just as I was putting the vegetables in the oven for Christmas dinner and they took me to have my head X-rayed. I was bleeding from one ear and the hospital admitted me straightaway as I was very giddy.

I awoke to see a Christmas tree in the corner of my ward with candles glowing and I started to cry – it was Christmas night and I was in hospital nursing a fractured skull and away from my children.

We'd planned to have Christmas dinner together, the Riley Street gang – Neddy, Brenda and her children, James and cousin Gloria Morgan and Mitchell Hamson and all our kids. The tables were set up in my flat. John King stayed and looked after my flat and the kids till I was on my feet again, then he took off for Melbourne. He took David with him to go fruit picking, but a week later David hitched home. He said John had got stuck into the grog and wasn't looking for any work. So Dave had jumped into the first truck that came along and come home. I said, 'Well good riddance.' I couldn't stay with anyone that was going to knock me around, I'd had enough before and didn't want or need any more of the same. I hid the truth from my kids – told them I'd fallen over and hit my head – I didn't want to start World War Three, and it would've been on for young and old if I'd told them about the shoe.

Early in 1972 I was in my small kitchen in Riley Street when there was a knocking at my door and I looked up to see Terry Priest, released from the Bay. I went to welcome him home then stopped – while he was walking towards me smiling, I could see my dead son Bill's spirit walking down the hall with him as much as to say, 'I'm gone, but I'm bringing you another son to care for,' and I cried happy tears. Dianne and Steve had come back from Port Kembla and they hugged Terry, and the kids came in and we all hugged Terry, hard to believe he'd done two years in the bighouse just for 'releasing' Dave from Daruk.

Then a letter came about Pearl's insurance, and I hurried to the solicitor. I received $4000 (payment for death). With legal fees and burial cost for the two funerals I was left with $2500, not much for a life and a terrible reason to be getting money. I had to think it was better than nothing, and just after that I got word about my Housing Commission home. I purchased a car for $300 and Steve drove it for me till it broke a crankshaft and was towed away.

I was overjoyed to finally have a home, and with the money I had left, I got Terry to drive me out to look at it right away. We had the keys but there was no power so I inspected it by torchlight and was so overcome I sat and cried.

Next day I went to the Smith Family furniture factory in Holt Street, Surry Hills, and bought a cheap lounge and three wardrobes, a dining setting, beds for four bedrooms and a few odds and ends. I hired a truck which charged $30 per hour, and sent Terry and David to lift the furniture off quickly so it wouldn't cost any more. We followed the truck in a taxi and when we arrived I yelled, 'Green Valley the Langfords have arrived, yippee! We're home, kids.'

'Yippee!' said the kids in what seemed a hundred voices.

15

Why we didn't 'Assimilate'

Green Valley

My first glimpse of the house left me with a lump in my throat. When the kids asked why I was crying, I said they were happy tears. We hugged each other and then the big job of moving in began. It was a four-bedroom house with a front porch and a lattice framework where I could put my pot plants.

The kids chose rooms and jumped on their beds and opened and closed their wardrobes.

There was a knock on the door next morning and I opened it to see my next-door neighbour who introduced herself as Mrs Jenkins. She invited me to her place to get acquainted over a cup of tea. I accepted and stepped over the fence and into her kitchen, where she had a fresh baked cake. She seemed pleasant and friendly, she had five kids too. I introduced my five.

David was unemployed then and living at home with me. Aileen started at Ashcroft High, and Ellen, Pauline and Jeff went to the primary and infant schools with the next-door kids. Nobby had come home from

Tamworth and was staying in town with Dianne and Steve.

After I got the kids off to school I started to dig a garden in the backyard. I planted chilli bushes, pumpkin, corn, lettuce and tomatoes. There was a mulberry tree and a tall pine in the back. Jeff climbed the pine tree and tied up a swing made of rope and a big tyre. Neighbouring kids asked if they could come through to pick mulberries. Everything seemed to be going fine.

Mrs Jenkins told me the house had been the first Aboriginal house in the Valley, and the people who lived there before me were the Phillips. When they moved in there was a welcoming ceremony, and an ironbark tree was planted to commemorate the first Aboriginal family to settle in the Valley. The radio and press were there. The ironbark, now twelve years old, was a tall well-established tree.

Mrs Phillips was a JP. Once, when she was away, her husband was smoking in bed when the mattress caught fire and the house partly burned down. Mrs Jenkins' boys had pulled him out. Henry Phillips had third-degree burns on his back.

The house was renovated before I moved in, but the burnt wood had never been cleaned out from behind the new walls. When we had showers the steam would cause the soot to seep through the walls.

Sometimes Henry Phillips came back to the house (when he was charged up) and he'd sit under the mulberry tree. The sons came too – to look around. One, who had the mellow voice of a crooner, was a radical who'd fired shots in Canberra to get the Queen's attention when she was on one of her tours, to make a plea for land rights.

I was glad to see the Phillips. It gave me a chance to talk about politics, but more important, at the time it gave me a chance to be with other black people. There were only three or four Aboriginal families in the whole of Green Valley.

These homes were the government's policy on integration. It meant putting us in among whites to see if we could live together, but because there were so few black families there in 1972 we felt very isolated from our friends and our culture. All my neighbours were white, and there weren't many black kids at the school.

I found out that you were not supposed to create a nuisance or disturb any of the neighbours. You also weren't able to have anyone come and stay without permission from the Commission. It reminded me of the missions. The rule was useless in our culture, where survival often depended on being able to stay with friends and relatives. Here I'd thought I'd got away from this, finally.

We couldn't afford to have the phone connected. If you needed to ring someone urgently most likely you'd walk for about half a mile before you found a public one that worked, as there were vandals everywhere, people with nothing to do but be destructive.

I was wondering one day why Jeff (who was six) took a different way to school each morning. He said there were a gang of kids waiting to belt him up. I was shocked but I knew there were adjustments to be made, so I said, 'Look Jeff, you can't be running away all the time from them, so what you do is, hit the one with the biggest mouth, and you'll find the others will shoot through.' I was to see the results of this action later in the afternoon.

He came in with his knuckles bleeding and his shirt collar ripped, but he had a grin from ear to ear. 'I did what you told me Mum, and it's true. They all ran away when I punched the big-mouthed one.' They didn't bother him again – it's a terrible thing that you had to encourage your young son to resort to violence, so he could go to school peacefully each day.

A week later the headmaster from Ellen's high school sent a message to say she'd been fighting in the school grounds. I said I'd come up. I found Ellie in the playground and we went to the office together. The headmaster looked at her.

'Why were you fighting, Ellen?'

'The girl I hit called me a dirty abo, so I decked her,' Ellie said.

The headmaster looked at me.

'I'm very sorry about this, Mrs Landford. We will not tolerate racism here.' Then he said to Ellie, 'You know you're not allowed to fight in the school grounds, Ellen. Next time you wait till you catch her outside, okay?'

My children were always brought up to be close, so if one of them got into a blue it was one out, all out. I taught them a long time ago that 'united we stand, divided we fall' and I'm very glad I did, this advice has come in handy on many occasions.

Our mongrel dog Devil took great joy in chasing cars up the street and barking loudly. I tried to keep him tied up but it was cruel to do it too much. As soon as I let him off the chain for a run he chased cars again. The neighbours complained and we had to lose a loved animal. Our yard had no front fence yet.

I was weeding the garden when my eyes caught a glimpse of a small animal running up and down the side fence and not making a sound. This happened a few times, then one of Mrs Jenkins' kids said that her mum had taken it to the vet and had its voice box removed. I found it hard to believe someone could be so cruel to a dumb animal.

Next day a row broke out over the kids fighting. I'd had enough of complaints from Mrs Jenkins so I ordered her out of her house. 'Come outside and fight as good as you can talk and complain,' I said, 'while you bastards were having your kids in comfort I was battling to raise mine in a tent where my husband had left me with a gutful of his next child – you don't own the land your house is on, my people were here first, so get off, come on and fight me if you're game you bitch.'

With that I started shaping up to her, and she ran inside and slammed the door shut. I didn't see her for days. There was never a dull moment – you had to fight to survive out there. The suburbs were nothing like the city and though I was glad to have my house we had trouble coping with the discrimination. If it wasn't kids fighting it was the grown-ups with their private wars. But no-one had any privacy, as the houses were built very close together. If Mr So-and-so caught his wife running around and they argued about it and raised their voices, the whole street knew probably before the rowing couple themselves.

One good thing, the Valley was a very sports-minded place with good facilities for swimming, netball, basketball and rugby league. The Valley was called Home Ground and the parents got great pleasure watching their up-and-coming football greats every weekend. Jeff started playing rugby for the Valley when he was six. He played for Mt Pritchard and Sadlier also, and kept on with rugby for seven or eight years. I was a football parent, I loved to see the kids running around and healthy.

But it got that way after a while that I was dying to see another black face like mine, someone to pass the time of day and yarn with, and if some relatives showed up for an occasional visit, when you went out to welcome them you could see your neighbours' curtains move and many eyes upon you. After a while I felt guilty about having visitors. I wondered who'd be dobbing me in to the Commission if the visitors stayed overnight.

My family and I were to live in Sadlier Green Valley for about eight years. The government policy of assimilation by absorption meant splitting up the Aboriginal communities, and I understand what this policy meant as I had four daughters and only one married an Aboriginal. My grandchildren are blond and blue or hazel-eyed, and within two or three hundred years there won't be Aboriginals in suburbia. So as far as the government is concerned, assimilation by absorption is working well, and in the end there'll be no Aboriginal problem whatever.

I have thought that one way we can keep Aboriginal culture alive is through the kids – having Aboriginal studies taught compulsorily in schools.

David was the eldest in the family when we moved to the Valley, and because he was the eldest and unemployed the rental was very good – for a four-bedroom house I was paying only $7 per week. When he got a job the rent was $9 a week – very reasonable – and the cost of living wasn't so severe then.

David's job was offsiding on a truck. He acquired an enormous chopper push bike and rode to the half-way shops where he was picked up by the boss each day. He pedalled like mad just to get the bike mobile. I saw him off each morning with his little overnight bag with his lunch in.

Aileen was now fifteen and decided to leave school. I tried to talk her into to going on but she wanted to do a receptionist course at Scotts College in Liverpool. I applied for a study grant for her and took her in to enrol.

My sister Rita was now doing her teacher's course there, and she said to me one day she hadn't seen Aileen at class for a while. I soon found out Aileen was catching the bus to Liverpool Station then getting a train to the city and spending all day in the movies – and she'd come home and make like she'd been in class all day.

When I questioned her she admitted to it and I was so furious after all my efforts I gave her a good thumping. She found other work later.

I was finding it difficult raising the kids and encouraging them to go on at school with no moral support from my usual friends. There were three Aboriginal families that I knew in the Valley – the Stewarts, the Munroes and the Delaneys – but they were settled all over, and the Valley was a big place with nine or ten suburbs.

Sometimes at weekends I went in to Redfern to Dianne and Steve and we went to the Empress to be among our friends. During the first few years in the Valley I put on a lot of weight. Whether this was some sort of protection against the grief of losing Pearl and Bill, or a combination of the beer and then the Valium the doctor prescribed for stress, I don't know. Maybe I'd got used to eating big meals when I was working hard in the bush.

I'd been on valium (2 mg) for over four years, since I'd buried my two eldest children. And I got that way I'd be drinking beer and I'd feel a bit uptight and pop a valium.

None of this was doing any good, and I joined a Weight Watchers group in Ashcroft. I lost one stone four pounds in a month, and won the sash for Queen of the Month. Two women had put on a few pounds and were put in the pig pen, where they had bibs tied around their necks. On the bibs was a picture of a big pig. They had to sit there by themselves.

One woman was told to get down on her hands and knees and bark like a dog. The other had to recite a nursery rhyme in a child's voice.

Watching these scenes I lost four stone in three months and ended up with heart palpitations and high blood pressure. The doctor told me to eat properly. I didn't know that alcohol and Valium was a deadly combination but between them I was nearly climbing the wall. So I gave up the pills and vowed I'd never take another anti-depressant as long as I live.

Then to my great joy, Neddy got custody of her grandchildren and was allocated a house at Ashcroft, only a few hundred yards away. We visited back and forth and on pension day we went shopping together at Miller Shopping Centre.

That summer Mrs Thomas from over the road gave me the rim of a twelve foot by three foot swimming pool. David bought me the blue vinyl and a ton of sand and rigged it up. The Valley was a hot place in summer and a long way from the beaches, so we cooled off in our new pool.

Nobby had come home from Tamworth and was living with Dianne and Steve in town. He had a job in a chocolate factory. I felt so glad that he and David were settled and had jobs – after their reaction to the deaths I wondered if they'd survive the system but they seemed okay.

One day I got a message from Dianne saying to come out and get James Golden as he was laying among the flagons in Lewis Street. I had no money, so I gave my wedding ring to the baker to hold for $20, caught a taxi to town and got him up. I told the nurse from the Aboriginal Medical Service not to give him any more needles and brought him home, where he stayed with me till he got situated. Since then he's never looked back. He gave up wine and only drank beer, which never made him sick. He bought a car we called the Grey Ghost and came around to take us out sometimes.

In 1973 I had to appear in Albion Street Court for David, he was there for stealing. I asked James to come with me – he was good at talking to the law. Dianne was living in Eveleigh Street at the time, so on the way to court I thought we'd go and visit her, and also see Nobby.

When James and I arrived, I saw Nobby's girlfriend with two big black eyes and I asked her, 'Who's done that to you?' and she said Nobby had. I was so disgusted with him – I didn't bring any of my sons up to be women bashers. They'd seen me with black eyes and bruises and knew I didn't approve of this. Nobby knew I'd be in town to go to court for David, he also knew I'd flatten him for doing this to his girl if I saw him, so he shot through and wasn't anywhere to be seen.

We went to court for David and while the evidence was being given the old magistrate dozed off and started to snore. All the court's eyes were on him till he woke up. Then James got to speak on David's behalf.

David had always had a good reputation among his fellows, he said, and he gave examples. He cited incidents in which David had played heroic parts, dating back fifteen years, although James himself had only known David for a few years. He entirely made up David's good reputation, though some parts were coincidently true, and at these times when James was speaking, David would smile and nod at him, as if encouraging him to invent the truth.

The light outside the courtroom started to fade, and James continued. He was still speaking after the magistrate had let David go and everyone was leaving the court.

We took David to Dianne's place and to the Railway View to have a drink before we went home to the Valley. As we settled in the lounge, there was Nobby coming through the door of the pub with about half a dozen of his mates, saying: 'Not now Mum, I know you're gonna give it to me, but not in front of my friends,' so I agreed, and he slapped a ten-dollar note on the table and said, 'Drinks for everyone, and anything my Mum wants she gets.' The drinks were coming so fast, the jukebox was blaring, and James Golden was being congratulated on his speech; my darling son got me so drunk that I forgot all about belting him one for what he had done to his girlfriend.

Not long after this, James was charged with drunk driving. He limped into court, displaying his war injuries, then he stuttered and stammered so much that the judge remarked on his 'undeniable speech impediment', and James walked away with another court victory. He should have been on the bench instead of in front of it.

One day there was a knock on the door and I opened it to see a very tall young bloke asking, 'Are you Mrs Langford?' I said I was and he handed me a note, saying: 'David sent me.' The note said, 'Mum, keep this bloke here, as he's my mate.' I could see he was hungry so I fed him and gave him a bottle of beer. He lay down on the divan and went to sleep. He looked exhausted.

When David came home he asked if this fellow could stay a while as he had nowhere to go. My house was full up most of the time but I said okay. I couldn't stand to see anyone without shelter.

What a contrast they were, this young man six foot four and David about five foot five. They got on famously. I wasn't to know till they caught him he was an escapee from Kirkonell Prison. His name was Steve Farrant, and I nicknamed him The Horse. Dave's old mate Sparrow came to stay and he and The Horse made a great pair also.

Ellen and Pauline were by now in high school and one night they wanted to go to a school dance. I refused to let them go without someone to look after them. Sparrow was elected, because he could dance too, in case they didn't get any partners. Away they went.

Meanwhile David and Steve were out the backyard with a light on an extension working on a bomb car I'd bought them for $25. It had some rego on it, and I'd bought another car the same model they could use for parts. The second car cost $5.

Suddenly the girls ran in and said, 'Mum, Sparrow's in a blue at the school, some blokes are getting into him!'

With that, The Horse dropped his tools and said, 'Quick, show me where he is,' and they took off for the school.

They were gone about half an hour and when they came back The Horse had his arm around Sparrow supporting him. He wasn't hurt bad, only a bit ruffled. Horse said, 'I fixed them up good, Mum,' and his sleeve was nearly off his shirt and his collar just hanging on.

The girls said, 'Boy, you should have seen them scatter when Horse came, he done the lot of them and they ran away.' David was still working on the bomb car and came in to see what all the excitement was about. He laughed when they told him, and said, 'Well you didn't need me then!'

Later that night The Horse said he could pinch any of Sparrow's girlfriends with no trouble, which made Sparrow spew. 'Go on,' Sparrow said to The Horse, 'you're big enough to hold an elephant out to shit, get your own girls!'

16

Nobby Goes to Gaol

Green Valley

In 1973 Nobby brought home a girl called Penny and asked my permission to become engaged. I thought he was too young at eighteen but I also thought it might settle him down, so I gave my permission. His friends organised a party and bought the food and we had a barbeque at home. One of Nob's mates, a young bloke named Maxwell, was bragging about a gun he had. Dianne looked at me sideways. We went to where Maxwell was standing and I said, 'Don't you have anything to do with guns. Guns kill.' He didn't say anything. The rest of the party went well, and we hoped Nob would be happy.

Then on the Tuesday morning after, I got a message from (son-in-law) Steve, saying Nobby had been gaoled for firing shots at police. I was shocked, but I got going and tried to find out what had happened.

Nob had heard that Penny was seeing another bloke, so he got blind drunk and asked his mate Maxwell to drive him home to the Valley. A friend of theirs, a fourteen-year-old girl, was in the back seat. Maxwell was driving negligently so the police chased them. Then shots were fired at the police car.

Nobby being the eldest copped the rap. The other two were sixteen and fourteen, and they went to children's homes, and Nob was to spend six years of a ten-year sentence in Long Bay. It began 21 June 1973 when they were charged and in court at Bankstown. I went to see Nob in the cells and he had two black eyes. We knew what this meant.

'I'm here, Nob,' I said. 'I'll do what I can.'

In court the case was adjourned for two months and Nob was put in the Bay on remand awaiting trial.

On the way home I bought a *Telegraph*. Page 10 carried the news: 'Two charged with shooting.'

'Two teenagers charged with attempting to murder a police constable appeared in separate courts yesterday … Langford was arrested at Rookwood Cemetery on Tuesday night after a high speed car chase.' And how must he feel, a kid who went handcuffed to his sister's funeral, who lifted his dead brother from the bath and laid him out, who drank to kill pain. Who was arrested in a cemetery.

It was a horrible two months of waiting. Then, in August, at Central Court twelve police gave evidence, though there'd only been two police in the car. A bullet had passed through the windscreen and through the headrest, an inch from the constable's head. The constable was there with his hand wrapped up, where the glass had cut it. His arm was even in a sling. Time after time 'evidence' came up that Nob had been seen leaning out the Valiant window firing shots at the patrol car. I stuck this out for three days, by then I felt sickened. I turned to Dianne and James, who'd come in with me, and said I was going home.

Nob was convicted and sentenced to ten years in Long Bay. I couldn't believe this had happened, and I must have been in a state of shock for months. James stuck by me through it all. He'd found a place of his own in the Valley.

Not long after Nob was put away, James came to visit with a woman called Juanita (Wannie). She came from Taiwan, he'd just met her at the pub. She worked at Inghams Chickens and had a letter from the Queen to show she was the first Asian bride to come to Australia. She'd married an officer in the army and they adopted a Taiwanese child. She lived in the same house with the officer, but they had separate arrangements.

I could see James liked her, and she liked him. He'd introduced me as his sister and after a few days she was calling me 'sit'.

'You like me to read your cards?'

'You read cards?' I said.

She took out a pack and started to shuffle. She said the cards had been in her family for a hundred years. I stood up and beckoned James out to the hall. When she couldn't hear us I said, 'How much did you tell her about me?'

'Nothing. Just said, you were my tribal sister.'

'Okay.'

Back in the kitchen Wannie put the pack in front of me. I picked up the top card, a nine.

'You have nine children,' she said.

A two.

'You lost two. Two kids dead. One boy, one girl.'

A ten.

'Someone you love, who loves you, behind a big wall.'

I looked at James. He shook his head.

Wannie said, 'He good man this one. When he come out behind wall he gonna be rich, plenty money.'

'Stop,' I said. 'That's enough for now.' Hair prickling the back of my neck.

Next day a friend of David's ran into my laundry while I was washing. I was startled as I didn't know where he'd come from. 'Mrs Langford, please hide me, the cops are chasing me and I don't want to go to gaol.'

Poor kid was crying. He'd come over the back fence. I grabbed him and pushed him up the manhole and said, 'Keep quiet.' I went on washing, my machine was just under the manhole.

Next thing the cops were at my laundry door.

'Did you see a young fellow go by here?'

'Yes,' I said, 'he went that way.' I pointed up the street and they ran off in that direction. After they'd gone I helped Robbie down and he thanked me and hurried away. I think he moved out of the Valley because he never came round again.

One winter afternoon of the next year, I was down at Miller Shopping Centre and I saw the headlines:

'GAOL BREAK!' I put down my shopping and grabbed a copy of the paper.

Photo exclusive. Police angry and astonished over the escape of seven convicts from Long Bay Gaol ... a 25 foot ladder ... three still at large ...

Nobby was out.

I got a taxi straight home and told the kids. We waited. I knew he'd try and call in, that he'd be here one minute at the most, that it could happen any time in the next few days. Then he'd head north. The kids always went north when they ran away. It seemed like unconsciously they were heading for Bundjalung country, but who knows. The weather up there would be better for sleeping out. I could feel my heart sinking. I sat down again. I sat in the chair and waited.

I must have slept for a while. The next afternoon I sent the kids out for a paper. 'MANHUNT FOR VIOLENT TRIO.' A photo of Nob and the other two. None of them looked happy.

Detectives have launched a massive manhunt for the three men and interstate police are on the lookout ... The five escapees used a 7.5 metre ladder made of bed ends lashed with sheets ... climbed over a 9 metre (30 foot) wall ... Langford, already convicted of shooting at police to avoid arrest, is considered the most dangerous.

I cooked tea and slept for a while. I was awake most of the night, then at daybreak a knock on the back door. Penny's sister came in and said, 'Nob's here, he can't stay long –' Nob at the door, then hugging me. 'Mum,' and crying. The kids came out of their rooms and hugged his legs. 'I can't tell you where I'm going because I'll bring you undone.'

'It's all right,' I said. 'Good luck.'

Four days later, Aileen went out for a paper.

GAOL ESCAPEE CAPTURED

John Leslie Jones, 22, was caught as he tried to run from a ground floor flat. Police believe another escapee, Gordon Allen Langford, 19, got away minutes before the raid … Langford is described by police as the most dangerous and they fear he will shoot if cornered –

I wondered where Nobby was, if he was in some small town reading this stuff about himself. I was so angry they'd describe him in this way. A few hours later a journalist knocked on the door. He wanted to know would I consent to an interview. I said I had a message for the police. I said my son had been portrayed as a vicious criminal, which he was not. The kids stood by me while I talked to the man.

The Saturday papers said:

POLICE RIOT ALERT IN GAOLS

More than 2000 top security prisoners have been confined to their cells …

The striking warders were calling for the resignation of the Commissioner of Corrective Services. The *Telegraph* concluded:

> *A full, and public, inquiry must be held to clear the medieval cobwebs from our dungeons.*

Next to this was a boxed article about me.

HE WOULDN'T HURT A FLY – MUM

'Don't shoot my son down like a mad dog,' Mrs Ruby Langford pleaded last night – Mrs Langford says she's certain the criminals who want to protect rackets within Long Bay Gaol will try to kill her son before he's recaptured by police.

He'd made up the last sentence, totally. I stared at it. He then described me and the kids in our 'Housing Commission home in Green Valley'.

> *Holding back tears, Mrs Langford said last night she never really expected to see her son alive again.*

On Sunday morning David disappeared. I thought he was going out to decoy, to get the police off the scent of his brother. He didn't come home that night.

Monday: 'POLICE HUNT ESCAPEE AFTER UTILITY CHASE.' I felt completely disoriented. I realised I was reading the papers to find out about my family. Dave had been caught in a utility in Chullora.

More than 30 uniformed and plainclothes police searched the Chullora area for the man who escaped. House-to-house searches were made –

I waited. David turned up after dinner looking exhausted. 'They got away,' he said, 'they're still free,' and flopped on the divan and slept.

Ellie went out for the afternoon paper.

ESCAPEES MISSED BY SECONDS

Two escapees broke through a police cordon and escaped by seconds after a dramatic chase through Bankstown early today ... after a chase by 11 police cars through suburban streets, the two men ran into a backyard and vanished over a fence –

Escaping. Vanishing over fences. The words went round in my head.

Two teenagers were taken to Bankstown Police Station and interviewed but were later allowed to leave.

So David wasn't being charged. I looked at him sleeping. Little black duck.

Nob and a man called Matthews had been free for eight days. The next day's headline:

CAPTURED!

Long Bay escapee arrested in 160kph city chase ...
Robert Matthews — Full story page 3. Police said the car
became 'airborne' while roaring down a one-way street
the wrong way.

I put my head on the table and moaned. I just moaned.
The kids made a pot of tea and we sat there, drinking,
nobody saying anything. Aileen put the salt shaker over
the picture of the crashed car in the newspaper.

I picked up the paper again when the kids had gone to
bed. Two teenage girls were in the car with Matthews.
Nobby was the only one still at large.

The following day Nob was caught in a backyard in
Lilyfield. A woman had seen him hiding under a car and
called the police.

Yesterday's capture followed a police stakeout which
began before dawn. Consorting squad detectives received
information that Langford would be staying in a house
in Ilka Street, Lilyfield ... They also arrested the other
two men and three young women who were staying in a
house in Ilka Street.

The next day James and Dianne came with me to
Central Court of Petty Sessions. Nob's hearing came up
at 10:30 a.m. Dianne had hired a barrister.

Nob was charged with escaping lawful custody and
stealing a utility at Five Dock on 5 August. He did not

plead. Mr M. Farquar, CSM, remanded him to Central Court on 22 August. He was remanded in custody and refused bail.

The hearing came up on 17 September. Nob's girlfriend Penny and her sister were there when we got out of the taxi in Liverpool Street. We went into the court. Nob, Jones and Matthews were heard first. Nob asked the magistrate if the police could be charged with assault, he said ever since they were captured they'd been getting bashings. The magistrate said no. Then came the two others, Harnett and Williams, who'd been recaptured the day of the breakout. They were handcuffed together in the dock. Just before the lunch adjournment, Harnett began swearing loudly and said that screws at Parramatta had threatened him with a flogging the night before. Williams was shouting too. He said he'd been in solitary confinement for two months. 'We're being treated like ANIMALS,' he said.

The Ds began to remove them from court when the magistrate called them back and sentenced Harnett to fourteen days gaol for contempt of court. It took eight cops to take them out.

The charges against the five of them were adjourned. Nob was remanded until November.

We waited outside for Penny and her sister, who had followed the police taking Nob back to the cells. In a while they came out crying. I shook Penny and asked what had happened.

'The cops were walking Nob along the corridor and then they threw him through a window. We were crying out, "Leave them alone". They didn't care that we could see. The warders and cops threatened to bash them again when they're back at Parramatta. Mum, they were calling out for help –' Penny sat down on the steps and we sat with her. Too shaken to move.

I didn't sleep much that night. In the morning I sent Ellie out for the *Herald*. There had been a riot in the cells after we left. Nob and the others were joined by ten prisoners from Bathurst, charged with offences related to the Bathurst Gaol riot in February.

The prisoners were armed with lengths of jagged wood and porcelain and with piping torn from the cell walls. After two hours shouting, stamping, screaming obscenities and banging on the walls they quietened down when threatened with tear gas.

The Bathurst men were all committed for trial. An ambulance had been called to treat a prisoner for a dislocated ankle.

As the third van left Central Police Station the prisoners pounded the sides of the van yelling 'police brutality'.

In November, Nob was sentenced to two years on top of his ten. With good behaviour he might be out in six. There was no way we could protect him from the police. Dianne got Ellie's second form Geometry Project book and pasted in the paper clippings. Then she wrote a page about Nobby. 'You are my big brother and no-one can change the love Mum, family and me have for you.' Then she wrote details about Nob. Date of birth 21 May. Complexion, fair. Height 6'2". Shoe size 11.

Over the next few months the project book took on a life of its own. She pasted in a page about her best friend Frances Hinton, who was in *Woman's Day*, modelling Carla Zampatti clothes. A picture of Sparrow boxing in the local paper. An article on Mum Shirl, the 'black saint' of Redfern. Our friend Harry Williams, 'the 23 year old left full-back [who] is the first Aboriginal to play soccer for Australia.' Harry worked as a field officer at the Foundation of Aboriginal Affairs.

Charles Perkins pointed out that: 'There are about 400,000 alcoholics in Australia today and 99.9% of them are white. Excessive alcoholism among Aborigines is a symptom of a deeper social deprivation ...'

A *People* article about Essie Coffey, a film maker who lived at Dodge City, a settlement outside Brewarrina. 'My Survival as an Aboriginal' won two prizes at the Sydney Film Festival. It was the first film by an Aboriginal.

Bookies were betting 5/1 on Tony Mundine's next fight in Paris, where he would be paid $100,000.

Then she pasted in pictures from our *Aboriginal Quarterly*. Steve and his mates fixing up houses in Redfern. Her friend Phillip Hall, a field officer. Her uncle Tom Williams, a social worker. Her friend Kevin Gilbert, a writer. Her uncle Lester Bostock, writer and radio person. We often spoke about the news we were getting which wasn't in the white papers.

I didn't hear from Nobby till February.

Parramatta

7/2/75

Dear Mum,

Sorry I haven't wrote before, but as we crims call it I've been doing it hard. I won't let on about my troubles as you have your own to cope with. How are all the family give them my love, well mum I've finally got sentenced I got two years so I won't be eligible for parole until 1978 but I promise you I'll never do a stupid thing like that again ... Mum could you rack up $15.00 and send it to me I need to buy a transistor and toothpaste ... I hear David's got a Falcon I bet he'll write it off before he's had it six months it's the biggest heap in Leichhardt I've been told. I should be going on escort within the next month so can David drive to wherever I go and see me?

PTO for a couple of jokes.

One day Jackie Jackie was sitting on this pole in the Sahara Desert
and along came this bloke in his car
He came to a shuddering stop and said
Hey Jackie Jackie, how far to the next town?
and Jackie Jackie scratched his head and said

How did you know my name?
And the bloke said I suppose I just guessed.
Jackie Jackie said, Well you can guess how far the next
town is.

… I was looking in a dictionary a month ago and read
the meaning of Nobby, I didn't like the meaning so I'm
Chico now OK.

Love to you all
Chico

I'd just finished reading this letter when Mick Porter, the Islander we befriended in Surry Hills, arrived at my door looking for a place to stay. I needed the money so I said it would be all right. He and James called each other partner.

Mick worked at the hospital, I think he used to rattle drugs because I'm sure he had two personalities. When he was drunk he'd say he was a devil worshipper. I was in no state for more stress. My hair stood on end.

One night I heard a noise in the kitchen. I decided not to switch on the light. I crept into the room thinking it was a prowler and reached for the switch when I saw Mick holding a pitchfork aimed right at me. He had a glassy look.

'Mick, what are you DOING?' I yelled. He realised it was me and said, 'I thought you were someone sneaking around.'

I nearly passed out with fright.

'Don't go walking around my house with that pitchfork, you could have stuck it into me.'

He mumbled an apology and went back to bed. He was starting to give me the creeps.

The next day he had Pauline bailed up with a knife at her throat. 'If you call the police I'll kill her,' he said. I was terrified. I kept talking to him and moved in with another knife behind my back. It was the closest I came to killing someone in my life.

Suddenly the glassy look left his eyes. He dropped the knife, pushed Pauline away and said, 'What are you doing here, Pauline? Go and play.'

I punched him hard and he went down. He didn't know what he'd done, and when I told him he cried like a baby, a vulnerable primitive crying, hard to listen to. When he calmed down I told him he had to leave. Now.

He went out the back door into the laundry. By the time I realised what he'd be doing, he'd swallowed a bottle of gamma wash. I rang the police to bring an ambulance to have his stomach pumped out.

I told the kids to pack, and we got on a train for David's place in Leichhardt. It was the school holidays, and we stayed a month. I lay in the grass under a peach tree reading and dozing. The kids knew enough to leave me alone.

Back home, there was a bad smell of burning. I looked in the backyard, piles of burnt clothes. My clothes, the kids' clothes. The house was an ambush of smashed crockery. The kids' toys, which he'd bought them, were broken. That meant he'd really gone. Dave and Sparrow and Horse said if he came back they'd kill him. He didn't come back. Not long after this, Horse went back to gaol anyway.

I was barely back on my feet again when an old friend turned up, Pommy Bob. His hair was prematurely grey from the chemicals he worked with. He helped me look after the kids and get the shopping in. One morning he handed me a photo of Bill, Pearl and Dianne in Luna Park. He'd taken them there years ago. I stared at Billy and Pearl's faces. 'You know I could see death in the kids' palms when I looked at them years ago,' he said. I remembered him reading palms. I sat down and cried. Then I remembered him coming to Portland Street when Pearl died, handing me a wreath and an envelope with $150 inside. He stayed for a while and then said he'd be back at Christmas.

Aileen, who was now seventeen, had gone to live with her fiance David Quintal in Bass Hill, and Dianne and Steve and Stevie boy moved in with me. Pommy Bob came back in December and told us he was going home to England for his sister's wedding. He'd been in Australia for eight years and at the time he was working for Johnson and Johnson at Botany.

We didn't have much to give him for a present so Steve and I gave him two killer boomerangs and a spear. We stuck tape on the back of the boomerangs and wrote: 'To dear Pommy Bob. These are genuine killer boomerangs. If this one doesn't get you the other one will.' We presented him with those and he was rapt. We waved him off at the bus stop and he held the spear and the boomerang like they were the crown jewels.

Horse wrote us a poem from the nick.

Dearest Mum and Family,
I remember, life before,
When things to me meant so much more,
I remember, correcting a wrong,
The soft sweet sound of a favourite song.
I remember, my new family's love
The glitter of stars so high above.
I remember, running away,
Finding a place where I could stay.
I remember the small white fence,
The grass in the garden that grew so dense.
The joyful songs in the month of December –
I remember! – GOD!! – I remember!!!
Your son and brother, Steven.

Neddy's son and daughter had arrived back and demanded she get out of her house. 'It belongs to our kids,' they said. Under threat of violence, she moved to her eldest daughter's place in Rose Street, Casula.

In May, Aileen had a son Billy, my second grandchild. At the end of the year Ellen who was fifteen left school. She was going out with Ron, whose mother got her a job with the Pink Ladies at RPA Hospital. Ellie moved in with Ron and his mother.

David showed up with a girl named Debbie, who was sporting a black eye. He asked if she could stay for a while as her family had kicked her out. He'd rescued her from her ex-boyfriend who had belted her up. I felt sorry for her and took her in. Pretty soon she and Dave were going together.

At Christmas we wrote to Nob and Horse and Allo who were all together in gaol. It was our biggest Christmas at the Valley. James Golden and Bronc (the Mad Scot) turned up. Then Ellen and Ron. Then Aileen and David Quintal and a couple of his army buddies. Debbie, Dave, Steve and Dianne helped me. I cooked for two days before. The table wasn't big enough so they took the door off Pauline's bedroom and covered it with bedsheets. It looked beautiful. Neddy and her children arrived and it was a happy day for all of us. Ron had his camera and for once we had some photos of the mob scene.

Dianne and Steve moved back to town, to the house Steve had been fixing in the Aboriginal Housing in Eveleigh Street, Redfern. It meant I had somewhere to stay and visit in town, though I missed them when they were gone.

In February 1976 Aileen was married at the School of Military Engineering. Quintal was a soldier there. His father and sister flew over from Norfolk Island but the mother declined as she didn't approve of her son marrying an Aboriginal. 'Norfolk Islanders are a mixture of Pommy and Tahitian,' I said to Aileen, 'and Tahitians are dark-skinned anyhow.'

'Don't fight it, Mum,' Aileen said.

She was eighteen. It was the first time she'd worn

make-up. She borrowed a dress and wore Dianne's veil, Quintal wore his private's uniform. The sergeants' mess did the catering, and James gave the bride away. He'd put a bride doll and white ribbons on his car.

At the reception I introduced George Quintal (Aileen's father-in-law) to my kids, to Mum Joyce, Neddy, Sparrow, Gert, James, Horse. 'I see you've got a whole crew here,' he said.

Sparrow was chatting up Quintal's sister, and as we were leaving the hall some bloke got jealous and knocked Sparrow down. Dave jumped in and lifted the bloke for hurting his mate. Steve tried to stop them and ended up swinging, and in the fight someone called the police who came and grabbed Dave and headed for the bull-wagon. Debbie ran after them and kicked their legs so they put her in with Dave and drove off. Dave went to gaol for three months over that.

Pauline was going out with a guy called Dave Mitchell and she decided to leave school. My last hope of getting someone through high school was Jeffery. In July we heard from Nobby again. He wasn't calling himself Chico anymore.

Dear Mum,

Peter Langford is up here with me we get on prity good I suppose but i tell you he is a sucker for tobaco last week i had to go without weed just to keep him smoking anyway i've given it up because it affect's my basketball this week we play an outside team i think we will win, as we've got

a real good team, we had a football competition last week
or should i say we started it last week and so far my team
has won three out of three we play the grand final this
week if we win we should be the best team in the Gaol
i think we will win, Tell Jeffery to keep playing football
maybe one day he might go of to the olimpic games as a
boxer or swimmer nothing would make me prouder what
about you?

So now my old husband was in gaol too.

Roberta was born to Pauline in June 1977 at Liverpool, and Ellen had Ronny boy in July at King George in Camperdown. Not long after, Aileen had a daughter she called Dianne.

It was the year of babies. It was the year my friend Jean Jebung turned up and we ran the house like a nursery. Jean's married name was Nixon. She came from Cherbourg in Queensland, it was a mission and said to be one of the biggest. I wouldn't know that as my knowledge of Queensland was limited at the time, but I heard it was supposed to be a trouble spot.

There was another friend of mine who also came from there, his name was Zac Martin. I'd met him at the Fijian Graws, a place where we used to go dancing down near Central a long time ago. I heard him and Jean talking about Cherbourg and I'd laugh at the name they had for it. They called it Gunna Gully meaning shit gully.

It sure sounded an interesting place. The mission where I grew up, Box Ridge, we called Hollywood, where all the movie stars lived.

Well, Jean had nowhere to stay so she came to live with the kids and me at Green Valley. She stayed for about a year. Her kids were grown up and living back at Cherbourg.

We had one room done up, like a nursery, for Roberta and Ronny boy. There was always a boiler full of babies bottles sterilising on the stove and the babies were bathed and fed before nine o'clock each day. We were pretty choppy, us old girls. Then on the weekend we'd relax and go and have a beer at Miller pub and listen to the bands there.

One bloke that Jean was knocking around with hit her, and she had skin off her face. 'The dirty rotten bastard,' she said, 'he knocked the bark clean off me, titi.'

She took Pauline down to Miller pub as there was a bloke named Shorty that was talking about her, she was wild about it. Pauline said Jean pulled him out of the pub and knocked him on his bum and called him a dirty unwashed bastard, and said, 'Don't you ever talk about me again,' and came home fuming, but she was a good mate and wouldn't put up with any nonsense from anyone.

I'd first met her one night outside the Empress Hotel when I was pretty drunk and couldn't find my way home. She took me to a flat she shared with a bloke she'd been living with for about seven years, and bedded me down, and that's how I met her. Later on she and her man – his name was John Hook – separated. It was a pity as they'd worked to help each other out.

So that's how Jean came to be out at the Valley living with us. At weekends Pauline and Ellen minded their kids and we took a break. One time we were going fishing with Bob McDonald up to Port Macquarie for a long weekend. We were following Ellen and Ronny into town in Bob's big F100 van. We had an accident when we rounded a corner and we were so shaken up we said, 'Stuff the fishing,' and got the taxi fare off Bob and headed home to the Valley where it was safe.

Some weekends we went up to Liverpool to the pubs near the railway. We joined in the sing-songs and had a good time. A mate of ours was named Greg Coe, and we christened him Mr A What. He worked further out at Prospect on a construction, he was a Koori like us, and he showed up with meat and bread to help us out. He was a good mate and looked after us if we were ever in a blue. He was a big bloke with tribal markings on his chest. I think he came from up Queensland somewhere. Any Kooris that came from up there we'd always ask, 'How's Joh Bjelke God?'

One weekend I went to the church in Redfern and saw Cyril Bailey (Donk) there. I took him home to try to straighten him out – he was drinking himself to death. I washed his clothes and made him take a bath, then I got some good food into him and he was on his way again. He never stayed long. It broke me up to see a fighter like him battling with the stupid bottle.

Not long after this my adopted son Allan Barrett, who Nobby and Dave had met in Daruk years ago, turned up on my doorstep. He had a friend with him, who he introduced as Patrick Cheshire. I made them welcome, thinking they'd been discharged from prison. I found out later they'd gone jogging from Cessnock Gaol and kept going till they reached home.

When Allan went to bed Patrick told me his story. His parents had died in a car accident when he was a kid. Big family. The kids were sent to relatives, Patrick to his uncle. The uncle was cruel to him and Pat laid him out with a side of planking, so the uncle put him in the boys' home. The same story as the others – boys' home to the bighouse.

I cooked up for them. Ron's dad worked at a bakery and he brought home heaps of sausage mince. Jean and I made pasties and huge sausage rolls for the boys, and they kept my back garden.

One afternoon I went into Eveleigh Street for Dianne and Steve's wedding anniversary and when I came home the police had raided the place and taken the boys back to gaol. If I'd been home I would have been charged with harbouring them. I wouldn't have given them up, if I had known they'd escaped from gaol.

All week we minded the babies and did our chores. The kids idolised Jean but she left crying, she said she was getting too attached to Ronny boy and loved him very much. She left to go home to Cherbourg and I haven't seen her for years.

In July a letter came from Patrick, who had been transferred to Matraville.

Friday
28th July 1978

Dear Mum,
Hi. How is the world's greatest mum going? I hope you are alright and have no more problems with the flu cause last I heard you were pretty sick, it was probably me that gave it to you if it was I'm sorry it's just my generous nature ... I miss you Mum, fair dinkum, while I was staying at your place I felt more at ease with myself and more a part of a family than any other time in my life, and I want to thank you for it, Pauline and the others all helped and I'll love them for it forever but I think it was mainly you and I'm eternally grateful –

There was a drawing of a flower at the bottom of the page.

Nob wrote to say he was making jewel boxes in Parramatta. He was being moved from gaol to gaol. One letter would begin:

Dear Mum,
Why haven't you answered all my letters –

Then he'd ask me to speak to someone for him, or not to mention so-and-so in my letter, sometimes angry and other times pleading. One letter ended:

Until somebody lowers themselves enough to write to me,

Your son,

NOBBY

And the next one began:

Hi Sweetheart, well how's my beautiful mother today.

James Golden was in for a drunk driving charge and Nob looked after him.

Parramatta

17/9/78

... Anyway Uncle Jimmy is driving me mad, he snores something terrible and is stealing all my aftershave, you'd think the old bastard had a woman stashed somewhere! ... Well I'm going to give Uncle Jim the pen for a while he wants to say hello OK!

On the back of the page in James' writing:

Hello Maud. I just read what Nobby put in the letter. Naragar. He talks about me having a woman stashed away, all he talks to me is about dubays, munie and durrying. But truly Maud as soon as he heard that I was here, he got me in his cell ... he lets everyone know that I am his uncle. He feeds and drinks me like a king ...

Nobby had added more at the bottom – he was happy now, and due for parole shortly.

At one time or another I had all my children and family staying with me. It had to be kept from the Commission. I felt like a criminal, the lies I told to survive in the Valley. Pauline and David stayed about a year, then David and Debbie and their two children stayed a year until they got a Commission house at Claymore.

In December 1978 Nob came out of gaol and was at my doorstep. I was so pleased that all his six years in prison were over I cried and so did Neddy. We bought two dozen beers to celebrate, and had a party.

It wasn't long before I could see the effects gaol had on him. He locked himself in the room for hours. Outside noises frightened him, he couldn't cope with hearing the babies cry.

I wanted to do everything to please him so I cooked his favourite meals. He said, 'Mum, don't fuss over me, please? Leave me alone.' I was hurt, but I knew he'd have to learn to cope all over again.

He wanted to go and visit Dianne in Redfern and was too scared to get on a train. He eventually went with one of the kids for company.

Back home he started to get sick. We found out he had hepatitis and that he was really ill. The police in Liverpool were always checking him out and wouldn't leave him alone. Not believing he was sick, they pushed past me. I didn't say anything till all four of them were in the bedroom, when I said, 'I hope you've all had your shots, he's got contagious hepatitis.' You should've seen those dicks fly out of the room, asking where the nearest doctor's surgery was. I fell about laughing and so did Nobby.

He lost a stone and a half with the jaundice condition. When he got better he found work on the North Shore and moved to Camperdown because the cops wouldn't leave him alone.

17

The Operation

Redfern, Erskineville, Mascot, St Peters

I decided to move out of the Valley. Jeff and I were the only ones left at home, and the Commission took a long time to do any repairs. Our days in Sadlier already felt like they were over.

I packed everything and went out to arrange transport. When I came home, most of the furniture was gone. A thieving end. I sat on a suitcase and stared at my feet. Some bad spirit had a stick. Every time I got up the stick would knock me down again. I was a big woman but I felt very small.

We asked Aboriginal Housing to put the rest of the furniture in the Vine Street factory, then we got a taxi to where Dave lived in Claymore. He and Debbie and the kids were there waiting. Now I felt like part of a family again. I was the mother. I didn't know how to be not-mother.

After tea I sat in the backyard with Jaymi and Davy boy, who were two and one. 'Look,' I said, 'the sun's shining on the leaves.' I pointed at their tree.

'Why?' Jaymi said.

'That's the job of the sun,' I said. 'To keep shining.'

'Why?' she said.

'Because if it didn't we'd all die.'

'Why?'

I changed the subject. But later Jaymi had been thinking about this. She had another question. 'Where does the sun come from?' 'It comes from its people,' I said. 'Its people live in another part of the sky. The sun goes there at night. That's why the night's black. It goes to its people for the night.'

She seemed happy with this.

The following weekend I went in to Eveleigh Street to stay with Dianne and Steve. I hadn't planned to go out, and had just got into my nightie and dressing gown and sat with Dianne to watch TV, when a loud knock came on the door.

It was Brenda's sister Joan saying, 'You'd better come quick, your two boys Nobby and David are killing each other down at the Clifton.'

I didn't bother to change. We jumped into her car and took off for the hotel. As the headlights turned into the driveway I saw the boys shaping up to each other, getting ready to come to blows. David was about five foot five and Nob six foot two standing with his legs apart so he could be level with Dave. They were circling each other when Nob spotted me getting out of the car.

'Hold it Dave, not in front of Mum.'

That was the end of the great fight.

David had an HE Holden he was doing up, and when they started to fight Nob had got a hammer and smashed all its windows. They were both very drunk and a large crowd had gathered.

While we were standing there someone rang the police. Nobby was on probation. David said under his breath, 'Nobby PISS OFF, here come the cops.'

'I'm not going anywhere. If they pinch you, bra, they can pinch me too.' Nob stood straight beside David.

The police went up to Dave and said, 'What happened?'

'Well –' Dave looked around at the crowd. 'While I was in the disco some dirty bastard smashed my windows.'

'Yeah,' Nobby echoed, 'some dirty bastard did this to my brother's car, the mongrels.'

When the police drove away I laughed into my hands. It didn't take them long to back each other up. Nob lurched forward and ran up the street yelling.

'I don't want anything to do with this family.'

It was getting near Christmas. One night Nobby appeared at Dave's place and handed him $200.

'That's for damages to the car – sorry Dave –' He started to walk away with his head down. Dave called him back and they walked into a hug. It was always like this.

I called them the long and short of it. Dave would say when he was half-charged, 'Mum, why couldn't you make me tall and six foot like those two buggers, instead of little and black?' And I'd say, 'I've got to have one of you like me, I'm little and black.' And he was satisfied with that and would walk away smiling.

After a week Jeff and I moved in with Dianne and Steve. I felt like doing the rounds. Aileen was there too. She'd broken up with Quintal and left him and her two kids on Norfolk Island and gone to New Zealand. Then she came home, broke. Ellen was also staying there, with her son Ronny boy. She'd broken up with Ron.

So Dianne's house had become the refuge. I listened to the girls' stories. I didn't want to think about Aileen leaving her kids behind.

I stayed there for three weeks but, with Aileen, Ellen, Ronny boy, Jeff and me all sleeping on the floor, it was a bit crowded. I looked around and got a one-room flat in Charles Street, Erskineville. It was a big room, so I asked Aileen and Ellen if they wanted to come with me, and they packed their things.

I rang Aboriginal Housing about my stored furniture and they said the factory had been robbed – my stuff was gone. I felt like laughing. I really felt like laughing.

We moved in, Jeff and I, with our clothes and some kitchen things, and our mattresses. I made tea and stood at the front door drinking it. There was a shop over the road. Outside the shop was a milk crate. I wandered over and picked it up. Back home I sat down with the tea.

In a while Micky Mundine turned up with tables and chairs and two wardrobes from the Smith Family. There wasn't room for anything else. The flat was one big room with a stove and fridge. The toilet and shower were in the backyard. But the girls helped me make a home of it and Jeff was off to Cleveland Street School.

Aileen met up with a Maori bloke named Dennis Dean, and he came to live with us.

They slept on the floor, Ellen slept with me and Ronny boy's cot was set up near Jeff's bed.

I was down at the Aboriginal Medical Service in Redfern one morning and I saw a notice about sewing classes. I decided to enrol. It turned out the co-ordinator was a friend of mine, Lily Madden. She was up from Byugil, another Bundjalung person.

The class was held in the top floor of the Aboriginal Medical Service, in an old convent next to Redfern Post Office. There were six Bernina machines and big cutting tables everywhere. The first person I saw was my mother. She'd got Parkinson's disease and was thinner but she seemed okay. She made me sit next to her. Ruby Leslie (from the Gunnedah Hill) was there too. I looked around and they introduced me to the ones I didn't know. Sarah, Muriel, Lily Coolie, Lola, May, Aunt Alma, Audrey, Minnie, Ruby de Santos, Millie and Vera.

I had a big overcoat from the Smithos, and I asked the teacher to show me how to re-line it. I did it with satin.

At weekends the girls went to the disco at the Clifton and they said the place was blacked out, Kooris everywhere.

Ellen's twenty-first was coming up. We made a cake and the All Black footballers turned up with Steve and Dianne. The publican from the Clifton came in, then Tony Mundine. Dave and Debbie came in from Claymore. Nob came over from Glebe. We spilt out on to the footpath, it was like old times.

I couldn't tell whether Ellen was missing Ron or not. They'd been apart now for seven months, he was living in Robey Street, Mascot. The following week Ellie came in crying. She'd heard Ron was in hospital. He was badly injured in a motorbike accident. She'd been in to see him and he was crippled up. His leg wouldn't straighten out, so he hobbled.

I sat her down and tried to talk to her. After a while she started to pack things and when Ron left hospital she went home with him.

About this time there was a letter from Allo, my adopted son.

P.O. Box
Goulbourn
29/5/80

Hi there,

How is the best mum in the whole world going? Still as beautiful as ever? Well mum I got your address off Dianne. Di tells me most of the kids have moved away to their own homes. But I'm happy that everyone is staying out of trouble. that's all that matters 'a' ... I sent a mother's day card to 'sadlier' but it came back that is why I wrote to Di and asked for your address. What I said in the card was:

Thankyou for caring and thankyou for always being around to help and listening to my problems. I appreciate all you have done over the years and I love you very much. So mum you just be happy and smile because you are never forgotten.

I remembered him turning up at the Valley with Patrick, how they'd gone jogging from Cessnock Gaol and kept going. In his letters Allo always said smile. Smile, mum.

I took myself out to the Clifton one night and hung around with my friends. Through the windscreen of the taxi coming home I saw Aileen doubled up in the middle of the road near the flat. I ran to pick her up.

'What happened?'

'Dennis kicked me with those heavy shoes of his in the stomach.'

'Where is he?'

'In the flat.'

I ran across the road and opened the door. He was eating his tea, not holding the fork properly because he was drunk.

'What did you do that to Aileen for?'

He said something but I didn't give him time to answer. I belted him and knocked him over the lounge and flattened him.

'I didn't raise my daughter to be bashed and kicked by bastards like you.' I threw him out. I don't know where I got the strength from.

He really wasn't such a bad bloke. He was always bringing home a quid. He worked at a food place and brought home heaps of frozen food. He and Aileen got together again later and moved into their own flat.

My lease was running out. Ellen and Ron's place in Mascot had three bedrooms and they asked us to stay there. I called round to tell Aileen the news and on her lounge was a bow and a set of arrows. 'Very professional looking,' I said. I looked to see if she thought she might be the target.

'Cup of tea, Mum?'

'Thanks. What's he going to shoot?'

'Foxes. We're going bush tomorrow, up to Warren.'

Jeff and I stayed at Robey Street a while. We had plenty of room. My sister Margaret (Mum's second family) lived down the road. I helped cook for barbeques and dinner parties, and sometimes I went with Margaret to the club. Nobby had bought a car and came to visit. On Friday he took us to the disco at the Clifton.

One week there was a letter for me from Aileen. Dennis was in gaol at Warren. He'd got drunk and was firing shots into the house of a fellow who owed him money. Aileen was stranded so I sent her fare and she came home to live with us.

National Aborigines Day was coming up and they'd organised a ball at Sydney Town Hall. It was eleven years since I'd been there, when Pearl danced with the Prime Minister. We dressed up as much as we could and Nob drove us in – Ellen, Ron, Aileen, Jeff and me. James Golden was there looking handsome. 'Darling Maud,' he said, scooping his arm round my waist. 'Now Jim, hands off my mother-in-law,' Steve said, appearing from the crowd with Dianne. Brenda Leslie came up with her mother, old Ruby Leslie, from the Gunnedah Hill. Regina, Brenda's eldest daughter, was making her debut that night. I let myself think about Pearl for a little while.

We squeezed as many of us as we could into the frame and the photographer yelled, 'Okay, grin everybody!'

I danced for a while with James and Steve then I sat out a few with Brenda. I asked her if she knew where Sam Griffin was these days (Sam was her brother).

'Coona, I think. You ever hear from him?'

'Never,' I said.

'You ever see Gordon?'

'Nuh. I heard he's in Sydney somewhere.'

Gordon was Aileen and Nob and David's father. He lived with Patty, Donk's aunty.

'You know Tracy's here, making her debut?'

'Who?'

'Tracy Campbell, Gordon's daughter he had with Donk's aunty.'

'I didn't know. She'd be Aileen and Nob and David's half-sister then. I should introduce her to Aileen.'

We looked around but Tracy had already gone.

We were having trouble paying the rent. Ellie and Ron moved in with Ron's dad until they got situated again. Brenda Morris had told me there was a house to let next door to her in May Street, St Peters, so I applied and got it. It had three bedrooms and was opposite Camdenville

Oval so I had a view of green. Sometimes I looked out and remembered the space in Bonalbo. Even though I missed the bush I didn't miss the hard life there.

Jeff and Aileen and I set up house, and Dennis came back from Warren and moved in. Not long after that, Dave and Debbie moved in and the two grandchildren, Jaymi and Davy boy.

By now I'd lost enough weight that I could have my operation. It was called a lipectomy (surgical removal of fat) and I was booked into the Prince of Wales, September 1981. Twice I was admitted and twice I was sent home, twice there was an outbreak of golden staph in the intensive care ward and they weren't operating till it was cleared. Each time I went in Nobby came with me and paced around the corridors waiting. He was so nervous about the operation he was more upset than me when it was delayed.

The third time he came with me again and I settled in. Then the night before I was set to be operated on there was a two-car pile-up, and the breathing machine I would have had to use was needed for the people involved in the accident.

The fourth time the operation went on as scheduled. It was major surgery and I was very overweight. They cut nine kilograms of fat from my stomach and sewed me up with eighty-seven stitches.

When I regained consciousness I saw a hand rubbing

the belly of a white china Buddha. I looked up and saw David smiling at me. Debbie sat beside him. The Buddha was a present – one fat belly to another.

Then Nob swam into my sight. He'd waited at the hospital while they did the operation. I couldn't talk much, too out of it.

Later Nob went out for my toiletries, Lo-Cal drink and flowers. He hired a TV, put a hundred dollars in my purse and every night he came to visit. His job at the picture framers was going well, he had a car and money in the bank. It really seemed like he'd survived gaol and would be okay. This was the first time Nob had been around to help when I was in trouble and I was glad to have him close.

I was on a strict diet of 600 calories a day and in the month I was in hospital I lost nineteen kilos. Even so, the doctor warned me, I'd have to come in for more surgical removal later on. In those days the doctor used to look at me and shake his head. Even though I'd lost weight I was still very big.

On the day I was discharged, Nob came to pick me up and took me on a grand tour around the city. He realised I'd be stir-crazy from a month in hospital so we sat near the harbour.

I hadn't healed properly yet, and the Home Nursing sent people to do my dressings at home. From my bed I could see out to the street, and I could hear Jeff and Aileen talking in the kitchen, or Debbie and Dave cooking for us all.

Sometimes when I looked out, I saw Jeff and David jogging in the park, and one day I saw a person walking by and nearly jumped out of my skin. It wouldn't have been that difficult to do with the big cut across my belly. I had been sliced nearly in half. The person going by looked just like Gordon. I yelled out for Aileen.

'Quick, that fella walking past, that's your father.'

'You sure?' she peered out the window.

'You go and look. If he's got a scar over his left eyebrow, that's him.'

Aileen ran out and I waited. After fifteen minutes she came in looking pale. I sat up in bed and held her hand. She looked all around the room and pulled her lips in.

'What happened?'

'I ran up to him and took his arm, I said, "Excuse me, is your name Gordon?" He said, "No" and kept on walking. So I kept walking too. I said, "Do you know who I am?" He said, "No." He wouldn't really look at me. So I went around in front of him and said, "I'm your daughter. My mother's name is Ruby." I could see the scar over his left eyebrow, it was him. So he said, "No, I don't have any kids." So I walked beside him again. He was pretty drunk. Then he sat down on a tree guard and I sat there too and I looked at his scar.'

I held her hand till she stopped shaking and she went out to make tea. I tried to remember some good things about Gordon but the last scene in my mind was him drunk and then disappearing from our camp on the river bank in St George. His blue and white car. I pushed myself to think. Then I saw him on the log near my campfire, playing 'Hang Down Your Head Tom Dooley' on the mouth organ. When Aileen came in with the tea I told her how he'd serenaded me. 'Yeah Mum,' she said. 'It's okay.'

She disappeared for the rest of the afternoon.

I had a food order from the Brown Sisters. It was Christmas 1982 and Allo and Brian Randall were the only ones home. I asked them to go to Flemings and off to Botany Road they went with the shopping list. It was ten o'clock. By three in the afternoon they weren't home.

Then Nobby was there with his car. I went out and told him I was worried the boys mightn't be able to get a taxi. 'Hop in the car and we'll pick them up,' he said.

When we reached Botany Road we chucked a U-ey in front of the Clifton Hotel, which was right next to Flemings, and lo and behold through the door I could see my two great shoppers playing pool.

They didn't see me alight from the car. As I came to the door of the pub they spotted me and dropped the pool cues. They ran past me apologising and into Flemings and boy it was the quickest my shopping had ever been done. In twenty minutes they were outside loaded up. 'We didn't realise what time it was,' Allo said.

'Thanks very much, it's the last time I send you two shopping. You buggers. We would've had no groceries for Christmas. And yous guys would have to starve.' I didn't even look at them. They were grinning at me sheepishly, like two saints, fair dinkum, I could have slapped them both and they were grown men.

Later I saw the funny side of it and went home chuckling to myself, with Nobby to help me unpack the groceries. He did it under protest but he was always there when a good meal was on.

Allo had been out of gaol a while and then Patrick came out and lived with us. One day when Aileen was mopping the kitchen I mentioned that the boys hadn't been home for three days. Just then they arrived and it turned out they'd met up with Darby Devine who'd had a case of Scotch. They'd spent three days dealing with the case then brought a bottle home for me. Allo held it out. His body didn't seem to have any centre of gravity, neither did Pat's. I stood there.

'Well Mum,' Allo said, 'Let's open it up. We'll have to help you with that.'

'No more. You're still drunk,' I said and headed off for the bathroom with the bottle. In a while Allo pushed the door open and tried to take the bottle from me. Making little jokes. I hosed him and he fell over in the water. I heard Aileen throw something, 'I'm not mopping up anymore!' she yelled.

Not long after this Dave and Allo got into a blue with some migrants at the Victoria Hotel in Enmore. They were outnumbered so they came home and got Bronc, Dave's bull terrier. Pat hobbled after them, he'd just had his appendix out. By the time they got back to the pub Dave had Bronc so wound up he was biting chair legs as well. In less than no time Bronc had cleaned out the pub and the boys came home for tea.

Every Tuesday I went to the sewing and craft classes in Redfern. I had finished the satin lining for my coat. I made pillow slips, mended and patched for the kids, and did machine sewing for the old girls who couldn't see well. We talked about families and grandkids, crafts, politics. We cooked damper and scones and hot meals for the staff at the AMS and we held fetes to raise money. We were saving up for a holiday in the bush, and we'd decided to go to Ayer's Rock.

I came home from the class one afternoon and Aileen was the only one home. We sat down to a cup of tea. In a while Allo came in drunk and wandered out into the backyard. It was just a patch of dirt. Then he went up the hall and disappeared.

Ten minutes later he came back carrying rolls of turf in his arms. The council had put them in the park over the road.

'What's he doing?' Aileen said.

'I don't know yet. Just watch him.'

Allo didn't notice us. He made the trip three times. Then he unrolled the turf in my backyard and being drunk lay down on it and fell asleep. The sun was hot. I put a towel over his neck.

When he woke up he said, 'Mum how could you let me sleep, this lawn has to be watered!' He jumped up and grabbed the hose. He was that sort of person. Always on the lookout for something kind he could do for you.

Soon after this Aileen and Dennis brought home their Kiwi friends Sherryl and Desmond. They both had guitars. By now Allo's turf had spread to fill the backyard and we lounged around there or in the laundry, which opened on to it, listening to them play. We christened the laundry the Empress II because of all the singing. Sherryl could play guitar and ukelele and Dennis had a very good voice. Brenda came in from next door with her man Mitch Hamson. Nobby came over and joined in, his head stuck into the amplifiers. He was rapt. Dennis sang 'Stairway to Heaven' and we all joined in. Another adopted son turned up, Charlie Jones from Coona. He moved in and got a job at Avis Rent-a-Car.

Debbie and Dave had got a Housing Commission home and moved there. Even so it was crowded with Jeff and me, Aileen and Dennis, Allo and Patrick and Charlie. We had a lot of parties and one night I got drunk and hunted all the kids out. I really wanted to be on my own for a while. 'Go on, get going the lot of you,' I said, waving my arms and shouting. They had nowhere to go but they could see I was serious, so they backed out. Charlie was trying to tie his stereo on the back of his motorbike. As soon as they walked out the door I started to cry loudly and they all came back. It was only the drink talking, I would've been lost without them, they were all I had.

It was about that time Brenda married Mitch Hamson and he was so possessive of her she couldn't move. We'd grown up like sisters but Brenda wasn't allowed to talk to me. Pretty soon he had all her kids in an uproar and took to firing shots at them in the house.

This was the man who had fathered three children to my cousin Gloria Morgan from Riley Street days, he was a bad marriage risk anyhow. I used to think Brenda would have a nervous breakdown.

On the street one day he threatened to run over one of my grandchildren. So to calm down I bought a flagon of Moselle and sat out the front drinking. He'd gone inside and somehow the look of his car made me so mad I started throwing glasses at it. Every glass I had, I threw at the car then went inside for another one.

He came out to see what I was doing and I shaped up to him. 'You're only good at fighting old women and kids, so fight this old woman,' I said. A thought went through me to protect the scar from my operation and to feint with the left hand where I'd broken my knuckles on Les Bourke. I feinted with the left then hit him hard with my right and knocked him onto his backside.

He jumped into his car and sped off somewhere. In the end Brenda had to hide out to get away from him, and eventually she divorced him.

About this time I became good friends with John King (the white one) who we met at the Cricketer's Arms. An argument had broken out over football. Two of the guys were going to punch on. I was frightened if a blue broke out the whole pub would join in, it had happened before.

I called out, 'Somebody please play the jukebox,' and a baldheaded bloke came across the room and put two dollars worth of twenty cents into it. He pointed for me to choose some songs, and I noticed he had the Koori flag tattooed on his wrist. The songs came on and the boys stopped their fight.

The jukebox man asked if I'd like a beer and I said, 'Thank you.' He sat down and introduced himself, said he came from Melbourne and his name was John King. We talked half the night. I thanked him for the beers and after that he became a regular at the Cricketer's.

He came home for a few beers and was very respectful. He told me he'd been brought up in an orphanage. We went out to the pictures and once to the Blue Mountains. He drove me past the house in Lett Street and I saw the potato beds had been returned to grass.

When John King went back to Melbourne he sent me $150 for a Christmas present. I was flabbergasted. Later he came back, and he always knocked around with Kooris, until one night at the Railway View some blokes robbed him and he just never came back anymore.

On the Sunday before my forty-ninth birthday Nobby arrived with half a dozen beers. I was at the sink and he said, 'It's your birthday tomorrow Mum, so leave the work.' We went out the back as he said he wouldn't be there tomorrow, and sat in the Empress II and started to have a sip.

Before long Pauline and David and the girls turned up, then Debbie and Dave and their kids, Ellen and Ron and Ronny boy, Patrick and Allan and Darby Devine, also Clem and Christine Thornton.

I didn't stop to think where all the drinks were coming from and here was Allo presenting me with Tabu perfume. He'd been climbing on a balcony to get me some roses and nearly fallen off. He gave me two roses and said, 'Smile, Mum.'

Early next morning there was a loud knocking on the door. It was the police, telling me that Allo was in gaol for robbery. I didn't realise as I was drinking and enjoying myself that my adopted son was stealing so I could have a good birthday. I would have called a halt to the celebrations, but too late.

I went to court for Allo for three days but it did no good – he was convicted and got three years in gaol. For a long time after I felt guilty, as if I was the cause of him stealing. I cried many tears over this boy. He would do anything for me if I asked, clean the yard, help around the house and put the garbage out without being asked. He brought me flowers. He had never met his own mother. Allo was a very obliging person and didn't deserve to rot in gaol.

Patrick got a job on the northside and moved over there. Dennis was working as a chef at Strathfield Station, so while we had a wage coming in, Aileen and I got the paper and found a place in Pritchard Street, Marrickville. There were five of these cottages in a dead-end laneway. We grew flowers in the front garden and everything was fine for a while.

Then Dennis and Aileen started to fight. One day he thumped her and she moved into a women's refuge in St Peters. Dennis got the sack and started to drink heavily and it wasn't long before he was in gaol.

When Jeff turned fifteen he asked if he could leave school. I tried to talk him out of it but it did no good. He wanted to be a spray-painter and eventually he got an apprenticeship at De Dona Smash Repairs in Surry Hills.

He was at this job for two and a half years – he won some money on lotto, bought David's Holden, went speed skating, played a season for the All Blacks, and grew up fast. He didn't venture out much though.

Aileen came over from the refuge at weekends. We went to the Cricketer's where the All Blacks supporters drank, and one Saturday she and Dianne decided to tell me a few home truths. 'I don't understand why Jeffery's gone so quiet,' I'd said. 'And lately he goes away every weekend.'

'Maybe he doesn't want to get air-raided by you every Saturday,' Aileen said.

'You come home drunk and then you really give it to him,' Dianne said. 'So what do you think?'

Well, I didn't think about it while I was in the pub but back at home I had a good solid hour of going back over things I'd said to Jeff and how I'd behaved. The girls were right, there was a definite pattern. I spent the next hour thinking about my health. I was always dieting and then I'd get low blood sugar, and alcohol made it worse. I'd started drinking when Pearl died and twelve years later it hadn't drowned my sorrows. Every morning when I woke up my sorrows were there again, worse if I was hungover.

So I decided to give it away; and I haven't been drunk since.

Not long after this Jeff came home with a girlfriend, Kerrie, and she brought him out of his shell. But she was jealous of his affection for me and it didn't work out.

All of the boys seemed to be having love troubles at the time. Nob was living with a woman called Roseanne. One afternoon after he'd been drinking at James Golden's place he was driving down the Hume Highway, playing 'Sweet Little Woman' on the cassette and he got pinched for drunk driving. It was the end of his romance with Roseanne. He did four months in Long Bay and when the time was up he came to my door holding a paper bag with his belongings in it.

I don't know how Nob managed to battle on, he lost everything while he was in gaol – his colour TV, a big stereo, all his books. His car. His share in an eight-acre farm in Bellbrook, near Kempsey.

A few weeks after he was released, I came home from sewing class and he was sitting at the kitchen table with his head in his hands.

'What's up, Nob?'

He wouldn't talk much. He couldn't find a job. He was depressed.

'You've got two good work references,' I said, 'so don't give up hope. Something will show up.'

He looked at me as if I was lying.

'Just have a little faith in your ability to cope,' I said.

'I can't keep going to the CES three times a week and sitting waiting. I need something to do.'

'Forget the CES. Go for a walk around the block. Go into every factory and ask.'

A week later I heard him come down the lane whistling and I knew he had a job.

'Data Mail,' he said, 'just around the corner.'

My small house was getting crowded with Nobby and Patrick. I saw the owner and got the place next door for them, at number 6. Not long after, Patrick came home with a girlfriend, Joanne.

At weekends we went to Bonnyrigg to see Dave and Debbie. Dave was working for Debbie's father carting bushrock. We swam in the pool and had barbeques, sometimes we went to visit Pauline at Fairfield. I found out that Blue and Margaret (from the mountains) lived nearby, so when Jeff came in from spray-painting on Friday I asked him to go next door and get Nob and Patrick and Joanne so we could go to Bonnyrigg. I hadn't seen Blue and Margaret for eight years. We went in Nob's car, Lizzie, the Valiant. On the way we called at the refuge for Aileen, then we called on David and Debbie. They piled into the car. Then to Pauline and her family. When we turned up at Blue and Margaret's – there was quite a tribe, just like the old days.

I was very content in the little house in Pritchard Street. I applied for an Aboriginal Home Loan to buy it, but the application was rejected. They said loans weren't available to pensioners. I knew people on the pension who'd got the loan, but they had insurance or other collateral to back them up. Where was my collateral? My biggest asset was the Smith Family.

I sat down and tried to write a poem about this.

A Home

A home is where the heart is
or so they say,
I wonder if I will own one
some sunny day
Or will all my efforts be in vain
and the whole battle be too much a strain
and put me in too much pain
hence I shall refrain from this endless strain
and pitch a tent.

There was a portulaca bush in the yard and some rubber trees. I planted flowers around them and I went round milking clippings for my pot plants.

Nobby worked at Data Mail for about twelve months and Jeff was still at De Dona Smash Repairs.

Then Nobby was in love again. Tracy was small and blonde and very good looking. She moved in with him next door. Tracy was drinking heavily and popping pills and a few times she took fits. It terrified Nob and me, our hair stood on end. It reminded us too much of Bill. I would hear Nob calling me through the wall, 'Come and look after her, Mum, I can't stand it.'

Nobby wanted to start fresh, and they decided to go to South Australia looking for work. Nob sold Lizzie and they bought a cheaper car and packed their gear. A few weeks later he rang and said there was no job there, and, being South Australia, they were drinking all the time. I told him he might as well come home and he rang off depressed.

One day he was at the front door. It was the middle of winter. He was wearing a tracksuit, no coat, and he had a blanket in a plastic bag. The job hadn't worked out. Tracy had taken a fit in the bath and nearly drowned. Nob jumped in the car and drove till it ran out of petrol. He left it there and hitched the rest of the way, it had taken him a week.

One night Nob and I went to the Courthouse Hotel to get among our people. There was a band there and a disco. I introduced Nob to Julie, one of Jeff's teachers from Cleveland Street. They hit it off well and started going out. I thought they were a perfect match – they were both tall and looked good together.

But they had some terrific fights. One weekend Nob came in seeming very low. I tried to talk to him, but he was too far down to hear other people. He said he needed a sleep and went next door. At tea time I went out and knocked on his door. Nothing. He'd locked himself in. I rang Julie and Ellen and the ambulance. When we got in, he was unconscious from an overdose.

The ambulance took him to Marrickville Hospital to pump his stomach out. It took me and Ellen and Julie and about five hospital staff to hold him down.

When he was okay he ran all the way home and he was sick for days. Not long after that, he and Julie separated.

At the end of winter David turned up crying. I could hear him next door in Nob's house. Debbie had shot through and taken Jaymi, and left Davy boy with him. They'd been smoking a lot of dope. Nob started to cry too, and by the time I got there and put the kettle on he was well into the story of Roseanne, Tracy and Julie. Those boys had a lot to cry about.

Watching them made me think about the time when I'd had boyfriends and how different it was now. How much calmer I was. There were certain things I missed, which I could remember very clearly. But I didn't miss all this crying at kitchen tables over one more abandonment. Bugger that. All the same, I felt sorry for the boys and made them cups of tea until they cheered up. I sat at the end of the table and chatted to Davy boy.

David moved in with Jeff and me. He signed Davy boy over to Dianne, as he had no job and no money coming in. At night he'd get drunk and talk to me half the night. He came into my room and curled up on the end of the bed.

'Why Mum, why? Why did she take my little girl away?'

I didn't know what to say to comfort him. He was the one of all my children who needed loving the most.

'I can't sleep without her beside me.'

Eventually he slept and I put a blanket over him. Tough times for the little black duck.

When Nobby moved to Clara Street in Newtown, Dave went with him. Nob had a Dobermann pinscher called Nappy (Napoleon). While Nob was at work, Dave kept house and walked the dogs. Napoleon was killed by a car and Nob got a new dog, General, a Staffordshire bull-terrier. Dave still had his bull-terrier, Bronc.

Bronc is now fourteen years old and lives with me. He sleeps on the lounge remembering his big night at the Victoria Hotel when he bit the chair legs in his frenzy. He bears the scars of many battles, nearly as many as me.

Patrick and Joanne were planning to have a big wedding and Nobby and Jeff were to be groomsmen. They started to save up. Some nights the boys took me to Newtown Leagues Club for the dancing and entertainment. Terry Priest my adopted son came over and took us for drives. On Mother's Day my house was filled with flowers and my neighbour was jealous as she only got one bunch. I told her that was the joy of having a large family.

18

Little Black Duck

Marrickville

In August 1983 Nerida was involved in a bad accident. At the time she was staying with her son Philip at Toongabbie, and came into town to visit my daughter Dianne in Eveleigh Street, Redfern. They weren't home, so she called into the Railway View Hotel and saw my son-in-law Steve there and had a beer with him, then decided to go back to Toongabbie. As she was about to board the train, on the last carriage, the train shuddered and took off, and down she went between the tracks, and the last wheels nearly took her arm off.

The doctors wanted to amputate but she wouldn't let them. She had about five operations on her arm and they cut a big piece of skin off her back rib cage to graft on to the arm, and took the flesh for the skin grafts on her hand from her upper thighs. She's very embarrassed about the arm and always wears longsleeved dresses or a cardigan. When she's asked questions about her arm she always says she's going to tackle the XPT next.

Nerida and I have been friends for about thirty-eight

years of our lives, and the only time we had a row was over a man, and we didn't think it was worth losing our friendship over. And it seems that our lives always cross, no matter where we go. She had a family of ten children and lost four boys and I had lost two, so we know what it's like to lose the ones we love the most of all, our children. She lost Happy in a shooting accident just before I lost Pearl, and the other two were only babies, but the last one was her eldest son Bill, who was found in the river at Dubbo. He'd been missing for three months, and I saw her anguish and tried to comfort her just as she comforted me when I lost mine.

All our children are grown now and raised, and we sit and talk about the past, and wonder what things would have been like if we were born rich instead of dirt poor and black as well, but I honestly think the rich couldn't have had as much fun and laughter as we've had even with our losses, and still come out smiling.

Neddy has been staying with me here for about seven months and will get her Housing Commission home soon, and I will miss her but she's only moving to Erko so she won't be far away, and we can visit back and forth and we will be content.

Around this time our sewing teacher left and the women asked if I'd take her place. I was a trained machinist so I said okay. We were still having fetes and selling lunches to raise money for our trip to Ayers Rock.

Jeff had lasted two and a half years at De Dona's then he had an argument with the boss over money. He was out of work for three weeks, then he landed a job as a trainee die-cutter. He was glad he didn't have to go to Tech.

After three months on the job his right hand was crushed in the machine. It chopped off the top of his thumb and index finger and mangled his hand in general. He was in hospital for only two days. They grafted the mangled bit of his thumb onto his index finger and he had pins in his fingers to keep them straight. When he healed he got his job back at De Dona's and was earning good money.

He came in one afternoon with a big grin on his face. Along with some workmates he'd won $4000 on the lotto. He bought a Valiant station wagon and spraypainted it bright yellow. One night he drove me down to the pub and I met up with an old boyfriend.

I'd known George for twenty years, he came from Moree way. I had met him in Queensland, when I was working on the fence lines. I'd gone into town for the dance and a bus-load of people turned up and the St George Kooris challenged the Moree Kooris to pick the best dancers. George was there jumping around on the floor. We had a few dances but even then he thought he was heaven's gift to the women of the world. Boy, I thought, what an ego, but he was nice looking and tall.

As Neddy said years later, 'Tall men are fatal.' Well, at the pub when we were reacquainted, George asked if he could spend Christmas (1983) with me and my family. I decided his ego had mellowed a bit or maybe I needed some loving, anyway I said yes and he arrived with bag and baggage and I was rapt.

I thought, after all this time of being alone it would be good to have a man around the house. I should have known his track record – he had kids but hadn't raised any of them. He went to work and paid board money and helped out, but he was a heavy drinker and gambler. I wasn't so much worried about tall men being fatal, but I had a record of attachment to men who drank or gambled, or both.

One morning George said he was going out to take his safari-suit to the dry cleaners and to get the money he owed me. I didn't notice he had an overnight bag in his hands. When he didn't come back I realised he'd gambled all the money he owed me and was ashamed to come and tell me. He just took off, the dirty coward. I thought, never again will anyone catch me. It makes you think something's wrong with you. I didn't want to feel bad about myself. But I should have known better, as I said to Neddy. Her reply: 'Oh, George. He always was a hit-and-run driver.'

On 16 June 1984 at the Holy Trinity Church in Dulwich Hill, Patrick and Joanne were married. Nob and Jeff were dressed in grey swallow-tails with top hats and gloves, and Dianne was matron-of-honour.

Then we went to Newtown Leagues for the reception. All my family showed up and we had a good time celebrating. Afterwards Jeff went outside and saw his mate arguing with a bloke who'd broken the aerial off his car. They started to fight and Jeff tried to pull his friend away. Just then Nobby came out and saw the struggle and thinking his baby brother was in a blue, stripped to the waist and was going to fight the world. He took some calming down. What a finale to a wedding. Patrick the groom also had a fight with his brother. It added atmosphere to the occasion. It all ended well.

After the wedding things were quiet for a while. Now that Jeff was the only one at home I had time to read the papers and find out what was going on in the world. I started noticing articles about black deaths in custody. There were ten Aboriginal prisoners for every one white prisoner. Many more black men died in prison than whites, and there were often suspicious circumstances – an inquiry that was held in the cell by one (white) man and was over in thirty-five minutes, and so on. There had been no real inquiries.

I knew quite a lot about what went on inside prisons. Nob, David, Steve, James, Patrick and Horse all had stories to tell, though they kept most of it to themselves. I knew that. But I knew Nob had been bashed by police, that tear gas was used on riots, that there was not adequate counselling for prisoners, that prison broke people's spirits, and it was killing our sons like a war.

When it rained the water lay everywhere. I went to hospital for a week with arthritis from the damp in the house. The landlord wouldn't be budged. Jeff went to change a lightbulb and the whole wiring came out. It fused every time it rained.

Ellen and Ron came over one day to tell us they were moving into a caravan at The Entrance. They were tired of the city. Ellie looked around at my buckets and saucepans and said we might like to take over their place in Henderson Road, Alexandria. It was $70 a week, so we agreed.

It was the best move we ever made. It had two bedrooms, an inside toilet, and a small yard. I saw my friends in the shops in Erskineville. We settled in and I decided to take Ellie up on her offer to go fishing.

At weekends I went to The Entrance. Ellen and Ron stayed in the annexe and I slept in the van. At night we took hand nets and torches and waded out after prawns. I slept with the sound of the waves splashing on the rocks.

When I got home Dianne rang to say Aunty Phyllis was in Prince Alfred with a stroke. I had an asthma attack, maybe from the shock, and I asked Di to go and say goodbye for me. I thought of Aunty Phyllis in the boat at Cabbage Tree Island, when we went to get the bananas. Her knitting. And then later in Sydney, her birthday party. Aunty Phyllis died two days later. She was buried at Box Ridge with my grandfather, father and Uncle Sam. She was my father's youngest sister.

I went to the doctor about the asthma and he said my chest would clear if I lost more weight. He sent me to the

Diabetic Weight Control Clinic near Prince Alfred. My diet, which was to last two years till the next lipectomy could be done, was called 'nutrition re-education'. We didn't use the word diet.

Next week at the Medical Centre I saw an Aboriginal newsletter about Cabbage Tree Island. It was now run by Kooris as a co-op, and they had made a big profit from the harvest. There were photos of the island.

When I came home Jeff introduced me to his new girlfriend, Michelle. I was glad to see him keeping company and going out to the club and the pictures.

Dave had been ringing Debbie at her mother's place at Liverpool, asking if he could see Jaymi. Finally she agreed and he brought her to my place to stay.

I came in from the bank one Tuesday and he had her dressed up in a tracksuit and sneakers. He swung her up onto his shoulder and grinned at me, happy again. 'Tell Nan where we're going,' he said.

Jaymi looked at me. They were going to McDonalds in King Street then over to Dianne's to see Davy boy. I hugged them both.

When they came home he got her showered and dressed in a nightie, then he made up the divan. They slept quietly, two sharp noses poking up in the air. They were so much alike – the dimples, the hair colour, even that squeaky little voice of Jaymi's. David was very content to have his daughter with him.

Nob had a new friend, Anna, who was living with him at Clara Street. They applied for a home loan and

Nobby gave up his job at Data Mail and bought a truck. He went into business as a contractor for All Purpose Messengers. He was all right. In the papers another black man had died in prison.

Jeff's friend Michelle moved in with us and not long after that Dianne rang to tell me my brother, Kevin Anderson, who lived in Newcastle, had been hit by a truck and was in a coma. Steve and Dianne borrowed the All Blacks van. Steve was half-tanked so David drove. We took Jaymi and Davy boy with us.

We went to the mission at Karuah, where Kevin's family lived, and also Steve's mother. I showered and left them there with Steve's family while I went to the hospital. Mum Joyce and sister Gwen were there with Deirdre, Kevin's wife and her sister and a heap of other friends.

When I saw Kevin I cried. He wasn't expected to live. Mum and I prayed hard every time we saw him. The doctor said if he made it past six days he might pull through.

We stayed with Gwen and Ron in part of the hospital where they had rooms for families. The next day David, Dianne and Steve, and the kids went back to Sydney and I stayed in Newcastle with Mum Joyce for ten days. When our money ran short we went up to Karuah mission to Kevin's place and looked after the kids so Deirdre could be at the hospital in case Kevin regained consciousness. His condition hadn't changed days later so I came home.

A few weeks later, still feeling shocked, I decided to go to Ellie's caravan for the weekend. I was getting into the car when I saw David come out and run towards the station calling, 'See ya, Mum.' He was waiting on a phone call at Glebe House from Debbie, about the custody of Jaymi.

When I came back after the fishing, I asked Jeff, 'Where's brother David?' He said he was at Glebe House helping Allo to paint. After a few days I started to feel worried.

On Wednesday 29 November I couldn't sleep. It was the first time I had picked up the pen to write this book, I don't know what compelled me, and I started by dedicating the book to all my children. I'd put Jaymi to bed and so I wouldn't disturb her I used the light of my power machine to write by.

I didn't realise the time until Jeff got up to go to the toilet and said, 'Hey old girl, what are you doing up so late?' I said I didn't know it was two o'clock. I decided to go to bed.

I dozed for about forty-five minutes then there was a loud knocking on the door. I thought it would be David coming home, that he'd forgotten his key. I said to Jeff, 'Don't worry, I'll get it.'

When I opened the door it was Nobby and his friend Phil. 'I've got bad news Mum, sit down.' I did. 'Brother David is dead.'

I didn't realise it then but the time I was writing in my book was the time they found him dead.

The story I was told by the police was that he'd gone out and got drunk the night before with his friends.

He was hungover and took Serepax to try and get some sleep, and didn't wake up.

It took me a long time to believe he was dead.

I had Bill's grave opened and put David to rest with his eldest brother, they will watch over one another.

It was a very big funeral and I'm still paying it off. I had no trouble arranging it, as the other two kids' funerals were paid off now. I couldn't help thinking, it cost you more to die than be born. The other two funerals cost $800, and this one cost $1,100. I wanted to get him a headstone, but that wasn't possible straightaway so I saved for it. Then the headstone sat in the backyard for months while Aileen's husband Mick cut the stone to shape and showed Jeff how to sand it down with the hose and wetstone. Then Mothro came in his ute and took Jeff and the stone. We followed them to the cemetery and put it up ourselves.

I got the coroner's report and it said there was no alcohol in his body. The cause of his death was classified as acute narcotism, which means heavy drugs. I don't know to this day who gave it to him, he had no money to buy this stuff. I went, in my anger, over to Glebe House to find out some answers. Everyone I spoke to was so pathetic, and all in their own private hells. I came away in tears, feeling sorry as they all needed help of some sort, so how could they have helped David when they weren't able to help themselves.

Jeff took David's death terribly hard. They were good mates, always fighting and wrestling about and having fun, and they had become closer after David came to live with us. Terry Priest also took it hard – first he'd lost his best mate Bill, then he stole Dave from the boys' home and did time for that, then he lost Dave.

I'd stuck to my vow to give up alcohol, so I had to take the full force of David's death. We all had to take Nobby's anger and hurt, the way he said, 'Oh Mum, why take Dave, I'm the crim, I'm the one who should've died.' I didn't tell Nobby about the coroner's report, I didn't think he could handle that piece of information at the time.

Jaymi and Davy boy went back to Debbie and we didn't see them for a long time. I missed those two, they were all we had left of David.

I'm glad he doesn't hurt anymore as he was heartbroken, 'Buckem in the heart' we called it in Bundjalung. I couldn't forget the night he woke me saying, 'Mum, talk to me, I can't sleep,' how I talked half the night to comfort him (God rest his soul). I used to call him little black duck. I named him David, which means BELOVED.

19

Uluru

Alexandria

In December 1984 after David's funeral, Jeff got into a fight at the pub and came home the worse for wear. Michelle and her friend Lisa had gone to the toilet and were stopped on the way back by the publican, who asked if they'd give him a blow-job. The girls went straight out to the main bar and told Jeff they wanted to leave. He asked what was wrong, and when they told him he went to the publican, 'What the hell are you on about?' he said. 'You've got no right to talk to the girls like that,' and soon the fight was on. The publican ended up in hospital and later Jeff had to go to court about it, but he wasn't charged. It upset him for a long time, he'd never had to go to court before.

Early the next year I decided to go for a holiday to sister Rita's in Brisbane. 1984 had been a bad year for our family and I needed the break. I asked Mum Joyce to come with me.

It would be the first holiday away from my children in thirty-three years, and I needed to stop thinking about them for a while, and calm myself.

It was also my first visit to Brisbane. Rita drove us up the Sunshine Coast to the Big Pineapple at Noosa Heads and then across the bridge to Bribie Island. I could feel the sun soaking through me and bringing me back to life, the hot sand under my feet, the look of the clear aqua water up there.

Rita was now an Advisory Teacher for the Queensland Department of Education. Her job was to collect information about Aboriginal resource material for use in schools, and she'd produced a booklet listing sources for school subjects at all levels.

At the beginning was a section called Evaluative Criteria where she discussed stereotyping, theories of human cultural development, ethnocentrism, terminology (e.g. 'piccaninny', 'witch doctor', 'gin') and exotic emphasis. All of which prevent white students and Kooris themselves from developing attitudes of respect for Aboriginals. At the back of the book was an appendix listing fifty-four Books Not Recommended for Use, which included *New Effective Social Studies*, Gregory, J. B., and *We of the Never Never*, Gunn, Mrs A.

The rest of the book was taken up with resource material for schools – books, slides, films, videotapes, cassettes, discs, charts, maps, pictures and kits.

Under her name in the front she wrote: 'To my big sister Ruby, happy reading, Rita.' I didn't know so many Koori people had written books and made films.

★

A few days later we went to Kilcoy to visit Cousin Midge and her family. I hadn't seen her for twenty-seven years.

'Remember boiling the clothes in the copper, and the metho iron? I used to do a whole day's washing and ironing to borrow a horse for the weekend,' I said.

'What about when it rained,' Midge said, 'and the water ran down the stock route like a river, and we'd get our togs on and slide in the mud all the way down to the creek.'

'Remember the hairy grubs,' Rita said, 'what were they called?'

'Spitfires.'

'And getting stung in the gum trees,' she said, 'and the swimming-hole near the butter factory.'

'And corn cook-outs.'

'And cattle sale days, sitting on the fence.'

'And the wild cherries at Gorge Creek.'

'Aunt Nell's cherry pies.'

We went on like this for hours, oblivious to the big women we were now, our minds inside those small girls' bodies jumping around in the bush. We hardly talked about the present, which was full of troubles – city life, operations, the boys in and out of gaol. We sank back in collective memory to Bonalbo, which we agreed was the friendliest town you could hope to be raised in, and had made us strong enough to deal with all the troubles later on.

When I got home and returned to the sewing class, someone had left a copy of a magazine called *Encore* on a side table. There was a photo of a Koori kid on the cover, and an article about a film called *Short Changed*. It was about an Aboriginal man, his white wife and their 'magpie' son; the marriage breakup, scenes in Redfern terrace houses, a custody battle, the father taking the kid to the bush. The (white) director was asked whether he considered the film would have broad commercial appeal.

He said: 'I've found the story is so enveloping and so big that I've become obsessed by it. I haven't thought about these things. I haven't been able to.

'It's an amazing thing to discover an entire race of people who keep walking into glass doors –'

Sitting there, not doing my sewing, I thought about the book Rita had made, how something as basic as language was a barrier, 'gin', 'boong', 'primitive'. How language was a glass door we walked into BANG all the time and not many white people could see it. There were a lot of books and pamphlets and posters here at the Aboriginal Medical Service (our sewing room was on the top floor) – and leafing through them you saw the endless photos of Kooris and their achievements – Best Practical Enrolled Nurse of the Year, a woman in South Australia gaining a law degree, people doing courses to become trade union reps, a woman going around remote country in WA in a four-wheel drive, teaching management skills in community administration, and learning about traditional Aboriginals. I thought how this kind of information hardly ever got printed in *The Herald*, *The Sun*, or *The Mirror*. You got historical articles with headlines like 'Aboriginals Treated as Vermin'. Occasionally white people who'd worked with Kooris would say, 'We as a white race are losing out on a spiritual journey.' Black achievements were the invisible glass door to white people. Not a barrier. Just invisible.

I'd been teaching the sewing class for two years now, and there were twenty-seven of us planning our trip to Ayers Rock. We cooked for the pensioner luncheon each month, made hot meals for the medical service staff, sold cakes, held fetes, and eventually we had $3000. Then we held a luncheon for the Aboriginal Arts Board and they donated $10,000 to our expenses. After that we approached TAA and they donated two return tickets to the Gold Coast for us to raffle. I'd make a boiler of spaghetti sauce and cook noodles and make three dozen rolls of garlic bread and sometimes I made chow mein, and it sold like hot cakes; anything to raise funds. Lily Madden banked the money and did all the arranging for the trip. My mother was coming. She'd never been on a plane. I kept telling her it'd be all right. I'd never been on a plane either.

A film crew from the ABC were coming to make a TV doco about us. Twenty-seven urban Aboriginal women seeing Uluru for the first time. We'd said okay, if they contributed towards our expenses. 'If you're gonna be shot, get paid for it,' Mum said.

Doctor Dianne from the Medical Service came with us. Our plane was to leave at 8:45 a.m. The crew filmed us in the departure lounge while we waited.

It would be the first time I'd ever seen our people in their tribal state. I wanted to see everything. I wanted to feel what it meant to stand near a big rock like that.

I can't describe my first impression of flying, well, very good, but I know I was waiting for that *feeling* of what it would be like to fly. I rushed into the plane so I could be near a window. And as we climbed I thought, this is okay, until the plane stuttered and shook, then it levelled off at 3,000 feet and the captain welcomed us aboard, some muffled voice, and I couldn't look out my window. Next to me was Millie Kemmester who peered around me and Ruby de Santos who lay back and enjoyed it, she'd been on planes to Europe and was a seasoned flyer.

The flight took two and a half hours. When I looked down I thought 'big', 'rugged', then I remembered reading in the paper that a writer should take to a cliche like a surgeon with a knife, but looking down on that country it seemed big and rugged. We passed over the Birdsville Track and Millie said, 'Ruby, what's that big thing sticking out near your window?'

'That's the thing keeping us up, it's the wing.'

The plane dipped its right wing for the runway at Alice Springs. Then it dropped like an elevator a few times and we touched ground. I coo-eed loud and Millie hit my arm and said, 'Shut up, can't you see you're scaring me?'

We were met by some men with a bus and a couple of cars from the Aboriginal Hostels Ltd. On the road to Alice we stopped at an all-Aboriginal rodeo. The dust flew, they sure could ride those Koori boys. It reminded me of the Khan brothers and the time we had Gwen buckjumping a steer and Aunt Nell cracking the whip.

We drove through Alice to the Melanka Lodge Motel in Todd Street and gathered round Lily for our keys. I teamed up with Aunt Monica and we went to our room for a bath and a rest.

The next day we went out for food. Alice looked full of tourists and souvenirs, I wondered where the Kooris were.

Next morning, the day we were leaving for a half-day tour to Stanley Chasm, I got up early and went outside. I could see a lot of tribal people sitting in the shade of trees in the Todd riverbed but I didn't go up to them. Then some young ones walked past the Lodge. I talked to some, and said hello, but they turned away. They were so shy.

The bus driver welcomed us aboard and said his name was John. He would point out things on the way. We stopped at Flynn's grave and you could see the colours of the McDonnell Ranges. I took photos, then the driver said this was the country where Namatjira painted. We stopped at the twin ghost gums.

At Stanley Chasm there were eight tourist buses there already. We paid a toll to enter. There were notices saying: DO NOT PAT THE DINGO (MULGA). The chasm was a small oasis in the desert – a cluster of houses, a kiosk, a garden with flowers blooming, picnic tables. We sat down for morning tea. Mulga followed us over and lay down not far from me. We took pictures of him but mine were taken from the back, I thought the clicking of the camera might disturb him.

On the way back to Alice the driver was making jokes back and forth with the women. Mum was in the front seat. Every now and then she'd laugh and hit the rail of the bus with her cane.

Next morning at seven-thirty the film crew joined us on the bus to Uluru. Looking out the window I wondered how our ancestors survived here. They must have been very strong people and I was proud to be just a portion of this race.

We pulled into a cattle property called Ebenezer Downs for morning tea. John said, 'Here we are, six thousand and seven hundred square miles, this property is, not acres, square *miles*.'

'Just imagine owning a property that big,' I said to Ruby de Santos.

There was a cafeteria selling food and drinks and Aboriginal artefacts. 'Freshen up, girls, we've got six hours straight travelling now,' John said (meaning go to the toilet).

The next property was Curtain Springs, 16,000 square miles, they were getting bigger, in the meantime the crew were filming our reactions, and did some interviews with six of us.

It was the first time I'd been interviewed for TV. I was wearing a Land Rights coloured hat, dark glasses and I hope it showed up good on film. The next property was

Erlunda, 26,007 square miles. All these cattle properties and I couldn't see any grass. It hadn't rained in eighteen months. John said the cattle fed off bushes and shrubs, saltbush. They looked fat anyhow. We came to a camel farm, some saltlakes, a big table-shaped rock formation called Mt Connor, then Uluru in the distance.

I sat completely still. It was like a huge animal that was asleep in the middle of nowhere. We came closer and I could feel the goosebumps and the skin tightening at the back of my neck. Everyone else was quiet. It made me think of our tribal beginnings, and this to me was like the beginning of our time and culture. Time was suddenly shortened to include all of history in the present, and it was also stretched to a way of seeing the earth that was thousands of years old.

We were going to stay at Yulara village for two days, Yulara which means 'the place where howling dog drinks'.

The first day we'd leave after lunch for a tour of the Olgas then come back and see Uluru at sunset. The second day we'd go to Uluru and do the filming.

At Yulara we had a barbeque tea in an enclosure big enough to seat about fifty people. This resort was a goldmine. If you didn't buy food there you'd starve. It put emphasis on how hard it must have been for tribal people to survive.

The Olgas, called Kutajuta in the tribal tongue of that area, were a cluster of rock formations all adjoining. My sense of time was beginning to slow.

Then the bus took us to the sunset viewing place for Uluru, seven kilometres from the rock. There were about thirty cars, vans and buses there, and you had to ignore the other people to enjoy what the rock was doing. It was true that it changed colour at different stages of the sunset. We watched and didn't say anything.

The next morning we were up early. Uluru means 'bald', and I was thinking how someone had said it was the magnetic centre and meeting place of all the dreaming tracks. The film crew met us at the bus. First stop was the Ranger's Office to get our permit to film. We had to have two tribal elders on board to show us where we could film and where we couldn't. Only one could speak English and her name was Barbara. They shook hands all round and were made welcome.

We circled the rock three times so the crew could film us coming and going. I stared out at the changing faces of the rock. It was huge. Everything else that you call huge shrinks by comparison. We could see people climbing up and when we stopped some of the women began the climb. There was a notice saying there had been nine deaths from this climb and the last was four months ago, so I didn't attempt it.

We bought some artefacts in a tent and ate some quondong fruit. Back on the bus we went to the garage and the store called Nginti. It was on their tribal camping area and there were signs saying: NO ENTRY AT ALL. I thought the people there were better off than us – they didn't have to pay high rents, or bother about keeping up with the Joneses. But city blacks couldn't survive there, and they couldn't survive in our half-black half-white world. It was very hard on both sides and for our survival we had to be strong mentally as well as physically. The next day I settled in to sleep for most of the way back to Alice.

Lily had organised for us to go to the radio station the next morning: CAAMA, which means Central Australian Aboriginal Media Association. First we stopped at the old radio station near the motel, and had freshly cooked damper with jam and syrup and cream. Then we went to CAAMA, which was housed in a nunnery, and was surrounded by grapevines and shrubs. We had a barbeque then the locals asked for two of us to be interviewed. No-one volunteered, so Audrey and I said we'd do it.

We spoke about the black movement in Sydney and our involvement with black rights; about the Medical Service and the All Blacks football teams. About four of us joined in giving opinions, and it turned into a good rap session. They videoed it too. Then we were taken back to Melanka Lodge and some of the women made good work of the gambling casino down the street. I dived into bed after a shower and was sound asleep in no time, and so was Aunt Monica.

The next day we packed and rested, and the following day we came back to 'civilisation'. Coming in from the airport I was writing up my notes for this book, and I wished at that moment I'd been born full-blood instead of the degree of caste that I was. I had a longing for the relaxed tribal sense of time and of looking after the earth, but I knew I enjoyed luxuries like not having to boil the billy for a cup of tea, or having to make a fire to do that – and the hot shower and watching TV. I'd become soft in the modern world.

One time I'd been as tough as I had to be, chopped trees for firewood and carried water buckets on yokes for drinking every day of the year, but that was when I was young and fit and strong as an ox, and had to be to survive with the kids. Now I was middle-aged. Those days were left behind.

At home I lay in bed thinking about the part of the rock that looked like a skull, and like tribal markings. It made me feel very humble and I could sense, even so far away, the spirit of the great rock we call Uluru. I remembered my mother going over with her cane slowly to the rock, laying her hand on it and saying, 'Now I can die happy.'

20

Reunion

Alexandria

In October 1985 my youngest daughter, Pauline, who had been living with the father of her children for eight years, decided to get married. Jeff's birthday was the nineteenth, and they planned the wedding for that day. She applied for a loan from AVCO for $2000 and they gave her $1500. I raised $150, Nobby loaned her $100 and the rest she saved from working the food stalls at the Easter Show. She bought her wedding dress, and dresses for Roberta and Kylie, her daughters, who were to be flower girls.

Mum Joyce and I went to her place at St Mary's two days before to cook the hot food. Nobby came out with Ellie and Ron to help.

The wedding cars were hotrods and the bride's car was silver. They made their vows in the gazebo at St Mary's Park. Her husband, David Mitchell, I called foghorn leghorn, he was a long streak of misery but okay, a good man. The photographer and video people arrived, and then we went to the reception, which was held between two soccer fields at St Mary's. Everything was blue and white, Jeff's favourite football colours (Canterbury). The groom's father made his speech then someone called out over the mic for the mother of the bride.

'I'm not good at making speeches,' I said, 'but I'm pretty good at air-raiding as my kids can tell you. David told me to put the shotgun away but on second thoughts I'd better re-load. There's a few more of my kids out there who have to walk down the aisle.'

I wished them well for the future and said 'God Bless'. I sat down, I'd done all the talking I was going to do. When I looked up, two men were carrying a huge birthday cake towards us. They set it down in front of Jeffery and we sang 'Happy Birthday' loud and clear across the soccer fields.

The dance had started. Horse waltzed with his wife Donna, Steve and Dianne joined in, then Nobby and Anna and the others. Sparrow's featherweight body moved in between them. Patrick and Jo didn't look too happy. Otherwise the place was jumping and the reception lasted ten hours, until at 2:00 a.m. We drifted across the field to the cars and the drunken ride home. Neddy sang in the back seat. Nobby went to sleep on Anna's lap in the front.

A week later Patrick rang. He was living at St Mary's and now had a baby called Jeffery David, after my boys.

'She's running around on me, Mum. I don't know what to do.'

'Well, if your marriage is worth fighting for, Pat, try to talk things out with her. Don't give up too easily.'

'Okay Mum. I'll try.'

After two days he rang again. He'd found out Joanne's boyfriend was his best mate. She refused to give him up, told Patrick she didn't love him any more and was always leaving the baby with Patrick and her brother to look after. Patrick gave her an ultimatum, settle down or piss off, so she went and took the baby.

Patrick followed her and got his son back. Then he went to his family in Queanbeyan to sort himself out. He came back to Sydney much thinner and moved in with me. The custody battle is still going on.

It gave me a shock. I thought Joanne was the ideal girl for Patrick, I thought they'd be happy. I misjudged her, they misjudged each other – I made the same mistake myself lots of times. It seems you get middle-aged before you take advantage of what you learn from those mistakes. And then you're tired of the whole rigmarole.

I decided to take Jeff on a holiday to a family reunion at Kilcoy. He'd never met Midge and her family. In the bus we had adjoining seats and were so squashed up I had a sore arm from Jeff's bony elbow where it was sticking into me all night.

The next morning we went through the Gold Coast and Jeff was looking up at the high-rise buildings and the women in bikinis on the street. Maybe it looked like some sort of paradise to him, his face was lit up.

In Brisbane I phoned Rita and she picked us up at the bus station.

We unpacked a large ham and a Christmas pudding I'd made, and talked about Rita's job for a while. She was divorced from Podge and had three daughters at home. Tania was at teachers' college, Shauna was learning to be an air hostess and Janna worked in a sheltered workshop.

Next day we hired another car for the kids. Jeff travelled with his three cousins, I went with Rita. We took him back to the Gold Coast, and stopped at Sea World. Water skiers went up and down like ballet dancers. Porpoises jumped and slid back into the water. A whale moved around like Uluru in a large aquarium. Slow, old. We watched a pantomime, then the kids got changed and went up the steps to the corkscrew ride. Rita and I sat in the sun and watched them whizzing down, yelling and tilting.

Back home, the girls cooked dinner and the next day we packed the car for Kilcoy. Jeff stared out the window at acres of pineapples, miles of pine forest. I stared myself, I never got tired of looking at that country.

Seven miles past Kilcoy we turned in at Hazeldean, Midge's property. Their house overlooked the Somerset Dam. There was a fowl run with about sixty chooks, and hills in the distance. Midge's girls took Jeff into town, and we sat yarning. There was a school reunion for Bonalbo in March, and Rita said she'd book us into the Bonalbo Hotel. That way we'd get a good view of the town. I was quietly feeling pleasure from the idea of being back at my belongin place in a few months, then at 2:00 a.m. Jeff came in and said, 'Hey Mum, they got me drunk,' and flopped on to his bed on the verandah.

On Christmas Day Rita came back from Brisbane with her girls, and we sat down to a huge meal. The kids had given me a miniature tape recorder for Christmas. I had it in my pocket with the record button ON.

Midge's son-in-law Peter Cobbin asked for a second helping of my pudding and said to her, 'You'd better put in your order for one each year.' He grinned at me, took a big mouthful and bit on something hard. Then he was holding his jaw.

'Ugh, what did you put in it?' he said.

'I dunno. It must have been a date pit.'

'It bloody near pitted my date!'

'I got all this on tape, you know.'

They were laughing so much we stopped eating for a while. When it got cooler we went to the backyard and talked into the night. I could hear the chooks occasionally move their feathers, and I could smell the tadpole-dampness off the dam. Night smells rising in the country. A cow mooed in the distance, and that set us talking about Daisy and Hobby and home. We told Bonalbo stories for the kids till it was late and the little ones were falling asleep.

Jeff went to Brisbane with his cousins for a New Year's fancy dress party. He went as a wizard, Shauna was a redback spider and Tania was a witch. When he came back to Midge's, her sons took him hunting and they got a deer. The next day the sons' mate rode in on a brand-new motorbike and gave him a ride. He was in his glee, he loved bikes and had several of his own at one time.

At New Year Gwen and Ron came up from Gunnedah and we talked ourselves out. The only one who couldn't come was Judy, Midge's younger sister. She was working at a refuge in Lismore so we rang her and took turns talking. We drank green ginger wine and lemonade and swapped stories till late.

A few days later Rita said we should go out to Bribie Island. She had friends there called Otto and Josie who had a greenhouse and a boat. We all agreed, and once we were there Jeff and the girls went down to the beach for a swim. I sat in the greenhouse happy as another plant with that soft light on everything and the tropical sun outside.

Our two weeks were over and Rita took us to the bus depot. Jeff was quiet, looking out the window. He'd seen the Gold Coast, been on the corkscrew ride, watched a whale, got drunk with his cousins, gone with a witch and a redback spider to a party, hunted a deer, ridden a new motorbike and swum on an island beach. No wonder he didn't say much.

When we were going past the Ballina road I told him to keep his eyes open as I could see the lights of Cabbage Tree Island. I told him that was the home of our Bundjalung tribe, they were the Richmond and Clarence River tribe. The river ran into the ocean at Evan's Head and we were approaching the turn off when we saw a big sign saying BUNDJALUNG NATIONAL PARK and I told him he was now in my territory, and that he was the only one of my children who'd ever been there.

Back home Mum Joyce rang to say she wanted to visit Kevin. He had come out of his coma after six months and part of that time he'd been clinically dead. We went up to see him and the doctor said his progress would be slow because he had to learn how to co-ordinate his movements. As soon as we entered the ward he hung his head. It was obvious he didn't want us to see him like that. I was shocked to see him reduced from a fifteen-stone footballer to a six-stone invalid. He'd tried to take some food, but had got a chest infection, he'd been fed by the drip for seventeen months now. He would speak but only in anger. The staff were force-feeding him. A few times he looked at me and said in a small voice, 'Ruby, where's Dad?'

I remembered babysitting him and Dennis when I was living with Dad and Mum Joyce, and working at Brach's. How we called him 'Plum with the black bum', what a sweet-looking kid he was. It looked like now he had no spirit to live. Mum Joyce and I were quiet coming back on the train, her face against the window looked as if the sadness would never go away.

In March I left Sydney at six o'clock on the Brisbane Express for the sixteen-hour train ride to Rita's. We were going to Bonalbo for the school's 75th anniversary along with 2,000 other ex-students.

On Friday Rita picked up a Terrago van from Budget and we went to an outer suburb where Midge and her family piled on board. Rita had brought country-and-western tapes – Dolly Parton, Tammy Wynette, Kenny Rogers – and we sang down the Gold Coast road to Beenleigh. We were going to meet Gwen, who was coming by coach from Gunnedah.

By five-thirty we were on our way to Bonalbo, cutting across country to the Mt Lindsay Highway. The van only had eighty kilometres on the dial and was shining new. We said to ourselves that the people of Bonalbo would think the Andersons and the Hinnett family had sure come up in the world.

'You painted up your lips
And rolled and combed your tinted hair –'

(My sisters looked at me sideways, they knew the stories of my four men, what had happened in each case, and they sang.)

'Ruby, are you contemplatin'
Going out somewhere –'

I saw behind their heads the Richmond Range around Mt Lindsay.

'The shadow on the wall tells me

The sun is going down

Ru – by, don't take your love to town.'

I turned on a high black mama voice and patted my chest. 'I took my love to town too many times!' and burst out laughing.

Then we were quiet and watching out the window. The timber was so very tall and the Taloome scrub so dense we couldn't have seen the mountain even if it wasn't in cloud. I remembered the sound of Uncle Roy's voice singing in the lingo about Mt Lindsay. This whole area was Bundjalung and Githebul. I heard there was a cleverwoman, Aunt Millie Boyd, who had become Keeper of the Rock. She looks after Taloome Falls, right back to Mount Warning, Nimbin rocks and that whole area.

We were at the border crossing the tick-gate and then there was a fork. The road to the left went to Kyogle where Mum and Gwen and Rita were born, and the right one went to Woodenbong where I was living on the mission and Bill had meningitis. So the Woodenbong road sank me back into a kind of futility, we'd saved his life at two, but then he died at eighteen. I wondered how I'd survived the anguish, or whether I had, sometimes I think I buried it while I was raising the other kids and now it was coming back to stare me in the face. I started to sing.

I sang louder than anyone else, it was Peggy Lee on the tape, the song where she spells out W-O-M-A-N.

Urbenville. We were thirty-six kilometres from Bonalbo. Rita and I were the biggest, we sat up front. The others in the back said we needed the weight to stabilise the van. I poked my thumb at them and pointed to the crosses in the ground. Bonalbo Cemetery, three miles out, and as we came around each bend in the road we saw the lights of Bonalbo and Rita and I called at the top of our voices: 'We're home, we're home.'

We pointed at the houses, remembering who lived in each one. Coming up around the hill we yelled and laughed and in a few minutes we were at the pub.

Bonalbo is a small town – a Post Office, a bank, garage, hotel, two restaurants, chemist, hardware store. The Butter Factory. The Memorial Hall. The school and four churches. That was how I remembered it. There were a few changes. An old people's home stood behind the hospital. The sawmill was gone, replaced by a municipal pool and a bowling club. But these things hadn't changed the town's layout.

We were looking for Mrs McGregor, the publican's wife, when I saw Midge cuddling a red-headed woman. I went over and she said, 'Do you know who this is?' I didn't. I looked harder and saw it was Nada Ramsey who'd lived next door in Dyrabba Street.

'I'm Ruby,' I said. 'I used to play your mother's piano when she was away shopping.'

Then she laughed and we were all hugging. Mrs McGregor gave us our keys and we went to the dining room for hot cross buns. The dining room was the same as when I worked here as a chambermaid when I was fifteen. I saw Aileen Parker, who I'd been to school with, and Dorrie and Ann Hedricks with their husbands. We talked for a while then Gwen and I went to our beds on the partition part of the verandah.

I woke up at six-thirty to the sound of someone moving around outside the partition. I sat up. There was a bloke carrying chairs and tables around to the front of the pub. I had a shower and dressed, and walked around the place. The kitchen. I remembered the smell of cattle sale days, peeling spuds while Mrs Watts made steak and kidney pies and caramel tarts. The publican's sister saying, 'I'll never eat butter or milk again' when the cow calved in the yard. I started to laugh.

Well that skinny fifteen-year-old kid was inside me somewhere, I could feel her all day. We had bacon and eggs and then back to the van for the ride to the school. It was only a few hundred yards away but we wanted to make a good entrance.

We walked up the hill to the school. I didn't realise how steep it was and I was out of puff at the top. Flopped into a chair then I saw the Cox brothers, Ken and Digby.

'I saw Gwen in a pub in Enmore once,' Ken said.

'It must have been me. Gwen doesn't drink, she's never been a pub habitee like me. Or like I used to be.'

Rita came back with our name tags and we went into the classrooms to look at the photographs. I was staring at the Hinnett family when a regal-looking woman stood in front of me and said, 'Hello Ruby, where are all the girls?'

It was Mary Parker our teacher. She'd been teaching in Bonalbo for thirty-four years and all told for fifty, and she was the guest of honour at the reunion. I called Gwen, Rita and Midge over, and she remembered us all.

I pulled out a pen and collected autographs in the back of a book they'd handed out: *75 years of Education in Bonalbo and District.*

Speeches of welcome were made, there was a tree-planting ceremony and we cut the anniversary cake. The whole of the playing field was full of people meeting old acquaintances, there was a lot of laughing and hugging. I was having such a good time I forgot to eat.

The photographer was calling, '1941 to 1950!' and we drifted to the chairs. 'Ladies, please remember you're in school,' he joked, 'come on, cover your knees!' Snap. Snap.

Rita and I sat under a lemon tree and looked at our books. She was in the 1951 5th and 6th class photo, Gwen and I weren't there.

There was a map showing the Taloome scrub, Gorge Creek, Bonalbo. Short histories of the schools. A page from a 1933 punishment book – quarrelling: 1 stroke; dirty or careless word: 2 strokes; breaking window: 2 strokes.

Old student recollections. A teacher once came in with a little basket and said she wanted them to draw a wicker basket. One boy drew Adolf Hitler.

'Listen to this,' Rita said, 'page 13. "According to scholars of Bonalbo, Alexander the Great was King of Macadamia." Wait – here it is, "The Ancient Sumerians

352

were astrologers. They studied the stars and made predicaments.'"

'I always wondered who made predicaments.'

'Now we know. Damn those ancient Sumerians.'

We lay back on the grass and laughed.

'Do you remember stabbing your milk bottle tops on the lemon tree thorns and dribbling the milk into your mouth?'

Later we went in the van to explore the town. Behind the school near the bridge were a couple of logs, the only things to show there'd been a sawmill there once. We crossed the bridge and headed out to Gorge Creek, where we used to swim. Past the Browns, the Noulands, the Johnsons, we turned into the road where the Grays lived. I searched for the Bulls' old place across the creek, but it wasn't there. The next day I was told it had been put on a truck and moved to Bottle Creek.

'Gorge Creek,' I said to the others, 'I used to get a lift with Clarrie Parker when he delivered the bread and mail on this run, and I'd go as far as the Grays' place then cut across country to the creek. Then I'd wade across to the Bulls' farm to get to work.'

'Gotta be better for you than commuting,' Rita said.

Back in town we went to the Butter Factory then criss-crossed every street, passed the saleyards at the back of the hotel, and drove up the stock route. It had been gravelled but we remembered when it was a mud flow to the creek.

'I ran into one of the kids who used to slide down in the mud with us today,' I said as the van climbed.

'Patrick Whalan, remember him? He's a crown sergeant now, lived near Liverpool in Sydney.'

'Notice how many of the people moved to Sydney?' Rita said. We drove up to the Khans' place. The Khan brothers hadn't come to the reunion, but the house was there. Then we were in front of Audrey Lee's place and the hill to Chiefy Pie's.

Back at the hotel I had a temperature and my blood pressure was up. Rita took me to the hospital, the doctor did an ECG and told me I'd overdone myself and I should stay there for the night. Because of the celebrations going on at the pub I agreed. He gave me a sleeping pill and a fluid tablet to bring my blood pressure down.

Before I went to sleep I looked out the window. This was the room where I'd given birth to Pearl in 1952. It had the same view of the school playground I'd seen when I worked here later, and in my mind's eye I could see Bill and Pearl playing and waving to me, and I went off to sleep peacefully.

21

Surviving Culture

Alexandria

Back home I visited Nobby and Anna. They'd applied for and been granted a $58,000 home loan and bought a home at Plumpton. Nob had landscaped the gardens and everything looked well cared for. I didn't say anything, but I thought that maybe now he was back on the straight path. Anna's kids ran up to him saying, 'Daddy, Daddy' – and he looked at me over their heads and grinned.

Then I got a phone-call from Anna one Wednesday night. She said he'd taken the day off and was going to potter round their new home, she'd gone out to a job interview and he'd had bad news – something about a solicitor. He decided to try working in the garden. He went into the garage for tools and there was Dave's pushbike, Dave's workbag, Dave's boxing boots hanging from a nail. Then he took off in his car with his dog Pip to run away.

He might have been heading into Sydney to me, Anna said. The car ran out of petrol and he started to fight with other people in cars. He wanted them to run him over

355

and kill him. He was in such a state he was fighting with a bloke in a semi-trailer because he wouldn't run over him. Head-butting a Mack truck.

He lay down in front of the semi and it took about five police to subdue him. He wouldn't tell them his name or talk to them. They thought he was a madman, but for some reason instead of taking him to a clinic for counselling they kicked him and put him in the cells at Flemington.

Annabella had bailed him out for $500, would I come out and see him?

The next day I went with Jeff out to Plumpton. It made my heart ache to see him, his hand was fractured, he was terribly sore and could hardly move. I couldn't understand what was going on.

'Why?' I said. 'Nob? Why are you punishing yourself so much?'

'I don't remember anything Mum. My mind's gone blank.'

Because he was broke Jeff gave him a hundred dollars and I gave him fifty. He lay on the lounge looking completely dazed.

I went into the kitchen and sat down with Anna. Now the details come out. The solicitor who was handling their home loan had embezzled $1400 of their repayments, and a letter had come from the building society to say the loan could not go through unless they came up with the money.

Nob had worked hard to get the home, and it was too much for him so he'd flipped.

I tried talking to him. 'You could have been killed,' I began, but he gave me an ironic look, as if that was the whole point, and I shut up.

At sewing class the next Tuesday a woman who had grown up with Nob, and who lived opposite Flemington Police Station, came and told me she'd seen him laying on the road begging the traffic to kill him. The woman said the police had him on the road with their boots on his head pushing him into the tarred road. They laid eight charges of resisting arrest on him, and eight of assaulting police. By the time it went to court, he had two assault police charges and three of wilful damage to vehicles.

He was remanded to 2 July and back at home I tried talking to him again.

I looked at him and wondered what would happen. I didn't think he could do gaol again. He'll nick himself, he's had enough, I thought.

The next month my brother Dennis rang to say brother Kevin had died. I went to see Mum Joyce who was looking very pale. We went together to the funeral in Redfern. The Aboriginal Legal Service people were there, the All Blacks, Kevin's wharfie friends and the whole family from Karuah. He was buried in Botany Cemetery, a hundred yards from David and Bill.

I wondered what would happen next, I didn't think I could take much more. Then Debbie turned up. She'd put a bit of weight on, but looked much the same. The kids were with her, hugging me. They stayed for the weekend and while I cooked Davy boy played with Bronc and Debbie talked about David's death.

'It should never have happened,' she said. 'If the people at Glebe House had got an ambulance he might have survived.'

'You saw those people. They'd be worried about bringing themselves undone if they had police or ambulance there.'

'They could've taken him out on the footpath and called an ambulance.' She said David's presence was always there for her. Touching her mouth, she said, 'I can feel him kissing me.'

At night she wouldn't sleep on the divan – that was Dave's. She put the kids in with me then climbed into the bottom of my bed and we all slept there.

Months later I had Pauline's daughter Roberta here and Debbie brought Jaymi for the weekend. The two girls were seven and eight. They slept in the front room where David used to sleep. In the night I heard Jaymi crying and went into her.

'What's up?'

Bertie was awake too. She sat up. 'Uncle Dave was here,' she said.

'Daddy was here,' Jaymi said. 'He covered us up.'

I told her to be glad he was looking after her, and not to be frightened.

The following Monday Gwen's son was in the newspaper under the headline ROOKIE ROOSTER WINS A CONTRACT:

Unknown winger, Ron Griffin, running around in park football a fortnight ago, clinched himself a contract with the millionaire Eastern Suburbs club with a champagne debut against Canterbury yesterday.

He was referred to as 'a clear winner' who had 'devastating style'. I rang Gwen and read it to her.

Jeff came in and I showed him the article about his cousin, then I noticed he was looking pale. He'd been getting chest pains and was often away by himself.

The next day Michelle told me she'd taken him to hospital for an ECG a while ago. He'd said nothing to me. I talked to him about it, and he admitted he wasn't well. I took him to the doctor for an overhaul and a talk. 'There's nothing wrong with your heart,' the doctor said. 'Because of the circumstances, you're suffering from stress.' Jeff looked at the floor. 'Just because you're unemployed doesn't mean you'll never get a job, you know that. You need to learn how to relax, and to have a little faith in your ability to cope.' I could see his spirit was lifted just by talking it out with the doctor.

I sat there thinking stress, at nineteen years old, how stupid. The doctor arranged for him to go to relaxation classes.

'It's not the end of the world,' I said when we got home. 'No-one's hiring people over the Christmas break anyway. Things'll come good in the New Year when the factories start back to work.'

'That doesn't mean I'll get work.'

'Jeff, you've got six trades to choose from – spray-painting, die-cutting, car detailing, panel-beating, plant operator and tyre-setting.'

He played with the things on the table. I knew work wasn't the real problem. Jeff was three when the older kids died and didn't understand about death.

'There's nothing we can do about David,' I said, 'only live our lives to the fullest, cram in as much laughter and happiness as we can. And fill our lives with meaning, then we'll be able to find contentment in ourselves.'

'David's death had no meaning.'

'But his life did, it had meaning.'

In the meantime Nob's case had been adjourned twice. He was travelling in from Plumpton to AWA in Ashfield where he worked as a storeman and packer. But Anna was forever watching him and he started to drink more. He went to stay with Horse for two days and back home he had an argument with Anna. She got frightened and called the police who threw him into the van and slammed the door on his leg and nearly hamstrung him.

He was released on his own surety next morning. He went to Mt Druitt police station and demanded to know who had done that to his leg. The police called him a smart-arse and took him into the station. They belted him up and charged him with offensive behaviour. That made three charges he had to appear for. By now he could hardly walk.

He demanded that Anna take him to a photographer to have pictures taken of his leg. When he came home he started to drink. Anna rang me to say she was taking the children to her mother's. I waited a while then I phoned him. His voice was muffled. 'Can you come out and get me Mum? Please?' It was about eight at night. I emptied my money box and counted out ten dollars for petrol, and when Jeff came home we left for Plumpton.

Nob opened the door. Tall, gaunt, his eyes black. He hobbled to the lounge without saying anything and sat down next to his dog, Pip. We put his clothes and a few things in the car. The dog climbed in and sat on the back seat.

When we went inside to get him, he pointed at the stereo and said, 'That's for you, Jeff.' We unplugged the stereo and put it in the car.

On the way to town he sat in the back cuddling Pip and crying to himself.

'If a house —' I said (wondering what was going to come out of my mouth) 'and its problems have done this to you it's best to walk away from it.' But to him I knew it meant another let-down. 'You'll have to learn to roll with the punches like I had to.' He knew what I meant.

Next morning I went with him to the Langton Clinic in Surry Hills. I waited an hour and a half while he talked to the counsellor. He had an appointment for the next week.

At home he seemed to be settling down. I cooked and spoilt him, then as court day appeared he began to panic. He came into the kitchen and said quietly, 'Mum I've got to be truthful to you, I'm not going to front court. I'm not going back to gaol.'

'You have to face it.'

'No.'

'You'll be running for the rest of your life.'

He sat down. I went to the next room and phoned his psychiatrist at the clinic. 'Don't worry,' he said. 'It's Nob's decision to run, he has to be prepared to take the blame if he makes the wrong decision. You've done the best for him and raised him. He's old enough to make up his own mind.'

Which is right. But it doesn't stop a person worrying.

That night he came into my room and told me he loved me, and kissed my cheek, and the next morning when I woke up he was gone.

It was Tuesday. Sewing class. I went out to wait for the van, and I was thinking about my book. It was nearly finished. I decided to go inside and get it, so I could read to the women at the Centre.

So I read them the Oinky chapter and they liked it and then we got on with our sewing. Mum sat next to me, watching me crotchet a Land Rights shawl. I decided not to tell her about Nobby.

She was very weak from Parkinson's disease. I noticed when she walked it was slower, and leaning more on the cane. Also she'd lost a lot of weight.

I knew she'd had a prolapsed womb. She'd been with the same doctor for seventeen years and he never gave her an internal. Eventually she'd had the prolapse fixed and later they diagnosed Parkinson's. From now on she was very frail and spoke only in a whisper.

362

She lived in Kogarah with Robert, a son from her second family. The following week Robert rang to ask if I could watch her for the day so they could have a break.

I propped her up on my bed and (thinking about my book) I said, 'Mum, I've got a tape recorder, there's a lot of things about you and Dad I don't know, will you talk into the recorder for me?'

'Yes, my girl.' Her voice was hardly there.

'Do you remember your first job in Bonalbo?'

'Yes – I worked for Tom Mills – and Dave Mills – I used to ride after cattle – and after sheep – and – brand the cows – all that. When I went to Bonalbo Show – the first time –'

'How long ago was this, Mum?'

'Oh, a long time ago.'

'How old were you then?'

'I was fifteen, sixteen. Fifty cents a week – five bob – when I finished I had a lot of money – put it in the bank – I went around for a while – I had appendicitis – couldn't work any more. The doctor – I had to go home, the doctor said.'

'And when did you meet Dad?'

'Oh, I met him a long time after – in Stoney Gully –'

'– he was born in Coraki, Dad.'

'Yeah – born Coraki' (she pronounced it Kooriki) '– and me and Aunty Katy was good friends, you know – and she said – my brother's coming up – to Stoney Gully this weekend – and he asked me my name – and he asked to marry me – and they wouldn't let us get married – you know. And then – he asked my mother – and they said yes – they're very strict you know – and when they say yes – you're not allowed – to go out with anybody else – or anything – gotta stay inside – they wouldn't let me go out to the dance – Katy used to ask me to go – but I wasn't allowed to go – unless your father was there to take me – very strict.'

'Very strict.'

'Very strict. They frightened me, you know –'

'Where did you get married?'

'Coraki – we had a big wedding – Aunty Pearl and Aunty Ruby [Dad's mother's sisters, the identical twins] made the wedding –'

'That's the ones I was named after.'

'Yes – and they – made the wedding and the white manager's wife Mrs English made me the wedding cake – and she was coming across – walking across the flat [the common at Box Ridge] with the wedding cake and she fell in the water –'

'I can remember the flat, where all the water used to lay after the rain ay, on this flat – and there was a big sheep dip.'

'– and she was soaking wet coming up the hill and – went back home to change her clothes –'

'And wet all the cake too?'

'She was wet but the cake wasn't.'

★

The next week Nob was caught. He'd gone to a friend, it turned out, who had loaned him a car and a gun ('to protect himself') – and then gone to Brisbane to stay with Rita. Coming back he was chased by the Highway Patrol and had fired shots at their car. He was back in Long Bay and three days later we were in court. He was refused bail and we didn't know when his case would come up. It was a serious charge (firing at a police car was like firing at police) – and nobody in the legal system seemed to understand he was having a nervous breakdown. I looked at my calendar. Nob had been caught on David's birthday, 10 August.

Meanwhile Mum's second family, the children she'd had with Eddie Webb, were looking after her as she had become more frail. The oldest, George, had been raised by the Webbs and had later died of a heart attack. The other three, Dorothy, Margaret and Robert, took turns to mind her. Then Margaret rang to say she'd been to Kogarah and Mum was not well. Maudie was there with her (Robert's wife). I said at the weekend I'd go visit her.

Next morning Robert rang and said she'd died in her sleep. She was sixty-eight.

I felt very sad about losing my mother. Her funeral was held in Mount Carmel, the Catholic church in Waterloo. Eddie Webb was a Catholic and Mum had raised the kids that way. A priest spoke about her life. She had one green eye and one red eye, he told us. This was for Souths – Margaret's boy played for them. The priest mentioned both her families. I was sad that Rita and Gwen didn't come.

My mother was buried in Botany Cemetery with Dorothy's daughter Suzie, who she'd reared. When they opened Suzie's grave I saw Mrs English holding the cake above her head as she sank into the water at Box Ridge.

I wrote in the book about my mother and then I took it to the sewing class. Some of the women were looking at photos of Uluru. I read the part about Mum laying her hand on the rock and saying, 'Now I can die happy.'

After that I read about Nobby and his troubles. Alma Skinner came and sat next to me. She said her daughter was studying at Tranby, the Aboriginal college in Glebe. There you could do maths, writing, Aboriginal studies and so on.

'You should go in there, Ruby, they've got heaps of books. You go on Thursday, look —' She took a leaflet from her pocket and handed it to me. HELP STOP THE KILLINGS. BAR-B-Q and VIDEO, it read.

'Below is a fortnightly program of discussions with Aboriginal activists and video showings for people interested in the Aboriginal struggle. Our aim is to ACT.'

Alma pointed to 18 September video, *Surviving Culture*. Aboriginal identity, both traditional and city dwellers, is alive and strong.

'That's this Thursday,' she said. 'Six o'clock.'

The street was terrace houses and iron railings. I paid the taxi driver and went into a dark red building like a large house. There were people sitting on the verandah.

On the left was an office, on the right a big room full of books by and about Kooris, Aboriginal culture.

Down the hall a common room and kitchen. In a classroom I watched *Surviving Culture* and felt the powerful feeling you get in a room of educated Aboriginals. One thing surprised me – the number of white people there – teachers, students, churchpeople – all interested in the betterment of our culture and people. The video was about life on the settlement at Papunya (140km west of Alice Springs). It opened my eyes to a lot of things not spoken about in books. The Pintubi sandpaintings were like maps and books of holy knowledge: they showed dreaming tracks, the waterholes, women's business, dancing, firebreaks, animals in certain areas. These things had a strong effect on me and showed me how most books in white culture have so little value. What is an autobiography compared to a dreaming track?

Then I realised the obvious. But that didn't increase my respect for books, at the time. The pen is mightier than the sword but the finger in the sand is mightier than that, in its own way.

In the meantime, in the city, the families of John Pat, Dixon Green, Eddie Murray, Tony King, were touring, speaking.

The next morning I sat in the sun at the front of my house and read through thirty pages of photocopies the Committee to Defend Black Rights handed out last night. There were prison statistics, case summaries, proposals for action ...

The committee had formed because of the acquittal of five police charged with the manslaughter of John Pat in 1983. They'd organised pickets, rallies and public forums on black deaths and land rights. They were calling for a Royal Commission. The cases I read about are now being investigated by a Royal Commission, which still has not given its findings.

The statistics are well known by now. Aboriginal people are gaoled ten times more than whites. In WA it's twenty times. The Northern Territory's gaols hold a greater proportion of blacks to the total population than any other Western nation except South Africa.

Then there were the case studies. John Pat sees a black man being hit by an off-duty policeman. Four other police join in, Pat tries to pull the black man away from the fight. A policeman punches him in the mouth. A witness: 'He fell back and didn't get up. I heard his head hit the road.'

Pat was picked up by the hair and kicked in the face. Witness: 'It was like a football kick.'

They threw him in the van and went to the police station. Cecilia Howard went into her front garden when she heard the commotion coming from the police station. She saw a group of eight policemen kick and punch a group of Aborigines till they went limp. Then the police dragged them into the station.

A forensic pathologist found that Pat died from head injuries which caused a brain haemorrhage. He had received ten blows to the head, half a dozen bruises above his right ear, his lips were cracked, there were scratches on his face, and he had two broken ribs and a tear in the aorta, the major blood vessel leading from the heart.

A month later the policemen's clothes have been washed repeatedly. There are traces of blood on the clothes and boots. There is an inquest and two court cases. The five police are acquitted and reinstated to their positions in the police force.

At this time the mining lobby has successfully raised white fears and irrationality about Land Rights. The Labor Premier turns his back on land claims. The Police Union issues dire warnings to the Premier about John Pat's case. Many people in WA, white as well as black, are fearful of the arbitrary control of the police. John Pat's case is not an isolated one.

Eddie Murray was hanged from a piece of prison blanket in his cell. On the fourth day of the inquest family friends and supporters stood on the steps of the Narrabri courthouse and unfurled a giant Land Rights flag. Inside, under cross-examination, police agreed that Eddie was so drunk he couldn't scratch himself. So how could he have hanged himself? There were serious inconsistencies in police notebooks: a highly detailed recording of events for 12 June, the day he died, but other dates out of sequence. Then the absence of records of large police actions in the area, as for the Land Rights occupation of Tulladulla Reserve.

The coroner said there was no evidence that Murray

took his own life but that he was inclined to believe that Murray could have formed a noose. 'He could find no evidence that an offence was committed by any person.'

I went inside and rang Aunt Alma. I told her I'd been to Tranby and seen the video. Then I told her about the case histories I was reading.

'Did you know how bad this is?' I said.

She did. She knew what was going on.

'I don't want to get upset any more about Nobby,' I said. 'But reading this, I'm getting upset about everyone.'

'Well, if enough people get upset and do something –'

'Yeah, maybe things will change.' But as soon as I said that I felt really hopeless.

'Maybe I better not read any more today.'

'Ruby, have a rest. Don't try and take it all in at once.'

'Thanks for talking, Alma.'

'Have a rest now, okay?'

I sat on my bed in the back room. My room was painted dark green. I looked at my typewriter, I looked at my Land Rights poster. Everything seemed like a horrible joke. But I couldn't stop reading.

Case 3. Robert Walker was assaulted in Fremantle Prison by five police, watched by a medical orderly. They hit him with a truncheon, on a grassed area overlooked by the cells. It was 4:00 a.m. The prisoners watched for twenty minutes. The medical orderly gave Walker an injection of the drug Largactil. The body went limp. He was handcuffed and carried away. At 5:15 a.m. the prison doctor announced that 'life was extinct'.

Months later, the coroner finds that 'death arose by way of misadventure'.

Charlie Michaels was handcuffed and tied with belts and a baton inserted and twisted until his head and feet were winched together backwards. The Perth coroner found that he died of a heart attack.

Dixon Green's front teeth were knocked out, top and bottom, there was sand in his mouth, a red mark around his neck. One eye was bruised. These things, seen by his brother just after Dixon died, were not in the pathologist's report. After the autopsy Dixon's body was returned to the family with the heart and brain missing.

I knew two of the Aboriginals who had died in police custody. One was B. T. Leslie, old Mum Ruby's son. The other was Allan Clayton Parker, a red-headed kid who went to school in Newtown with my kids when we lived in Fitzroy Street.

I couldn't read any more. I didn't feel like talking to anyone for days.

22

She's very impressive, Mary

Allawah ('Sit awhile'), Granville

I was working with my editor on rewrites of the book, and keeping my eyes open for anything relating to Kooris and writing. I'd read Charles Perkins' autobiography, *A Bastard Like Me*, and James Miller's *Koori, A Will to Win*. Now I read Mum Shirl's biography, a book by Margaret Tucker called *If Everyone Cared*, and then *My Place* by Sally Morgan.

There were ads in the paper for the Second National Playwrights' Conference, where they'd be talking about black issues and writing, and workshopping the plays. I wanted to go, thinking I would learn a lot from this, but it wasn't possible at the time. One afternoon I was cleaning up the newspapers and I saw a headline: EVERYONE SAID THEY HAD THE SAME DREAM. Another heading mentioned SACRED ROCKS. I knew Aunt Millie Boyd had been made Keeper of the Rock in Bundjalung-Githebul country near Nimbin.

I sat at the table and spread the paper out.

Millie Boyd, 86, has always lived at Mulli Mulli mission, near Woodenbong, just below the Queensland border.

An elder of her Githebul people, she is known tribally as a 'cleverwoman' ... She is the spiritual custodian of Nimbin Rock, an Aboriginal sacred site shrouded in mystery, superstition and death.

Whites who have visited the site have experienced a series of accidents not dissimilar to events that befell Lord Carnarvon's team of archaeologists who opened the tomb of the Egyptian king Tutenkhaman in the 1920s ... A classroom of schoolchildren who went on an excursion near the site all experienced the same dreams that evening ... There have been other events which no conventional white logic can explain.

It turned out the kids had 'Aboriginal dreams' about goannas and snakes and spirits. One boy dreamed of a warrior, 'a big fellow with a shield and spear. It was as if he was guarding the rock. It scared me. I had a sense of overwhelming power.'

Millie wasn't surprised by the story of the dreams. 'That's given to them by the spirits,' she said.

Other people have seen the warrior spirit. One man was sitting on a hill facing Nimbin Rocks when the warrior appeared. 'He was looking away from me and he turned and smiled. There was a silver and blue quality about him.' A Thai Buddhist monk, who was staying with a friend near the rocks, said that one morning when he was meditating he saw a white light shining out of the top of Cathedral Rock. Nimbin gets its name from Nymbunje, the Wee-Un or cleverman who is buried near the rock. The area is traditionally male-only, but the spirits are worried the old ways will die with Millie's generation.

Three clevermen who died in the past few years made her the Keeper of each of their sacred areas.

Millie is a high priestess of Aboriginal culture, and with other cleverwomen and men is the equivalent of the white world's highest university-educated people. A professor of anthropology has compared the cleverwomen and men with the great yogis of Tibet.

Millie has an apprentice, Lorraine Mafi-Williams. The women had never gone to the male-only site till concern over rainforest logging in 1982. Lorraine said the rocks were so sacred that clevermen who went there for initiations brushed the soil from their feet before leaving.

When Millie took the journalists from the *Sunday Telegraph* to the area, 'She would sing out in dialect to her mother and grandmother who belonged to that territory and who, she says, are living there in spirit. She told the Spirits we were coming and asked for protection for herself and us.'

Then there was some news about people from the Richmond River Historical Society at Lismore, where I'd written for information on Grandfather Sam and Uncle Jim Morgan. They had lots of records about Bundjalung and Githebul people. A woman called Marjory Oakes, a collector of Aboriginal history, had learned the Bundjalung language from Lyle Roberts, the former custodian of the rocks. She had written, 'The district is alive with spirit beings ... only white people pretend they don't believe in them.' Mrs Oakes had known about the Nimbin-Lismore area. Her friend Marjorie Henderson knew the Evans Head area. 'In 1962 she began agitating for the protection of what is now the Bundjalung National Park.' This was the park I'd pointed out to Jeffery when we were coming back from Rita's. The paper said there are many Aboriginal artefacts here and a 'clever cave' where the wee-uns held ceremonies.

'Mrs Henderson says numerous people she has taken there have heard Aboriginal voices ... Aboriginal cleverpeople claim to have power over the elements ... Mrs Henderson believes this since working with the Keeper of Goanna headland at Evans Head, Mary Cowlan.'

The hair was standing up on the back of my neck. Here was information about a culture I had lost when I came to Sydney. Only it wasn't lost. There was a direct line from Uncle Ernie Ord to the woman singing in the lingo at Yamba, calling the porpoises in, to people like Aunt Millie Boyd and Lorraine Mafi-Williams and Mary Cowlan.

Mrs Henderson had said that Mary Cowlan can talk to the wind. 'We have sat on top of the hill there and the weather changes and storms blow up.'

The main thing was that political action could come from such powers. The Bundjalung area was now protected as a National Park. The traditions of the rock was being handed on. Logging of rainforest was (as much as possible) being prevented.

I sat there for a long time thinking about the difference between city knowledge and bush knowledge. What happened to blacks in cities, particularly to people like Nobby, made me despair – and then I would find something like the story of Aunt Millie Boyd and I would feel connected again, not just to my Bundjalung origins but to positive forces happening now, to these people who carried the culture and kept it strong, who were concerned with ecology and spiritual health.

White people had given us all kinds of technological comfort, but the tribal ways still need to be strong. I thought of the difference between white people saying 'I own this land' and blacks saying 'We belong to this land'. I looked out at the street and the tall weeds in the railway yard opposite. The phone-lines, the traffic. And I wondered who had been the custodian of Henderson Road, Alexandria. The Eora tribe. Eora country was at La Perouse but it reached this far into the city, to Redfern.

In Botany Road in the old Winn's building is the Eora Centre, next door to the CES. You can do courses there in painting, dramatic arts, music, photography. It's an off-flow of TAFE.

★

A few days later Annabella rang to say that Nobby's request for bail had been moved up to 18 December (1986). I had an appointment that day with Mack the Knife, my surgeon Doctor Graham, to be assessed for more surgery on my mountainous stomach. I rang and cancelled, and sat down to write something in support of Nobby.

On that day we took the lift to the thirteenth floor of the Supreme Court in Macquarie Street. We asked if we could get a clean shirt to Nobby. While we waited for his solicitor from the Aboriginal Legal Service to show up, Anna and I decided what each of us should say.

Then we decided to sit in on a few bail applications, just to see how the magistrate was reacting. Out of five cases he only granted bail to a Vietnamese thief. The other were drug traffickers and dealers.

Court adjourned for lunch. Nobby's solicitor came in and said we were on at 2:30 p.m.

The room was large. I could see Nobby looking very dignified in his navy suit, sitting between two gungabul. He looked strained but when he saw us he waved and smiled.

Then the charges were read out by the police prosecutor, a beautiful blonde woman in her middle twenties. She read out all the times Nobby had escaped from custody, as far back as the children's homes. All his record was read out.

I held my breath. Why was all this coming out now? He'd served six years for this same charge (shooting at a police car) fourteen years ago. Ironic. Futile. He was being judged on a record he'd already served time for.

Then Nobby spoke. He'd had a nervous breakdown, he said, and thought if he went away, 'I'd be able to get myself together and come back and face the music when I felt better.'

'Where did you get the gun?' the magistrate said.

'A mate gave it to me to protect myself,' Nobby answered, '– in my condition I didn't know what I was doing, I wanted to die. I was grieving over my brother David's death. My family found me laying on his grave, he's buried with my eldest brother Bill. And later I was found by the police, fighting with a man in a prime mover.'

He told how the police had not taken him to the psychiatric centre, but kicked him on the road and bashed him at the station. 'I came out looking like the Elephant Man, my face was so swollen.'

Later he said, 'I realise I need help and I want to have counselling.'

'You saw a psychiatrist in Maitland,' the magistrate said.

'Yes. But he only stayed half an hour and all he did was look at his watch. I'd been in custody nearly five months and that half hour was it.'

'What's to stop you from doing this again in another fourteen years? With your psychological problems you might snap again and I wouldn't feel good if I let you out in the community again. Bail refused.'

I tried to interject but they wouldn't hear me. As they

were taking Nobby away he turned and said, 'They still won't listen, Mum.'

'Hang in there son, we'll win one day.'

Anna had given a good account for him, but to no avail. I was so angry I yelled out, 'I wonder if a half-caste will ever be given a chance – or will white Australia ever understand –'

I left the court in tears and didn't bother to bow.

I had been reading in the newspapers in National Aboriginal Week (27 September 1986) that finally a Royal Commission would be held into the treatment and deaths of Aboriginals in police or prison custody.

We have known for years that police in some country towns can be as brutal as they like to Kooris, and get away with it. People who try to protest and get help are persecuted or run out of town. In some places they herd old blackfellers out of town like they were dogs. I have witnessed this.

I had been checked out for my second operation and was booked in to hospital for 27 March. Aileen came with me and stayed while I was operated on, and she came to visit nearly every day.

They cut thirteen kilos from my belly and sewed my muscles back in place. After the gut-busting work I'd done I was now really gut-busted – the scar ran from near my kidneys right around my stomach to the other side of my back. I looked like I'd been sliced in half, and I thought of the Bodiless Woman at the sideshow. There were 180 stitches and 86 metal clamps holding me together.

I was there for a month. Horse and his family came to see me, and all my kids except Nobby. The doctor said I was likely to feel depressed and under stress for the next six months.

At home the nurse came to change my dressing every day. I felt weepy and low, though I was glad to be home among my books and Land Rights posters and the family calling in. Neddy came to visit and we swapped our latest stories. She'd applied for a Housing Commission place at Wreck Bay, the mission where some of her kids lived. She asked me how Gert and James were. And she'd stopped drinking.

I was too unwell to work on my book, so I read and researched. An alternative network magazine called *Maggie's Farm* had an article called MISSING LINKS – A SEPARATE REALITY, about Aunt Millie Boyd.

Continuing the Maggie's Farm series with Aboriginal shaman/storyteller Lorraine Mafi-Williams of the Bundjalung tribe in northern NSW. The following is an interview with her teacher, elder/custodian Aunt Millie Boyd, 89 years, of the Githrabaul Tribe.

Lorraine asked her to explain about totems.

'Wherever the old tribal Aborigine was born that place was their totem. What's in the water, what's in the mountain, was given to us by the old tribal people ... our

totem is the goanna and the bullock.' (Aunt Millie later
explained the spirit of the bullock totem 'wandered in'
from a distant tribe. It is suspected it might be a buffalo,
an Amerindian totem.)

'Is the Willy Wagtail bird also a totem in your
family?'

'Yes, that's our messenger, brings us messages. But
when the Williams who married into our family die, you
see, the main totem will be goanna. If we see a young
goanna dead we know we're going to lose young men or
young girls, that's how our totem comes and lets us know
things.'

'And when you're sick yourself do you send your
spirit —'

'We send our spirit just like a fog travelling in the
morning. Just like that!'

I lay on my bed wishing I could send my spirit somewhere
so my body could heal. The drain was messy, I felt low
and mopey and had no energy. I read on.

'… Are there any "clevermen" still living in this area?'
'Yes, there is one "cleverfellow" who is Githrabaul.'
'What's his work?'
'Everything. If he wants to travel a long way his spirit
can go. He travels in the form of a giant bee —'

I must have gone to sleep then, and my dreams were full
of the wings of the giant bee ranging across the hills of

Mulli Mulli, Woodenbong, Box Ridge, Yamba, Lismore.

When I woke up I read about a woman years ago who was a master of jumping long distances.

'Her name was Denargu and she lived up in Blue Knob (behind Nimbin),' Lorraine said. 'Denargu used to sing out to the wind, call the wind. She could travel on the wind the same way a tornado picks up things. No matter where she wanted to go she could be there in an hour.'

Aunt Millie: 'Even when her husband was in the tribal wars she would sing out and call the wind to turn the other tribe back from the foot of the mountain.'

The paper's interviewer said, 'A line of fire across the mountain in the rain?'

Lorraine: 'You see Mary W, the one I told you about, even now she can whip up a good storm. She's very impressive, Mary, she's the one that drowned all the bulldozers down at Goanna Headland when they tried to peg it out for development. They were going to put a tourist resort ...'

'So she's the custodian of that place.'

'She's no lady to play with, old Mary,' Lorraine said.

I slept again. I seemed to be able to sleep for days ... I could read, and think about these things, but I had no energy for other activities ... The operation and a series of stressful family events had laid me low. I went back to sewing class a few times but then it took another day to recover.

I managed to find another solicitor for Nob. Her name was Kathy and she seemed genuinely concerned about his case. She went to Long Bay to see him, and engaged a barrister. They said that he should not be in gaol, and they'd work for free.

They prepared his case, I wrote a letter for the judge and a psychiatrist wrote a full report. On the day, Kathy came for Jeff and Shelley, I wasn't well enough to face more court.

'He'll be out by Christmas,' they shouted as they came in the door with Anna. I made a pot of tea.

'The judge took into consideration,' Anna said, 'that he'd had a breakdown, that he should never have been taken to the cells, that he was bashed. We showed pictures of the house. I spoke for him too. I said he was a good man and a good worker.'

He was given a three-year sentence for the charge of firing at the police car, with an eighteen-month non-parole period. By August he had already done twelve months. He was to get remission for his work in gaol, for the courses he'd done, for playing football.

On 4 August 1987, Kathy rang to say he would be out by 17 September. 'Surviving culture,' I thought, 'I hope Nob survives.' It was a great relief to know he'd be free.

I was in and out of hospital during this time for chest infections and other problems, no-one seemed to know what was really wrong. It was four months since the operation and some sort of long, slow recovery was taking place.

At sewing class I'd heard about an Aboriginal hostel in Granville for people who'd raised their families and didn't want to become live-in babysitters for their kids. It was the first of its kind.

I moved there on 11 August 1987.

The place was called Allawah, meaning 'sit awhile'. It was a huge house with rose gardens and stained-glass windows and a hallway big enough to swing ten cats. I had a room of my own and a sunroom off that for a study.

Six or seven other people lived there – I'd known them all at various stages of my life and they all had their stories to tell. It looked like someone had pointed me in the right direction if I wanted to do more writing. I felt at peace here. Not hemmed in.

I unpacked my books and bought a typewriter (my other one had packed in), a desk and a filing cabinet. Outside my window a hibiscus opened its buds and the noise now was not traffic but birds.

One of the men was an actor, and the next morning a car called to take him on location. Word had got round I was writing a book, so there was teasing talk about how if they didn't look out this place would turn into an artists' colony.

Someone had left the *Telegraph* and a copy of *Land Rights News* on a coffee table so I took them to my room to lie down and have a read. On the centre page of the Land Rights paper was a photo of a woman talking into a microphone. This was Helen Boyle, who had gone to Geneva to talk to a UN working group about the deaths in custody. She was chairperson of the committee who had put out the leaflets of case studies I'd read.

Every time I picked up a paper the numbers had gone up. The committee had 101 deaths in custody recorded, and feared there were many more. Fifteen this year so far. Averaging one a fortnight. Underneath there were lists of national actions that people could go to.

White journalists were now picking up on the issue and making fairly radical statements, particularly now the Bicentenary year was coming up. People felt something had to be said. In the *Telegraph* an article called 200 YEARS OF INDIFFERENCE talked about how the white race 'have learned nothing, and lack the maturity to be a nation ...'. It was honest and well-written and I sat to write and thank the journalist for this article. I read it out to a few people around the house. Then I typed another one out real deadly and sent it to him.

On black Friday, 13 November, Nob was released from the Bay after fifteen months, pissed off and ecstatic. Something had finally gone right for him. A good solicitor and the Shadow Attorney General as his barrister, and both had worked on his case for free because this imprisonment had been so unjust and we had no money. Some white people you couldn't knock, but you had to find out who and where they were. We were very lucky this time. Fingers crossed this would be the end of Nob's career of doing time.

The next week I had a phone call from the All Blacks asking if I'd make twenty dampers for their football presentation dance. My reputation for dampers was still around. Mrs Christian and I used sixty pounds of self-raising flour, four large tins of Sunshine Milk and water, with half a pound of table salt. This time I had mod cons and a big kitchen. I'd never used a Kenwood Chef and the first damper came out so hard the general opinion was to take it outside and bury it, so we holed that one. The others were fine and on the big night we went to Souths Juniors at Kensington – Brenda Leslie and her old man Nicko, Mum Ruby, Aileen and me.

Max Silver and his band Black Lace were playing the All Blacks song 'We keep the ball in motion/Just like a rolling ocean' and later they played 'Midnight Special' and the place was jumping.

My manuscript was almost ready for the publisher. I knew when I finished this book a weight would be lifted from my mind, not only because I could examine my own life from it and know who I was, but because it may help better the relationship between the Aboriginal and white people. That it might give some idea of the difficulty we have surviving between two cultures, that we are here and will always be here.

Glossary

AIM – Australian Inland Mission
AMS – Aboriginal Medical Service
bagel – man
Big E – The Empress Hotel, Redfern
binging – turtles
bra – brother
bundung – bum
bunning – porcupine (echidna)
burbi – bear
captain – a bloke that you can con up for money or food
Do wana nanarabi – You are not of my meat
doorie – urban Aboriginal word for sex
dubays – women
durrying – sex
Go ngudam – sleep
goom – metho
gubb – urban Aboriginal word for white person
gulay – wine
gungabul – policemen
gungys – police (constables)

gunyum muggul – cheeky arse

gunyam – bum

guyahny – possums

hummed – cadged

jarahny – frogs

jarjum – child, kids

joogy-happy – chicken hungry

jum – smoke

jung – bad

Koori – Aboriginal person

moggi – ghost

munie – pussy

naragar – bullshit

ningana – don't do that

nunyars – my, mine

Nyaiwanyi bumanyi – I'll hit you

nyathung – grandfather

tita or **titi** – sister

waddy – stick

Acknowledgements

I started this book on 23 May 1984. It is a true life story of an Aboriginal woman's struggle to raise a family of nine children in a society divided between black and white culture in Australia. It is dedicated to my children – living and deceased: Billy, Pearl, Dianne, Nobby, David, Aileen, Ellen, Pauline and Jeffery. Also to my adopted children who I collected along the way - Allan, Doug and Pat Barrett, Steve Farrant (Horse), Terry Priest, Steve Freeman (Sparrow), Charlie Jones, David Jarrett, and Darby and John Devine.

Dedicated also to every black woman who's battled to raise a family and kept her sense of humour.

I want to thank Billy Marshall-Stoneking for reading the first draft of my manuscript and for writing a letter recommending I get funded.

I want to thank the Aboriginal Arts Board of the Australia Council and the Australian Bicentennial Authority's National Aboriginal and Torres Strait Islander program for grant money received to work on this book.

The publishers gratefully acknowledge permission to reproduce the following: 'Ruby, don't take your love to town' to EMI; 'Ghost riders in the sky' to EMI; 'El Paso' to Castle Music/Belinda Music and Acuss-Rose; 'Black Woman' to Roberta Sykes, first published by Saturday Centre Press, Sydney; 'A Song of the Rolling Earth' by Walt Whitman in *Leaves of Grass* to Airmont Publishing Co. Inc.; Extract from the *Telegraph* to the *Telegraph*; Extracts from *Maggie's Farm* interview with Aunt Millie Boyd by Lorraine Mafi-Williams to *Maggie's Farm*.

Every effort has been made to trace all copyright owners. The publishers would be grateful to hear from any copyright holders not acknowledged or acknowledged incorrectly.